JANE GREY SWISSHELM

JANE GREY SWISSHELM

An Unconventional Life,
1815–1884

Sylvia D. Hoffert

The University of North Carolina Press

Chapel Hill and London

Designed by
Jacquline Johnson
Set in Legacy by
Keystone Typesetting, Inc.
Manufactured in the United
States of America

The paper in this book
meets the guidelines for
permanence and durability
of the Committee on
Production Guidelines
for Book Longevity of
the Council on Library
Resources.

Library of Congress Cataloging-in-Publication Data
Hoffert, Sylvia D.
Jane Grey Swisshelm : an unconventional life, 1815–1884 /
by Sylvia D. Hoffert.
p. cm.
Includes bibliographical references and index.
ISBN 0-8078-2881-5 (cloth : alk. paper)
1. Swisshelm, Jane Grey Cannon, 1815–1884. 2. Feminists—
United States—Biography. 3. Women social reformers—
United States—Biography. 4. Women newspaper editors—
United States—Biography. 5. Women in politics—United
States—Biography. I. Title.
HQ1413.S95 H64 2004
305.42′092—dc22
2004003682

Portions of this work appeared earlier, in somewhat
different form, as "Gender and Vigilantism on the
Minnesota Frontier: Jane Grey Swisshelm and the U.S.-
Dakota Conflict of 1862," *Western Historical Quarterly* 29
(Autumn 1998): 343–62, reprinted by permission of the
Western History Association, and "Jane Grey
Swisshelm and the Negotiation of Gender Roles on
the Minnesota Frontier," *Frontiers: A Journal of Women's
Studies* 18 (Winter 1997): 17–39, reprinted by permission
of the University of Nebraska Press.

08 07 06 05 04   5 4 3 2 1

CONTENTS

ILLUSTRATIONS

JANE
GREY
SWISSHELM

Jane Grey Swisshelm may have been married to a farmer, but she was no ordinary farm wife. Nor did she, like most farm wives, pass through life quietly and in relative obscurity. During the mid–nineteenth century, her name appeared in newspapers across the United States. She supported the antislavery and woman's rights movements from the podium and in print, and, despite the fact that she was a woman, she actively participated in local, state, and national political affairs. She was so well known as a journalist and a reformer that when she died in 1884, editors and their readers chronicled her life, extolled her virtues, lamented her death, and did what they could to preserve her memory.

> *When a good and gifted woman—one who has blessed humanity with her devotion to grand principles—passes away, she leaves a space that is not easily filled. Especially is this true when that woman's name is a household word, because of her love, not only for her sex but for all humanity.*
> Frank G. Thompson to the Chicago Evening Journal, *July 24, 1884, p. 2.*

> *There is no other woman including Apassia among the ancients, and Pompadour among the moderns who exerted so powerful an influence on contemporary events as has Mrs. Swisshelm.*
> "Mrs. Swisshelm," St. Paul Daily Globe, *July 26, 1884, p. 4.*

The story that they collectively told was both dramatic and compelling. Jane's background was humble. She was born in Pittsburgh, Pennsylvania, in 1815, the granddaughter of a weaver and the daughter of a Scotch-Irish Covenanter Presbyterian chair maker, Thomas Cannon, and his wife, Mary Scott Cannon. Jane grew up in a tightly knit, rigidly orthodox Calvinist community whose members believed in original sin and the inevitability of eternal damnation for all except God's chosen few.

When Thomas Cannon died in 1827, Mary, who had three children to support, put Jane to work painting on velvet and making lace. Eventually, Jane found employment as a schoolteacher.

Jane married James Swisshelm, a farmer, over her mother's objections in 1836. Conflicts over matters of conscience and what she perceived to be the insensitivity and greed of both her husband and his mother doomed the marriage. Two years after their wedding, Jane and James moved to Louisville, Kentucky. Already a woman with abolitionist sympathies, she came face to face with the realities of slavery. Against her husband's wishes, she returned to Pittsburgh in 1839 to care for her dying mother. Aware of the problems that characterized her daughter's marriage, Mary Scott Cannon made legal provisions that prevented James from having access to his wife's inheritance. Enraged, he threatened to file a claim against Mary's estate for the loss of Jane's domestic services during the time she nursed her mother.

> *In 1838, at the age of twenty-three, she went to Louisville, Ky., and there, seeing slavery in all its horror, increased her hatred of the system and no doubt nerved her pen in her grand warfare against it a few years later. Her domestic experience with a tyrant husband was more bitter and must have been the secret spring which nourished her intense hatred of the wrongs heaped upon woman by custom and law. . . . Mrs. Swisshelm, after such experience with a despotic husband, devoted all her energy to the overthrow of such legalized injustice.*
> "Mrs. Jane Grey Swisshelm," New York Herald, July 23, 1884, p. 10.

During the 1840s, Jane began to write poems, stories, and essays for publication in local newspapers. Editors' willingness to print her submissions, their regard for her opinions on matters of public interest, and her desire to promote the cause of social reform encouraged her to use the money bequeathed to her by her mother to begin publishing a newspaper called the *Pittsburgh Saturday Visiter* in 1847. In her columns she supported temperance, the abolition of slavery, and the emerging woman's rights movement.

> *She wrote most passionately, but with rare ability, for the freedom of the negro slave and of the white wife.*
> "Mrs. Jane Grey Swisshelm," New York Herald, July 23, 1884, p. 10.

> *Mrs. Swisshelm's was a life of great usefulness and devotion to the cause of the weak, suffering, and helpless.*
> "Jane Grey Swisshelm, Eminent Philanthropist and Journalist," Louisville Courier Journal, July 27, 1884, p. 11.

Her pen was used to oppose slavery, befriend working women, and other friendless classes.
"Jane Grey Swisshelm," New York Daily Tribune, *July 23, 1884, p. 5.*

There are few women in the United States who, by sheer force of personal character, have made their influence more strongly felt during the past thirty or forty years than has she. She early turned her attention to the consideration of affairs of national or great social importance, and from deep convictions entered heart and soul into the work of doing what lay in her power to remedy certain overshadowing evils.
"Death of Jane Grey Swisshelm," St. Cloud Journal Press, *July 24, 1884, p. 2.*

Born in an obscure station . . . she yet extricated herself unaided, and solely with her vigorous common sense, her strong convictions and unflagging energy, she made herself a power during a period when gigantic events were the rule, and the existence of great minds was not an exception. Slight, delicate, fragile as a thistle-down, she did not hesitate to encounter giants, and generally to the sorrow of the Goliaths, who scorned her diminutive figure and her simple sling.
"Mrs. Swisshelm," St. Paul Daily Globe, *July 26, 1884, p. 4.*

In 1850, Horace Greeley, the editor of the *New York Tribune*, offered Jane a job as a freelance reporter. She spent two months in Washington, D.C., sending letters back to the *Tribune* describing and commenting on political life in the nation's capital. Her employment as a regular correspondent for Greeley ended when her *Pittsburgh Saturday Visiter* published an unsubstantiated and highly inflammatory story libeling Daniel Webster.

Her articles were copied far and wide, and she sprang at once into an honorable fame. . . .
In 1850 [the Visiter's*] editor had gained such a reputation that Horace Greeley secured her as a correspondent to write letters to the* Tribune *from Washington. She was the first woman who had ever been regularly engaged in this business, and she opened the way for woman reporters by inducing [Vice] President [Millard] Fillmore to open the reporters' galleries in Congress for her.*
"A Staunch Foe of Slavery: Death of Jane Grey Swisshelm, the Philanthropist," New York Times, *July 23, 1884, p. 5.*

Jane left Washington and returned to Pittsburgh to resume her editorial duties at the *Visiter*. She continued to write poems and stories, which she published between columns dedicated to social reform.

Her style was vigorous and caustic and her views of reform radically advanced.
"The Death of Mrs. Swisshelm," Washington Post, *July 24, 1884, p. 1.*

She rebuked the advocates of slavery in her own vigorous style, which stung where it hit.
"Jane Grey Swisshelm" (letter of Rufus Blanchard to the Chicago InterOcean [clipping], Harpel Scrapbook, vol. II, p. 147, Chicago Historical Society).

> *Mrs. Swisshelm was a vigorous writer, clear, logical and incisive, and she had an inexhaustible armory of ridicule, in the use of which, when engaged in controversy, she was unsparing. She cared little for any discussion in which there was not some principle at stake, and then she enlisted on the side where she believed right to be with the whole ardor of her nature.*
> "Death of Jane Grey Swisshelm," St. Cloud Journal Press, *July 24, 1884, p. 2.*

In 1852, she and James had a daughter, Mary Henrietta, affectionately called Zo or Nettie. Determined to be an attentive mother, Jane gave up her responsibilities as the editor of the *Visiter*, but within months, she was back in her office, tending to her newspaper business.

By 1857, Jane had spent more than twenty years trying unsuccessfully to please her husband and combat her mother-in-law's hostility. Finally willing to admit that her marriage had been a mistake, she deserted James and with Zo in hand fled to frontier St. Cloud, Minnesota. Jane lived there for almost six years, making her living as a printer and newspaper editor. She continued to champion the cause of women and slaves and participated actively in the political life of her adopted state. Shortly after her arrival, her freely expressed and often inflammatory opinions so enraged the sensibilities of local Democratic leaders that they broke into her newspaper office, destroyed her press, and threw her type into the Mississippi River. With the financial support of her friends, she bought a new press and resumed her editorship. In 1858, she turned the *St. Cloud Visiter* into the *St. Cloud Democrat*. She eventually became a supporter of the Republican Party in Minnesota and was deeply involved in its activities. She also lectured throughout the state on the issue of woman's rights.

> *These were stormy times in Minnesota, and Mrs. Swisshelm's editorial bombshells brought mob violence upon her at one time.*
> "Mrs. Jane Grey Swisshelm," New York Herald, *July 23, 1884, p. 10.*

> *She entered the field alone to war upon established institutions, perfectly organized factions, and recognized interests. She was tabooed by society, threatened by power, menaced by murder, visited by violence, but she moved on undisturbed, and as serene as if all the elements clamoring about her had been gentle-voiced breezes, aromatic, and harmless.*
> "Mrs. Swisshelm," St. Paul Daily Globe, *July 26, 1884, p. 4.*

> *Her path was a thorny one, but despite threats, and even mobs, she confronted her enemies not only in the columns of the* Visitor, *but took the lecture field in a defiant attitude.*
> "Jane Grey Swisshelm" (letter of Rufus Blanchard to the Chicago InterOcean *[clipping], Harpel Scrapbook, vol. 11, p. 147, Chicago Historical Society).*

In 1863, after the end of the Dakota Rebellion, she left the *St. Cloud Democrat* in the hands of her nephew and moved to Washington, D.C., to offer her personal advice to President Abraham Lincoln regarding his Indian policy. She earned her living as one of the first female clerks in the quartermaster general's office and spent her free time nursing Union soldiers in the field hospitals surrounding the city.

> *Her career as a nurse in the hospitals during the war is not the least interesting portion of her life. There, she exhibited the hate of shams, red-tape, and inefficiency which she had shown in all other portions of her life. She defied regulations, she insisted on saving men whom science had given up to die, she revolutionized all with which she came in contact, and, after her own convictions, and in defiance of rules, and precedents, she carried on her reforms.*
> "Mrs. Swisshelm," St. Paul Daily Globe, *July 26, 1884, p. 4.*

During her sojourn in Washington, she exacerbated a controversy over the administration of an orphan home in Georgetown. In December 1865 she began publishing another newspaper, *The Reconstructionist*, and concentrated her editorial efforts on monitoring the course of President Andrew Johnson's Reconstruction policies. She finally gave up her role as a newspaper editor in March 1866 when an arsonist tried to set fire to her pressroom and living quarters.

Left with no source of income and a daughter to support, Jane returned to Pittsburgh. On the advice of her friend, Secretary of War Edwin Stanton, she sued her ex-husband for fraud and won her case in the Supreme Court of Pennsylvania in 1868. The court granted her possession of the Swisshelm homestead, Swissvale. After she had made improvements to the house, she and Zo moved in.

Jane spent the last fifteen years of her life moving from place to place, trying to make her living as a freelance journalist and public speaker. Based at Swissvale and at a country cottage in Indiana County, Pennsylvania, she often visited her sister in St. Cloud and spent considerable time in Chicago, writing for the *Chicago Tribune* and composing her memoirs.

> *Some time later, a successful suit gave her possession of a valuable property at Swissvale, the old homestead. The years between 1865 . . . and her death, were spent at St. Cloud, at Chicago . . . and at Swissvale, with one year in Europe. During this time she was a contributor to a number of leading daily papers and lectured occasionally on the labor problem and other questions of current interest.*
> "Death of Jane Grey Swisshelm," St. Cloud Journal Press, *July 24, 1884, p. 2.*

> *She has written for many of the leading papers of the country, and whatever came from her pen was read with eagerness.*

> *"Death of Mrs. Swisshelm," Chicago InterOcean (clipping), Harpel Scrapbook, vol. II, p. 146, Chicago Historical Society.*

> *In every public crisis she threw herself into the breach, and when she spoke through the columns of the leading newspapers of the country her words rang out clear and unmistakable in their meaning after bringing light to the subject that had not been evoked by any other one.*
> *"Jane Grey Swisshelm" (letter of Rufus Blanchard to the Chicago InterOcean [clipping], Harpel Scrapbook, vol. II, p. 147, Chicago Historical Society).*

In 1881, Zo Swisshelm, an accomplished pianist who did not seek the public limelight, married a Chicago insurance executive. Three years later, Jane died at Swissvale.

> *Mrs. Swisshelm came from Chicago, where she had passed the winter, a few weeks ago and went to her home in Swissvale, the suburb she christened years since. On Saturday the 12th, she was taken ill with a complaint common in the summer season. . . . [Y]esterday [she] finished dictating a letter for the Commercial Gazette, on whose writing staff she has held a position for a long time. Her daughter Zo and son-in-law, Mr. Allen, have been with her.*
> *"Passing Away: A Great Mind Losing Its Hold on Earth," Pittsburgh Commercial Gazette, July 22, 1884, p. 4.*

> *All that was mortal of the gifted writer and true friend of the oppressed—Jane Grey Swisshelm—was yesterday carried to the grave and forever hidden from the view of those who were endeared to her. Since her death became known, the four roads that intersect in front of her rustic home have been continually alive with carriages, buggies and pedestrians all centering towards the abode of the dead writer, there to pay the last earthly respects. Yesterday, long before the hour for the last rites to be performed, the old log cabin creaked and groaned under the heavy weight of sympathizing friends, the stillness being only broken from the subdued whispers which conveyed from mouth to ear the many sterling qualities of her whose lifeless body lay ready for the grave.*
> *"In Her Grave: Jane Grey Swisshelm Laid at Rest," Pittsburgh Commercial Gazette, July 25, 1884, p. 2.*

Jane Grey Swisshelm's life spanned most of the nineteenth century. Her story, full of personal drama and emotional conflict, is compelling in its own right. But it also offers a unique opportunity to explore what it meant to be a woman in an age in which gender distinctions were becoming less rigid.[1]

Jane lived in the age of the so-called self-made man. In her day, reams of paper and millions of dollars were dedicated to the glorification of men whose pluck and luck allowed them to achieve some degree of personal autonomy, political power, and economic success. But in the nineteenth century, self-making was culturally defined as a male activity. Because men's nature was viewed as malleable, they were expected to take the initiative and "make" something of themselves. Their claim to manhood was often measured by their ability to overcome circumstances that might inhibit their pursuit of wealth, social status, and influence.

Women in the middle and upper classes did not have to fulfill those expectations. Their "feminine" nature presumably dictated who they were and what they did or did not do. Considered inherently weak rather than strong, passive rather than active and competitive, and emotional rather than rational, women were expected merely to fulfill their biological destinies by marrying, bearing children, keeping house, and deferring to their husbands' authority. As a result of such assumptions about women's nature, Jane had to go about the process of self-making in ways that differed significantly from those of men. In so doing, she found it necessary to transgress gender boundaries. As an unconventionally ambitious woman who publicly critiqued and successfully challenged social conventions that restricted her personal behavior, limited her political and economic opportunities, and attempted to silence her voice, she provides a model through which we can explore the connection between gender ideals and the construction of individual gender identities.

> She was true to principle, and in sunshine and storms she braved everything for anything that her conscience approved of, and although a woman *she did not hesitate but rather courted the privilege of meeting in the intellectual arena the ablest opponents of the sterner sex.*
> Frank G. Thompson to the Chicago Evening Journal, *July 24, 1884, p. 2; emphasis added.*

> *The unusual vigor of her style and her reputation as a controversialist were the cause of disappointment to nearly all who met her for the first time.* Instead of finding a woman of masculine form and manners, *they saw one of slight figure, of less than medium height, with pleasant face, eyes beaming with kindliness, soft voice, and winning manners.* What was masculine was her intellect and her courage. *Clear and positive in her convictions, she hesitated to attack no man no matter how high in position he might be, and no interest no matter how strongly intrenched which she believed to be wrong. The great battle of her life was that all men, black as well as white, might be free and equal before the law, and going into the contest as one of the little handful of Abolitionists, she lived to share in the final victory.*
> "Death of Jane Grey Swisshelm," St. Cloud Journal Press, *July 24, 1884, p. 2; emphasis added.*

The significance of gender prescriptions as well as the distribution of social, economic, and political power were as contested in the nineteenth century as they are today. As a result, Jane Swisshelm's efforts to choose from a variety of overlapping, sometimes contradictory models intended to prescribe what it meant to be a "true woman" has a strikingly contemporary resonance. While she struggled in private to be a dutiful daughter, wife, mother, and housekeeper, she negotiated a place for herself in the male world of commerce, journalism, and politics. This book's central concerns will be how she created a personally satisfying and very public feminine identity for herself; what expressive devices she used to do so; what social, economic, and political tensions resulted from her efforts; and how they were resolved.

What follows is the story of her life, written not in the typical linear fashion—chronologically from beginning to end—but instead in a format that is both asymmetrical and circuitous. Like the strands of a braid, parts of the story will appear, disappear, and then reappear. I will present my narrative chronologically, but I will do so by focusing on a series of discrete topics. My major concern is to describe the life of a remarkable woman. At the same time, I will show how Jane dealt with the constraints imposed on her by middle-class gender conventions. The story will start with her childhood and end with her death. But in between, I will place her efforts to define what it meant to be a woman in various contexts. In the first chapter, "That Olde-Time Religion," I discuss the influence of religion in general and Covenanter Presbyterianism in particular on Jane's life as well as on her attitudes toward gender and the role of women in American society. "A Marriage Fraught with Conflict" and "The Troublesome Matter of Property" explore the gendered dimensions of marriage, separation, divorce, and property ownership. "Woman's Work in a Man's World" deals with adjustments in the work environment that became necessary when women transgressed gender boundaries and imposed themselves on male work spaces. "A Different Sort of Politics" discusses Jane's role in partisan politics in the mid–nineteenth century. "A World in Need of Improvement" examines Jane as an advocate of temperance, abolition, and woman's rights and explores the contradictions and tensions that she exposed in her pursuit of social reform. The last chapter, "Respectable but Not Genteel," concerns class issues and discusses Jane's struggle to integrate the meaning of respectability into an expanded version of what it meant to be a "true woman" in U.S. society.

*I was born on the 6th of December, 1815, in Pittsburg, on
the bank of the Monongahela, near its confluence with the
Allegheny. My father was Thomas Cannon, and my mother
Mary Scott. They were both Scotch-Irish and descended
from the Scotch Reformers. On my mother's side were
several men and women who signed the "Solemn League
and Covenant," and defended it to the loss of livings, lands
and life. Her mother, Jane Grey, was of that family which
was allied to royalty, and gave to England her nine day's
queen.*

*This grandmother I remember as a stately old lady,
quaintly and plainly dressed, reading a large Bible or
answering questions by quotations from its pages. She was
unsuspicious as an infant, always doubtful about "actual
transgressions" of any, while believing in the total depravity
of all. Educated in Ireland as an heiress, she had not been
taught to write, lest she should marry without the consent of
her elder brother guardian. She felt that we owed her
undying gratitude for bestowing her hand and fortune on
our grandfather, who was but a yeoman, even if "he did
have a good leasehold, ride a high horse, wear spurs, and
have Hamilton blood in his veins." She made us familiar
with the battle of the Boyne and the sufferings in
Londonderry, in both of which her great-grandfather had
shared.*

Jane Grey Cannon Swisshelm, Half a Century, 10–11.[1]

Jane Grey Swisshelm was immensely proud of her religious heritage and deeply in awe of the courage and martyrdom of her forebears. Throughout her adult life, she tried to follow their example. She typically recalled their image when she felt the need to defend her opinions or her actions. And she incorporated into her personality both their admirable qualities and their shortcomings.

The old Scottish Covenanters that she heard about from her grandmother were immensely brave, fiercely stubborn, and rigidly principled as well as infuriatingly single-minded and self-righteous. And never was any group of religious zealots more convinced that what they did they did for the glory of God. As staunch Calvinists, they believed that every individual was born with an innately sinful nature and that most people would spend all eternity burning in the fires of hell. The Covenanters believed that God, in his infinite wisdom, had chosen some to go to heaven. The only problem was that they could never be entirely sure which of them he had chosen for salvation. So they found themselves caught between despair and hope, constantly evaluating their relationships with each other and with God, hoping for some assurance, some sign that might relieve the tension caused by their spiritual lives, knowing all the while that seeking assurance was presumptuous in the extreme. They were willing to die for their religious beliefs, and they did. They were seventeenth-century Covenanter Presbyterians, and Jane Grey Cannon Swisshelm was a latter-day version of them.

Religion profoundly influenced nineteenth-century U.S. society. Shortly after the American Revolution, a series of revivals engulfed the former colonies. Known as the Second Great Awakening and led by charismatic evangelists from a wide variety of denominations, these revivals resulted in the conversion of thousands of men, women, and children. This phenomenon marked a turning point in the history of religion in the United States. As religious enthusiasm spread, the influence of Calvinism, with its emphasis on the depravity of humankind and its insistence that salvation was exclusively in the hands of God, began to decline. Evangelicals preached that Jesus had died for the sinful and that individuals could claim a place for themselves in heaven by choosing Christ as their savior. Having done so, converts were obliged to join a church and do what they could to prepare the world for the second coming of Christ.

The result was that the converted flocked to join their local churches. After making a denominational commitment, the converts turned their attention toward reforming the world. By the 1850s, social reform movements were flourishing. Men and women alike joined missionary societies, tract societies, and Sunday schools to convert the unchurched. These reformers raised huge sums of money to help the poor and organized temperance societies to fight drunkenness and abolition societies to end slavery. A few even supported a woman's rights movement.[2]

Jane Grey Cannon Swisshelm eventually joined efforts to reform society, but unlike other reformers, her religious identity did not derive from the evangelical tradition. Instead, it grew out of the actions of a group that traced its roots back to seventeenth-century Scotland and prided itself on its ability to preserve the Calvinist traditions for which so many of its adherents had died. Her link to that past and those traditions was through her maternal grandmother, Jane Grey Scott, wife of Hance Scott, a Scotch-Irish weaver. At her grandmother's knee, young Jane Grey Cannon heard stories of loyalty and sacrifice, heroism and martyrdom, suffering and death by both women and men whose commitment to God and their version of his church constituted the determining focus of their lives. Because of their dedication to what they considered to be the true church, her forebears had been among those who had rebelled against the authority of King Charles I, fled from Scotland to Ireland to escape religious persecution, and eventually suffered martyrdom at the hands of James II at the siege of Londonderry. These ancestors and their friends and neighbors had lost their property and their lives in an effort to sustain their spiritual integrity. Because the chronicle of their suffering became so much a part of Jane's sense of who she was and was so critical in determining what she became, it bears repeating in some detail.

One result of the Protestant Reformation was that the Scots were relatively free to reject Catholicism and to create their own form of Protestantism. They refused to adopt the hierarchical type of church government composed of bishops and archbishops favored by the English and instead established churches, which were governed by democratically elected synods, presbyteries, and a national assembly. Each Scottish congregation chose its minister and organized church services around scripture, praying, and preaching rather than around what its members considered to be the popish liturgy found in the Anglican Book of Common Order. The Scots established criteria for church membership and the rules under which church members could be disciplined by the local church session. The Scots demonstrated their abhorrence of the ritual and trappings of Catholicism by refusing to kneel and by forbidding ministers to wear vestments. In short, these Presbyterians refused to allow the English to impose royal authority, bishops, and Anglican forms of worship on the national Church of Scotland.

When James VI of Scotland ascended to the English throne in 1603, following the death of Elizabeth I, Scottish resistance became increasingly difficult to sustain. As the head of the Anglican Church, he considered it his duty to impose his spiritual as well as his secular authority on all of his subjects. Charles I, who followed James to the throne, was similarly motivated. The Scots did what they could to thwart the English Crown's efforts to interfere with the way they practiced Christianity. In 1638 Scottish nobles, landowners, ministers, merchants, and common folk signed the National Covenant, documenting their resistance to "popery" and warning the English that the signers would oppose any attempt by the Crown to impose bishops and the Anglican form of worship on Scottish churches.

Charles I responded to this public challenge to his authority by declaring war on the Scots. It was an unfortunate decision on his part. The Scots turned back his attempt to invade, and he found it necessary to call Parliament into session to ask for money to raise another army. A power struggle between the English Crown and Parliament ensued and led eventually to the rise of Oliver Cromwell and to the English Civil War. Taking advantage of the turmoil in England, the Scots signed another document in 1643. In what they called the Solemn League and Covenant, they pledged to do whatever was necessary to guarantee that Scotland remained Presbyterian. Jane believed that her forebears were among the signers.

After Cromwell died and Charles II ascended to the throne, the new king tried to reclaim royal control over the Scottish Church by authorizing four bishops to go to Scotland to impose an episcopalian form of church government on the rebellious Scots. When the bishops arrived, they stripped the Scottish presbyteries, synods, and sessions of their authority and fired all the ministers who refused to acknowledge the king as the head of the Church.

About three hundred ministers and thousands of ordinary Scottish Presbyterians refused to accept the authority of the Anglican bishops and began to abandon their churches to hold services in homes, barns, and open fields. The king and his bishops responded by imposing fines on those who did not attend Anglican services. When this measure proved ineffective, Anglican officials sent soldiers to arrest the stubborn Scots.

Continually hounded by English authorities, the Covenanters finally rose in armed rebellion in 1666. Poorly led, with few weapons and even less money, they were finally defeated in 1679 at the Battle of Bothwell Bridge. The "killing times" followed: many of those who refused to submit to episcopal authority went into hiding as British troops scoured the countryside. If caught, the Covenanters knew that they might well be tortured, tried for treason, and sentenced to die. Some were banished and transported to the New World. Others, including Jane's forbears, fled to Northern Ireland, hoping to escape persecution.[3]

Jane's ancestors settled in Londonderry, a pleasant town surrounded by a low wall and built in the shape of a cross on a hill above the River Foyle. Life was good in Londonderry. English Episcopalians and Scottish Presbyterians lived together in peace, focusing their hostility on the Irish Catholics who lived in the surrounding countryside. Londonderry's wharves were busy, and the townspeople prospered.[4]

But peace and prosperity for the Covenanter Scots were interrupted by events beyond their control. Their faith was tested one more time. In 1689 Irish Catholics rose to support James II, who arrived with troops and ships and laid siege to Protestant strongholds. Never a garrison town, Londonderry was not easy to defend. Its wall was low and overgrown with a tangle of weeds, wildflowers, and dark green moss. The drawbridges were inoperable. Moreover, Londonderry was surrounded by hills, which gave the enemy a decisive advantage. The food supply was limited, and refugees flocked into the town, further straining its resources.

When the king's forces began firing on Londonderry on April 18, everyone from soldiers and artisans to tradesmen and servants rushed to the walls to man the guns. Women and children dodged incoming shells to carry water and ammunition to their defenders. Jane's forebears saw their homes destroyed and their friends and neighbors killed and maimed but stubbornly refused to surrender the town to James and his Catholic allies. Unable to break through the walls, the king's troops resorted to a blockade. They closed off all roads leading to the city and blocked the river with a wooden boom reinforced with cables. When food supplies ran low, the city's defenders began to eat their horses.

Relief seemed imminent when, on June 15, ships sent by people in England who hoped to keep James from reclaiming his throne appeared at the mouth of the river. But these vessels lay at anchor and made no attempt to sail upriver. The sight of the furled sails tormented the people trapped in Londonderry as their situation became more and more desperate. Supplies ran out. Lead-coated brickbats replaced cannonballs. The inhabitants were reduced to eating their dogs. A whelp's paw sold for five shillings, six pence. Sickness and casualties decimated the population. The cellars filled with bodies because no one had the energy or the opportunity to bury their loved ones, and the stench of the dead and

dying filled the air. At the end of July, after more than a month of ago-
nized waiting, two merchant ships accompanied by a frigate finally broke
through the boom and arrived at the quay with food and supplies. The
blockade was broken, and Londonderry was saved, but James II was not
yet defeated.[5]

Jane Grey Cannon's great-great-great-grandfather continued to sup-
port the Protestant cause. When William of Orange eventually defeated
James II at the Battle of the Boyne in July 1690, her ancestor was there.[6]
James fled to the Continent, and peace was restored. The English Crown
established the Anglican Church and imposed a test act, which provided
Presbyterians in Ireland with toleration but did not grant them equality.[7]
The Scots in Londonderry went about the business of rebuilding their
lives and worshiping God as they wished. And they proudly passed down
from generation to generation the stories of their courage, devotion to
God, and resistance to English tyranny.

The port of Londonderry grew into a bustling urban center whose
prosperity was based on the production of linen. Jane's maternal forebears became weavers. It is unclear when they emigrated to America, but
they may have been among the thousands of Scotch-Irish who, dissatisfied with the religious settlement and suffering from a slump in linen
production in the 1770s, found return passage on ships that transported
flaxseed from the American colonies to Ireland.[8] Arriving in such ports as
Philadelphia and Baltimore, many of these immigrants headed to western Pennsylvania, where they settled around what had been Fort Pitt.[9]
Little differentiated them from their frontier neighbors except their commitment to learning, their dedication to their religion, and their sense of
community.

Jane's maternal grandparents, Hance and Jane Scott, settled in Pittsburgh on the north side of Sixth Street between Wood and Smithfield.
There Jane's grandfather built a small log cottage and set up his looms.[10]
The Scotts joined the Oak Alley Covenanter Church, which had been
organized in 1800. The Covenanters in America were no less politicized
than their ancestors in Scotland and Ireland had been. After founding the
Reformed Presbytery of America in 1798, they denounced the U.S. Constitution as an immoral document because it did not establish God's law as
the highest law of the land and because it sanctioned slavery. And in 1800,
the Presbytery passed a resolution forbidding its members to own slaves
or have fellowship with those who did.[11]

On Sundays, Hance Scott and his family attended morning and afternoon services characterized by psalm singing, long prayers, and preach-

ing. During the week, they subjected themselves to Church discipline strictly enforced by their minister and the members of the session. They sat in their pews and watched while those who broke the rules were "sessioned," or publicly humiliated by having their names read from the pulpit, and then suspended from the Church community until Church authorities had been satisfied that the wrongdoers were sorry for their transgressions and had repented their sins. And the Scotts welcomed Church elders into their home to supervise family worship, catechize family members, and, when the time came, determine whether to admit their children to Church membership.[12]

The Cannon side of the family also immigrated from Ireland. Jane's paternal grandfather, Thomas, settled in Pittsburgh with his wife, Agnes, and their children. Jane's father, also named Thomas, was born in 1783.[13] Things did not go well for the elder Thomas in the next few years. In 1787 Agnes abandoned him, and he found it necessary to announce in the *Pittsburgh Gazette* that he would not be responsible for her debts.[14] He apparently remained single, and when his namesake reached adolescence, Thomas Sr. arranged for his son to apprentice as a chair maker. But the boy was willful and rebellious and ran away before his apprenticeship was over. At some point he must have completed his training, however, because he became a master chair maker.[15] In 1806 the younger Thomas leased a piece of land on Water Street between Market and Wood and set up his shop.[16] Two years later, he married Hance Scott's daughter, Mary, in the Covenanter Church in Oak Alley.[17]

The Cannons had seven children, but only one son, William (born in 1812), and two daughters, Jane (born in 1815) and Elizabeth (born in 1821), survived the consumption that plagued the family.[18] Like their parents, Thomas and Mary had their children baptized in the Covenanter Presbyterian Church. And like good Calvinists, the Cannons exposed the children at an early age to the idea that humans were sinful by nature and would never be able to earn a place in heaven through their own efforts. For as long as she lived, Jane was haunted by that thought.

What we know of Jane's spiritual life, we know from the autobiography, *Half a Century*, that she published in 1880, four years before her death. Much of what she wrote about her childhood involved her awareness of her own depravity and her fear of damnation. She remembered being sensitive to the precarious state of her soul as a young child. As she recalled, she learned to read the Scripture, could recite her catechism, and understood the implications of original sin by the time she was four years old. One of her earliest memories was of having a "great awakening" to a sense of her own potential for sin and the unlikelihood that she had been chosen by God to claim a place in heaven when she died. She was, she wrote, "struck motionless" by the conviction that she could never escape from God's "All-seeing Eye" and could never win his approval. She was convinced that "Divine Law was so perfect that" she "could not hope to meet its requirements—the Divine Law-giver so alert that no sin could escape detection."[19]

Churchgoing was an important part of life in the Cannon household. Parents and children regularly attended services at the Oak Alley Church, located only a few blocks away from their home. Smoky Pittsburgh was not a healthy place to live for a family susceptible to tuberculosis, however. So in 1816, shortly after Jane was born, her father subleased his Water Street property for a hefty $450 a year and moved his family to the countryside.[20] In the little village of Wilkinsburg, seven miles outside Pittsburgh, he bought property where the turnpike leading to Harrisburg crossed the road leading to Philadelphia. The routes were heavily traveled, especially in the winter, when wagons carried freight between Baltimore, Philadelphia, and Pittsburgh. Thomas built a log house, whitewashed it, and turned half of it into a general store. In the basement was a spring. A trumpet vine grew all over the chimney side of the house, and the yard was full of lilacs and wild roses.[21] Wilkinsburg had first been settled by Dunning McNair, a Scotch-Irish Covenanter who bought the land in 1789. He laid out the town and built a large stone house and six small stone huts for his slaves sometime around 1790.[22] Until the day she died, Jane had very fond memories of her early childhood in Wilkinsburg, describing it as a sylvan paradise where pink blossoms fell on her as she sat underneath an apple tree in the springtime.[23]

Wilkinsburg may have been a pleasant place to live, but it had no Covenanter Church. Its absence complicated the Cannon family's religious life.[24] The rigid rules of the Covenanter session forbade what was called "occasional hearing": simply put, it was not permissible for Church members and their children to attend services at another church. Mary and Thomas Cannon had previously been sessioned for this transgression, so they spent most Sabbaths during their sojourn in Wilkinsburg at home in serious religious contemplation.[25]

Despite previous punishment, however, the Cannons occasionally flouted the rules and attended the nearby Beulah Presbyterian Church, where services were led by the Reverend John Graham. The Beulah church had a large congregation and conformed closely to the religious regimen established by the Reverend John Black, the Covenanter minister in Pittsburgh.[26] One Sunday when Jane attended this church, the Reverend Graham gave a sermon on the text "Many are called but few are chosen." On the way home, Jane's older brother, William, announced that he "did not believe God called people to come to him while he did not choose to have them come. It would not be fair; indeed, he thought it would be mean." That evening during catechism, he expressed his doubts to his father, and Jane continued to discuss the issue with her brother. The thought that he might be denied entrance into heaven because of his disbelief troubled her, but the issue remained unresolved.[27]

By 1820 western Pennsylvania was in the midst of an economic depression. After the Crash of 1819, the value of Pittsburgh real estate plummeted, and Thomas's title to the Wilkinsburg land was unclear because McNair had mortgaged his original land grant to the Pennsylvania Population Company. Standing on the verge of bankruptcy, the Cannons returned to Pittsburgh in 1821, moved in with Hance and Jane Scott on Sixth Street, and resumed their attendance at Black's church.[28] From then until his death in 1849, Black served as Jane's spiritual mentor.[29]

Born in Ireland in 1768, John Black graduated from the University of Glasgow in 1790 and immigrated to western Pennsylvania in 1797. He was ordained and installed as the first minister of the Pittsburgh Covenanter Church in 1800.[30] A man of great integrity, he was plainspoken and direct. When he preached, Jane wrote, he "seemed always to talk to *me*, and I had no more difficulty in understanding his sermons, than in mastering the details of the most simple duty."[31] Black considered himself as responsible for the intellectual life of his congregants as for their spiritual and moral well-being. A staunch abolitionist, he used communion as an occasion to testify to the sinfulness of slavery. Before he served up the body and blood of Christ, he announced that anyone who had broken any of the Ten Commandments was barred from celebrating the Last Supper. Slowly and systematically, he went through all ten. "When he came to the eighth," Jane wrote in her memoir, "he straightened himself, placed his hands behind him, and with thrilling emphasis said, 'I debar from this holy table of the Lord, all slave-holders and horse-thieves, and other dishonest persons,' and without another word passed to the ninth commandment."[32] Jane remembered him as "a man of power, a profound logician, with great facility in conveying ideas. To his pulpit ministrations," she wrote, "I am largely indebted for whatever ability I have to discriminate between truth and falsehood."[33] The Reverend Black conscientiously tended his flock during good times and bad, comforting them in their bereavement and celebrating births and weddings with them.

Shortly after the Cannons moved back to Pittsburgh, Jane's sister, Mary, died of tuberculosis, and her father began to suffer from the first stages of the dread disease that had already carried away four of his children. When he was no longer able to work, Jane's mother began to spin flax into linen thread. Thomas died in 1827, leaving his wife with a son and two daughters to support. Before he died, he lost his Pittsburgh property because he was unable to pay the ground rent. And when he died the title to his house in Wilkinsburg was still disputed. His estate included only the contents of his chair-making shop and warehouse.[34]

After the funeral, Mary Cannon put Jane to work making lace and painting on velvet. William contributed the family income by making and selling small chairs. And Mary spent her time coloring leghorn and straw bonnets. When the title to the Wilkinsburg house was settled, she moved back to the village and opened a general store.

When Mary became a widow, she was subjected to the scrutiny of Church elders, for there was no longer a man in her household to regulate its affairs, discipline its members, and monitor its spiritual well-being. Jane's brother, William, was about fifteen at the time, on the threshold of manhood. He helped his mother run her store and did the heavy work around the house. An imaginative young man with an interest in technology, he spent his free time fiddling with tools, making fire engines, waterwheels, and other sorts of machinery. He even built a small foundry so that he could cast kettles and toy cannons. But Church leaders, who felt it their duty to advise Thomas Cannon's young widow, were determined that William should learn a trade. Deferring to their authority, Mary apprenticed William to a cabinetmaker.

Like his father, William found his circumstances as an apprentice unendurable and ran away. He boarded a steamboat and headed down river only to die of yellow fever in New Orleans. Jane and her mother were devastated. Until the day she died, Jane held the elders of her Church responsible for his premature death. She deeply resented their unwelcome interference in the life of her family. Their rigid piety, she believed, had interfered with their humanity, and their determination to serve God had prevented them from serving others. Jane wrote in her memoir that William's unhappiness as an apprentice and his tragic death were "dreadful, irreparable, and . . . wholly due to that iron-bedstead piety which permits no natural growth, but sets down all human loves and longings as of Satanic origin."[35]

Jane grew up in a relatively insular environment. The Covenanters did what they could to keep their society closed to outsiders, and as a result she was relatively ignorant of the spiritual lives of those outside her own religious community. Not until her mother enrolled her in the Edgeworth School in Braddock's Field, about twelve miles from Pittsburgh, did she confront the reality that not everyone took religious devotions as seriously as she did.

Founded in 1825, the Edgeworth School was the first educational institution for girls west of the Allegheny Mountains. Intended to produce well-bred young ladies, the school was run by an Englishwoman, Mary Gould Olver, and her husband and attracted students from as far away as New York, Virginia, and Maryland. The students lived and studied in a large brick mansion with wings at either end of the hall and a grand staircase just inside the entryway. The classrooms, dining room, and parlor were on the first floor. The boarders shared whitewashed, sparsely furnished bedrooms on the second floor.[36]

The Covenanters valued education, and Jane was well prepared to continue her studies at Edgeworth. She enjoyed being at the school but was deeply distressed when she saw the young women with whom she attended classes walking on the lawn on Sunday afternoons rather than praying and reading the Bible in their rooms. From her point of view, their behavior was "a desecration of the day." She remained silent but nevertheless understood that her failure to admonish her new friends to give over their free afternoon to the worship of God was a serious moral failure on her part. She later wrote that for her "own share in the violation" she "was painfully penitent."

Feeling penitent was not a new experience. She wrote in her memoir that she experienced much of her early life as "a dreary treadmill of sin and sorrow" during which she spent most of her time repenting for her sins of omission and commission, large and small. "I never could see salvation in Christ apart from salvation from sin, and while the sin remained the salvation was doubtful and the sorrow certain," she wrote.[37]

Jane had spent only about six weeks at Edgeworth when her mother sent for her to come home. She had developed a cough. And because her family had a history of consumption, her mother was concerned about her health.[38] So she returned to Wilkinsburg to continue her schooling with her faith intact, relatively uncorrupted by the secular influence that pervaded Edgeworth.

When Jane was about sixteen, she began to seriously contemplate joining the Church. That possibility brought on a great spiritual crisis. She knew that she believed in Christ but was not sure that hers was what the Covenanters considered a "saving faith." Both willful and stubborn, she

was unwilling to submit to God's judgment but could not face the possibility that she might go to hell. "My whole soul flew into open revolt,"
she wrote. And as she lay awake agonizing over the state of her soul, she
felt increasingly guilty about questioning God's wisdom. She had learned
her Calvinist lessons well. She was, she wrote, convinced that if God was
willing to take care of her, no one could hurt her. But she also recognized
that if he was not so willing, she was on her own. And she truly believed
that "to be accepted by him was all there was or could be worth caring
for." But she did not know how she could receive his grace when her
"heart [was so] full of rebellion."

In the end, she followed the example of her forebears and made a
covenant with God to resolve this problem. His obligation was to prepare
a place for her in heaven and assure a place for her brother, William, as
well. Hers was "to spend my whole life in any labor he should appoint,
without a sign of the approval of God or men." Having given up any
thought of independent agency and made her pledge, she reported that
she fell asleep and "woke in perfect peace," convinced that her proposi-
tion had been accepted and that when it came time for her to die, she
might have some hope of receiving God's grace. She seems to have been
quite aware of the price she might have to pay for her hope of assurance.
It would be no less than that which was demanded of her martyred
ancestors. "I should have all the work and privation for which I had
bargained," she wrote. "[I] should be a thistle-digger in the vineyard;
should be set to tasks from which other laborers shrank." As long as she
did God's bidding, she was convinced that she would never be alone. And
if she did his work well, she would die expecting to "at last hear the welcome 'well done.'" She told no one of her agreement, joined the Church,
and took her first communion listening to the Reverend Black's admoni-
tion, "Let others do as they will, you are to follow the Lamb, through
good and through evil report, to a palace or to a prison; follow him, even
if he should lead you out of the church." In retrospect, she wrote, "no
other act of my life has been so solemn or far-reaching in its consequences, as that ratification of my vow, and it is one I have least cause
to repent."[39]

The first test of her spiritual strength came after her marriage to James
Swisshelm, who came from a Methodist family. His father, John, had
donated the land on which the Methodist meetinghouse stood, reserved
space on the family farm for a camp meeting ground, and opened his
house to circuit-riding preachers who between sermons and revivals conducted baptisms, weddings, and funerals for all the Methodists for miles

around. James's mother, Mary Elizabeth, prayed aloud and shouted during Methodist services when the Holy Spirit moved her to do so. Despite the evangelical nature of that denomination, James was not a church member when he proposed marriage, and he promised Jane that if she married him, he would set up a household separate from that of his parents and allow her to conduct her spiritual life however she saw fit.

Shortly before their November 1836 wedding, however, James became a zealous Methodist. After he and Jane married, he refused to move away from his family's farm to the town of Allegheny, as he had promised, and began insisting that Jane convert to Methodism. Jane was so upset that she refused to move to the Swisshelm family farm and continued to live with her mother. James came to visit her there once or twice a week. The more Jane rejected her husband's pleas to change her religion, the more James and his mother worked to save her from what they considered "the toils of Calvinism." "My kith and kin had died at the stake, bearing testimony against popery and prelacy; had fought on those fields where Scotchmen charged in solid columns, singing psalms; and though I was wax at all other points, I was granite on 'The Solemn League and Covenant,'" she wrote.[40]

Not until 1842, six years after her wedding, did Jane agree to live with James in his mother's house. After moving to the Swisshelm farm, which she called Swissvale, she again found herself pressured to become a Methodist. Circuit-riding preachers who boarded with her mother-in-law earnestly engaged Jane in theological debate and tried to convert her, but she publicly denounced Methodism as a form of "will worship." Methodists, like other evangelicals, rejected the elitism of Calvinism and preached that everyone had the power (or will) to choose God and be saved. True religion, Jane argued, had less to do with individuals and their free will and more to do with obeying "God's law." Methodist churches, she complained, did not have Bibles in their pews, their members were largely uneducated, and many of their ministers could not "repeat the Ten Commandments."

Jane's "heretical" religious opinions and her opposition to the idea of free will offended many of the Methodists who attended the Swissvale chapel, and the circuit-riding ministers came to believe that her outspokenness on religious issues threatened to undermine their control of the Swissvale congregation. To diminish her negative influence on their congregants, the clergymen proposed that a new church be built in Wilkinsburg to replace the small frame meetinghouse that stood on the Swisshelm farm. The prospect of putting some distance between herself and the Swissvale Methodists appealed to Jane, so she did what she could to help raise money for the new chapel. But James and his mother took great pride in the fact that the center of Methodist life was located on their land and opposed the move. Mary Elizabeth in particular was furious at the thought that, as Jane put it in her memoir, the building "which had been to her all that the temple ever was to Solomon, would be left to the owls and bats. . . . Those walls, made sacred by visions of glory and shouts of triumph, would crumble to ruin in the clinging silence." Mary Elizabeth could do nothing to stop the move, and convinced herself, according to Jane, that Jane's "evil" influence had removed the chapel at Swissvale from the center of local Methodist life.[41]

As the tension in the Swisshelm household rose, Jane engaged in a period of tortuous soul-searching. What had she done, she asked herself, to bring down God's wrath on her in this way? In her memoir, she described the anguish that she suffered as her relationship with James deteriorated even further.[42] She eventually concluded that there were two reasons for the difficulties that plagued her.

After the death of her father and brother, Jane had convinced herself that God had taken them from her because she "loved them too much."[43] She now looked to her feelings for James to explain why her marriage had turned into such a nightmare. Jane's God was a jealous God, and she believed that he was "scourging" her "for making an idol" of her husband and "bowing down before it." Such punishment, she maintained, was as "just" as it was painful. The only comfort she could find was in the words "Though he slay me, yet will I trust in him."[44]

Jane also convinced herself that God was punishing her for collaborating with the local Methodists, whom she pejoratively called "Black Gagites." In 1840, shortly after Jane and James married, the Methodist General Council meeting in Baltimore had passed a gag rule in an effort to hold the northern and southern branches of the church together. Under this rule, black church members could not testify against white church members in church trials in any state where it was illegal for blacks to testify in courts. James had attended the conference and returned home deeply disturbed by the new rule, which he considered unjust and un-Christian. He even refused to worship with those who had voted for it. In this matter, Jane agreed with her husband. But as part of her wifely duty and in an effort to put as much distance between herself and the Methodist congregation as she could, she had advised the members of her husband's church about how to raise the funds needed to move their church from Swissvale to Wilkinsburg. She came to believe that because she had helped these Methodists, who put Church politics above Christian duty, God was punishing her.[45]

Covenanter Presbyterianism and her personal relationship with God had a profound impact on Jane's life. They were both a blessing and a curse. Her covenant required that she sacrifice herself in the pursuit of God's work. And while it did not assure her of salvation, it did give her considerable self-assurance. The terms of her covenant set the agenda for her life's work and convinced her that she was ultimately accountable only to God. But accompanying that self-confidence was a distrust of personal attachments and a fear that they might somehow diminish her ability to fulfill the terms of her agreement. Such distrust complicated her personal relationships and made it hard for her to carry out her reform efforts in collaboration with others.

The legacy of the Covenanters gave her the courage to transgress gender boundaries in pursuit of what she believed to be God's will. At the same time, however, this legacy burdened her with a good many conventional ideas about gender. As Calvinists, the Covenanters believed that both men and women were born with inherently sinful natures and were equally likely to receive God's grace. The Covenanters believed that it was presumptuous to try to predict who was ultimately headed for heaven. Therefore, they were obliged to regard each man and woman as potential candidates for salvation. On a spiritual level, then, men and women were equal. Therefore, it was not surprising that Jane's spiritual role models were the "thousands of female martyrs [who] had sealed their testimony with their blood," as she put it.[46]

But despite the belief that men and women were equal in the sight of God, the Covenanters were also social conservatives, and as a result Jane believed that men and women were fundamentally different. She was convinced, for example, that there was such a thing as "feminine delicacy" and that it was not just "an offspring of conventionality, but a principle of nature." She maintained that women were definitely the weaker sex and that while their weakness was often due to what she called the "habits of life," it nevertheless existed. Because women were weaker than men, she believed that they should not be expected to do work that was either heavy or dangerous.[47] She opposed abolishing all legal distinctions based on sex because men and women had different needs. As long as differences between men and women existed, she argued, "there should be a difference in the special enactments intended for each." At the same time, however, she maintained that because women were innately weak, their rights should be guarded and expanded. Only with such tools as the vote would they be able to redress the wrongs imposed on them.[48]

Jane's belief that women should be loving, nurturing, and self-sacrificing completely conformed to prevailing feminine ideals both in the Covenanter community and in much of the country at large. She believed that women were meant to marry and have children. And as a young bride, she did not question the idea that women should accept a dependent status in their households and should submit willingly to their husbands' authority in all matters except those of conscience. She believed that women should be educated in part so they could read their Bibles, worship God, and help their husbands teach their children Christian values. She idealized marriage, believing that it should be a partnership based on mutual respect and emotional compatibility. And because she took literally biblical gender proscriptions, she grew to adulthood giving little thought to women's role in public life outside the church except in matters of charity and benevolence. The idea that women should play a prominent role in partisan politics and should speak out on matters of public policy was not initially a part of Jane's definition of how women should behave. As she put it in 1880, she entered womanhood willing to break her engagement if it meant that her name would appear in print.[49]

Jane's ideas about what constituted "true manhood" were equally conventional. She admired men with imposing physiques, assertive personalities, and good business sense. She idealized those whose sense of civic duty encouraged them to sacrifice their self-interests in pursuit of the public good. And she had a high regard for men whose strength of personality was counterbalanced by sensitivity for the feelings of others. Like her contemporaries, she defined manliness in terms of moral and physical courage, responsibility, sobriety, thrift, hard work, and economic success. And she believed that because men were privileged in American society, they had the obligation to protect the interests of those who were not. Abuse of power on the part of the opposite sex she considered unmanly. "People instinctively judge of a man's quality by his courage and faithfulness in taking care of and protecting women, and instinctively he is felt to be a paltroon in proportion as he uses his strength for her oppression. . . . God has planted in the heart of man an instinct for woman's protection, and in the heart of woman the instinct to claim it, as a counterpoise to the possibility of violence to which her sex subjects her," she wrote.[50]

Jane argues that as a young married woman, she did her best to fulfill conventional gender expectations. Like all "true" women, she married, bore and nurtured a child, and took pride in keeping house. She demonstrated her piety by reading the Bible and attending church as regularly as she was able. In deference to her husband, she gave up activities that gave her personal pleasure, such as painting portraits and reading literature. She claims that it was only in matters of conscience that she refused to submit to his authority.

Despite her good intentions, however, her attempt to conform to prevailing gender conventions failed. As she grew older, she became increasingly disillusioned with the idea that men could be counted on to represent the interests of those in need of their protection. They had certainly done little to protect the interests of slaves, and many women seemed little better off as a result of whatever concern men might have shown.

That growing disillusionment, combined with her difficult personal circumstances and the self-assurance she derived from her covenant with God, encouraged her to thwart or subvert conventional ideas about women's proper place in American society. In her attempt to negotiate a personal definition of what it meant to be a woman, she found it necessary to resolve the conflict between dependence and submissiveness on one hand and self-reliance and assertiveness on the other. Her attempts to carry out God's work allowed her to cross gender boundaries and encouraged her to try to expand women's public role.

But while her religious background may have given her the self-confidence to transgress gender boundaries, it also ensnared her in a web of bigotry. The stories about Covenanter martyrdom at the hands of Anglo-Catholics combined with her religious parochialism made her oblivious to the benefits of religious diversity, deeply suspicious of the power and authority of the Catholic hierarchy, and almost totally ignorant of Catholic theology and ritual. In this she was, of course, not alone. Anti-Catholicism had deep roots in American culture. The Protestants who originally settled the English colonies in the New World were outspoken in their hatred and fear of "popery." Maryland was founded by the Catholic Lord Baltimore, but by the time of the American Revolution, Protestants outnumbered Catholics even there. Widespread concern about the influence and power of the Catholic Church did not appear until the 1820s, when Irish immigrants began to arrive in large numbers. From that time on, anti-Catholic propaganda combined with scattered acts of violence against Catholics and their property fed American Protestant religious prejudices. The result was the rise of a particularly virulent form of nativism. Suspicion of immigrants in general and Catholics in particular took political form when the Know-Nothing Party was organized in 1853. The party's political power was short-lived, but its early successes established a political context in which anti-Catholicism could be expressed.[51]

In 1847, Jane became the editor of the *Pittsburgh Saturday Visiter*. She had previously had little to do with Catholics, and during the first years of her editorship she carefully avoided engaging in sectarian religious debate. In desperate need of subscribers and advertisers, she pledged to respect the religious beliefs of all her readers. As a result, she initially established relatively cordial relationships with the Catholic bishop in Pittsburgh and the editor of the *Pittsburgh Catholic*. In January 1849, for example, she complimented Bishop R. R. O'Conner on his "naturally fine mind" in a review of one of his public lectures and thanked the editor of the *Pittsburgh Catholic* for printing a copy of the *Visiter*'s "Prospectus."[52]

But in the early 1850s, O'Conner came out in favor of using public tax money to support Catholic schools. Jane opposed this plan, arguing that a public school system was necessary to perpetuate republicanism and good citizenship among the whole population—whether it be Catholic, Covenanter, Baptist, or Methodist. She claimed that public funding of Catholic schools would lead to an increase in sectarianism and would drive an even larger wedge between Protestants and Catholics.[53] Despite the fact that she was the product of a religious tradition that was inherently anti-Catholic, she publicly denied that she bore any ill will toward the Catholic Church or its members. "We have," she wrote, "hitherto looked upon that peculiar sect without any more distrust or prejudice than we have felt for other sects differing from us in what we consider non essentials. . . . [W]e have thought its members as free from bigotry as other people." The bishop's campaign to raid public coffers to support parochial education, however, served as a warning. "It can no longer be doubted," she told the readers of her newspaper, "that the policy of the Head of the Church, and of the clergy generally is totally at variance with free institutions."[54]

When the bishop failed to persuade the citizens of Pittsburgh to support Catholic schools with their taxes, he turned his attention to building a cathedral to serve as testimony to the power of the Church and the prosperity of its members. St. Paul's, a physically imposing structure, was completed in 1855. In June, he and his clergy held an elaborate dedication ceremony to celebrate its completion.

By this time, Jane no longer owned the *Pittsburgh Saturday Visiter*, having turned it over to Robert M. Riddle, who changed its name to the *Family Journal and Saturday Visiter* and paid her to write for the editorial page.

The dedication of the cathedral was a newsworthy event, so Jane bought a ticket to the proceedings, attended the ceremonies, and collected material for her weekly column. In her report, she insisted that she had gone to the festivities merely intending "to witness the Catholic mode of worship" and that she had approached her experience with "an earnest desire to look without prejudice" on what she saw. Given her religious background and the nativism that permeated American society, however, it was impossible for her to be a neutral observer. She was both appalled and astonished by the rituals and ceremonies she saw. She arrived early, she wrote, to see outside the church "a little group of men and boys, about a dozen, wearing black petticoats, some with white lace skirts, heavily embroidered, worn over the black [skirts] and descending to the feet." Two boys, she reported, held up "unusually long candles," a man carried a large, highly ornamented cross, and another carried a "gilt crook." "In the center was a little fat man in petticoats with what appeared to be a large, showy cradle quilt pinned around his shoulders. . . . On his head there was a pasteboard cap running up in the shape of a smoothing arm; and not far, we judged from eighteen inches high." From the back of his cap hung "two wide streamers." The "little fat man" held "a gilt ball, the size of a large apple, fastened on one end of a round stick, and the other end he held in his hand." As he walked along he made passes at the walls of the building with the ball, and when he did so, it "emitted a little shower like a watering pot."

Jane further criticized the Catholic dignitaries' appearance, behavior, and rhetoric, describing some of the participants as "ugly" and their facial expressions as "sinister" and "snaky." She characterized their behavior as comical, saying that during the ritual of dedication that took place in the cathedral later in the day, the participants processed to the altar, only to pad "about, hurrying and worrying, weaving in and out, and back and forth, sweating and fussing, nervous and anxious looking, moving sofa, chairs, candles, books, and censers hither and thither, dressing and undressing, bobbing down upon their knees and jerking themselves up again, making signs of the cross as if in a hurry to be done with it."

In addition, she charged that the visiting bishop's sermon of dedication was devoid of intellectual or theological merit. "Bishop Hughes dwelt entirely upon the importance of forms and the beauty of the building," she wrote. "This was his sermon, nothing more. No word about the beauty of holiness, the duty of doing justly, loving mercy or walking humbly with God. No allusion to inner life, or nobler life, or any duties to God and man, except believing in these forms. Of the small matter of salvation from sin he said not a word." At the end of the service, she contended, no one in the procession or in the crowd had "the slightest appearance of devotional feeling." Astonished by the grandeur of Catholic ritual and the pretensions of the clergy, she ended her description by appealing to God to "save us from the power of these men who pretend to represent the majesty of God in their own persons by donning the toggery of a ball-room or buffoon . . . and protect us from the political influence of the men who erect *bonafide* thrones in our land." Unable or unwilling to reflect on the meaning of symbolic action, she dismissed Catholic liturgy and ritual as meaningless and characterized the spectacle as a religious "farce." Those who attended had paid a dollar per ticket. The actors, she said, looked "pompous." And the spectators, hoping to be entertained, she claimed, were there only out of curiosity.[55]

A response from editor of the *Pittsburgh Catholic* was not long in coming. Predictably, he found her description and its publication offensive. For her readers, she excerpted his comments regarding her impressions, a response that focused on the words she used, the vanity and self-absorption that she exhibited, and the degree to which she abdicated her claim to "true womanhood." Describing her article as a "very unlady-like" one, he wrote, "If this woman has a husband, and her tongue is like her pen, the unfortunate fellow deserves to be pitied." He speculated that the cause of her "bad temper" and the impropriety of her criticism was that her "baby" had kept her up the whole night before. And as for her description of the participants, "Who, but a silly girl, perfectly conscious of her own beauty, would enter a Church for the purpose of seeing how handsome, etc., were the people, and make it afterward a matter of conversation?" he asked.[56]

Initially, Jane appears to have been somewhat stunned by the Catholic response to her characterization of the dedication ceremonies. But it would have been out of character for her to have apologized. She took personal pride in her reputation for being unlikely to back down from a fight, particularly when the primary weapons were words. So as the criticism directed toward her mounted, she took an increasingly defensive stand and escalated her insulting rhetoric. She argued that given her Protestant background, her readers could hardly expect her to appreciate or fully understand the symbolic and spiritual implications of what she had observed. As far as she was concerned, her only offense was to have innocently used the wrong words to describe what she saw. She had intended to give her readers, particularly those who were not Catholic, a clear picture of the ceremonies, she explained. So she looked for a way to describe them in terms that non-Catholics could understand. Most of her readers, she pointed out, "live in or in the immediate vicinity of the 'laundry, the bedchamber, and the kitchen,'" so she took it for granted that they would understand what she was saying. If she had used the term "cassock" to describe the garment worn by the celebrants, most of her readers would not have known what she was talking about. But they certainly knew what a petticoat was and could picture a man wearing one.

The real problem, she said, was that her critics were more concerned about form and appearance than about the more important matters of morality, piety, and the quality of their devotional services. "An article which, as a 'petticoat,' is disgraceful and ridiculous in the last degree, as a 'cassock' becomes 'grand, imposing, august' and stupendously magnificent. A thing that is a badge of reproach when called a pasteboard cap, is the emblem of knightly authority when dubbed a 'mitre.' A garment that is disgusting by the names of blanket, quilt, or bed comfort[er], is the very representation of Diety when you call it a 'cope.'" Whatever the name, she argued, the article remained the same.

Jane understood the power of words, and few editors were more facile in the use of them, so it seems inconceivable that she did not understand that names are fraught with meaning. By pejoratively calling a cassock a "petticoat," a mitre a "pasteboard cap," and a cope a "blanket," she discounted these items' sacred and symbolic role in Catholic ritual. Yet throughout the controversy, she disingenuously maintained that she did not understand why anyone would object to her use of the petticoat analogy in her description of the ritual clothing of the Catholic clergy. "There is nothing ridiculous in wearing petticoats," she wrote. "We have worn them over thirty years, and know a great many excellent people who have gone about publicly in the same description of garment, and never think of being injured by a statement of the fact."[57]

Like others in her day, Jane was sensitive to the significance of dress as a gender marker. While she may have been willing to blur gender boundaries in other ways, she was not willing to do so in the matter of dress. The issue had come up a few years earlier when woman's rights advocates such as Elizabeth Cady Stanton, Susan B. Anthony, and Lucy Stone had begun wearing the loose-fitting bloomer costume, arguing that it was a sensible alternative to corsets and tight-fitting dresses with crinolines and hoop skirts. This costume immediately became a symbol of female rebellion against social convention and women's demands for more rights.[58]

Jane opposed the dress-reform initiative for three reasons. On a practical level, she found bloomer dresses ugly, inconvenient, and uncomfortable. The trouser legs irritated her by flapping against her ankles when she walked. And she complained that not only did she have to hold her underwear up by using straps or buttons but that the skirt dragged on the ground when she bent over.[59] She was also convinced that dwelling on the subject of the length of women's skirts diverted attention from more important woman's rights concerns. She was willing, she said, to defend the cause of woman's rights "single-handed against the united armies of a world," but she was not interested in trying to convince other women to wear bloomers. "Those who want to go to Pantaloondom, let them go in welcome," Jane wrote, "but they shall not hitch their burden care to the locomotive of female emancipation if we can prevent it."[60]

Her third objection was based on the same theology that she would eventually use to criticize the apparel of the Catholic clergy. "The law prohibiting one sex assuming the dress of the other was written by the Creator himself . . . and we have no wish to see it repealed," she wrote. "In the animal and vegetable kingdoms the difference of sex is marked by external appearance, and it is altogether proper that man should make no attempt to be an exception."[61] She believed that biblical injunction had established dress as an important gender indicator and that distinctive dress for men and women served as one of the bases for establishing moral and social order. "Who does not see that if sex were not indicated by dress, the most unbridled liberty would be given to the depraved, and to the weak to become so? What would be the state of society if one could not tell whether his neighbor were living with his wife or his brother, or whether the two gentlemen who lodged in No. 72 were a gentleman and a lady, or a pair of maiden aunts to the two gentlemen who lodged in the room adjoining?" she asked.[62]

So in 1855, when she observed members of the Catholic clergy in ritual costumes that resembled women's clothing, she could not help but express the same sense of outrage that she had voiced during the early years of the bloomer controversy. Jane had no tolerance for men wearing women's clothes or the gender ambiguity that the apparel of the Catholic clergy implied. She considered their "long sweeping skirt[s]" to be "womanly apparel." In Corinthians, she pointed out, Paul had specifically designated the sort of dress to be worn by men and by women while at worship. His instructions did not condone the practice of men wearing women's clothing. Moreover, in Corinthians II he had written, "Every man praying or prophesying with his head covered dishonoreth his head." The bishops who presided at the dedication had had their heads covered. Were they men or women? she asked. "If they are men, it is plain they are acting in defiance of a Scripture rule." She also believed that what was good for the goose was good for the gander: "So long as men, and especially Catholic priests, condemn women for wearing pantaloons, there must be a manifest impropriety in their wearing petticoats."[63]

The Catholic clergy in Pittsburgh were not the first to be subjected to the lash of Jane's pen, nor would they be the last. Skilled in the use of sarcasm tinged with biting wit, hyperbole, and satire, she often wrote with a viciousness that was as disturbing in its effect as it was impressive in its power. Rebecca Broadnax Hicks, editor of the *Petersburg (Virginia) Kaleidoscope*, acknowledged the damage that Jane could inflict with her editorial pen, writing, "The lady editress of the *Pittsburg Visitor*, is down upon the Roman Catholics in her last leader. We should not like to be attacked by Mrs. Swisshelm—She wields a pen whose strokes tell wherever they fall. Her pen is cudgel, probe, spear, scarification, long-shooter, blunderbuss, cowhide, or whatever else MRS. JANE SWISSHELM may desire it to be. At all events, it is a powerful weapon, and with it, the lady has just succeeded in flaying and scalping some Roman Catholics up her way."[64]

Whether "flaying" Catholics or "scalping" slaveholders, Jane saw the world through the lens of Covenanter Presbyterianism. Her grandmother's tales of the courage and steadfastness of the Covenanters tied Jane irretrievably to the past and helped to determine her future. Through those stories, Jane became an actor in a drama that spanned three hundred years. Her actions as an adult were in part an attempt to fulfill her personal obligations to God and to live up to the standards set by the Covenanter heroes and heroines who had come alive when her grandmother spoke of them. Whenever Jane seemed to stand alone or to confront what seemed to be overwhelming odds, she would remind herself of the kith and kin who had gone to their deaths singing psalms and thinking only of their duty to God. When principle was involved, she was as uncompromising and obstinate as her forebears. When fighting to defend the rights of those she believed to be in need of her protection, she tried to be as fearless as she believed the old Scottish Covenanters had been. Her "brickbats covered with lead" were her pen, her voice, her press, and the often vitriolic hyperbole and satire that spewed forth from them.

Jane interpreted everything she did and everything that happened to her from a Covenanter reference point. Her religious beliefs gave her a framework for understanding and making a place for herself in the world. They provided her with a set of values with which to critique the society in which she lived and to judge the people with whom she came into contact. And her religious tenets provided her with a literary per-spective and vocabulary that she could use to describe herself and her place in the world to others.

Her ties to her Covenanter heritage both empowered and crippled her. Her religious impulses combined with a highly developed and rigid sense of right and wrong helped to assure that she would make her mark on the world. But they also made her difficult to live with and sometimes impos-sible to deal with. As a result, she was beloved by some but loathed by others, a generally well-meaning but inflexible woman whose judgment was sometimes clouded by a rigid adherence to principle that did not measure the cost to herself and others.

CHAPTER TWO

A

MARRIAGE

FRAUGHT

WITH

CONFLICT

Whenever two are really weary of each other, they are no longer married; and nobody can marry them. . . . It is a base prostitution of the name and object of marriage to bind two to live together contrary to the will of either. Nor can we see how society can possibly be benefitted by an arrangement which compels the semblance of marriage where the reality does not exist.

When families are reared without the ligaments of genuine wedded love between the parents to bind the members to home and one another, they will be a curse rather than a blessing to the community. We sincerely believe, twenty divorces for every one we now have would greatly benefit the parties most concerned, and society in general. We can see no reason why a mistake in forming a marriage partnership should effect any ones reputation a bit more than an error in any other partnership; but whatever blame is due to making *a union that is a libel upon truth and nature,* breaking *it must be a duty. If it be necessary to protect the public from laxity in marriage laws, let the unfortunate victim of misalliance be condemned to imprisonment, exile or simply hanging— something less than the capital punishment of spending a life in a mockery of marriage with an unloved, hated object.*

We cannot tell how any one could wish to retain a legal claim to the person or society of a companion, when all heart interest is gone! We would not, could not live with a husband we thought would rather be free! Could not bring ourself to retain a claim upon him which his heart repudiated; but would sew the button on his clothes, pack his trunk, give him free papers and our blessing any day. Mutual consent forms the bond of marriage, and when that ceases the marriage is at an end! No legal enactments can bind them together and make their lives any thing else than legal prostitution; and the State cannot be benefited by what is a crime in the individual!

Jane Grey Swisshelm, "Marriage," Pittsburgh Saturday Visiter, *August 18, 1849, p. 122.*

Jane Swisshelm did not sew a button on her husband's jacket, pack his trunk, and send him away. Instead, after more than twenty years of marriage, she gathered together her own belongings and with her five-year-old daughter in tow deserted the man with whom she had pledged to spend her life. Considering herself "the unfortunate victim of misalliance," she would not "be condemned to imprisonment." She would take no part in "base prostitution." She gave James his "free papers"—but in the process, she gave them to herself as well.

James Swisshelm was a farmer, hardworking, tall, and strong, who loved the land that his young wife called Swissvale. By all accounts, the farm where he spent most of his life was a beautiful piece of property, nestled low in a valley dotted with trees. The house where the Swisshelms lived was a two-story log cabin with three first-floor rooms, each with its own fireplace. It had a good kitchen. A stream ran by the house, through the millrace, and then down a spillway overflowing with catfish. In the yard, willows waved gracefully in the breeze. And not far away from the house, a good double barn sheltered the livestock. Nearby were a mill and smith shop. In the spring, the orchard was filled with the delicate fragrance of the blossoms of two hundred apple trees. It was a quiet and peaceful place. Only the rush of water, the songs of the birds, the chirp of the crickets, and the rustle of the breeze in the trees disturbed the silence on a quiet day. It was a place where a man could see the sky, hear himself think, and plan for the future. There James and his three brothers and two sisters grew to adulthood. James's goal in life was to be a good Methodist, to work the land, to improve it, and finally to inherit it. His 1836 marriage to Jane Grey Cannon was held hostage and then sacrificed to achieve those ends. He was in his mid-sixties, married to his second wife, with whom he had a son, James, when his mother finally died and he became master of Swissvale.[1]

If ever there were two incompatible people, they were James Swisshelm and Jane Grey Cannon. Even in appearance, they were an incongruous-looking couple. He was a big man—over six feet tall, well built, and muscular. His eyes were black, and his hair and whiskers were as dark as his eyes. His swarthy face was long, his countenance grave.[2] She was delicate looking, small and slender. Her forehead was broad and high. She wore her dark brown hair pulled back from her face and wound in a bun at the back of her neck. She had large, light, gray-blue eyes, a rather prominent nose, and a small mouth with thin lips.[3]

James and Jane were equally dissimilar in temperament. A man of few words and little imagination, James relied on God, experience, practical

Jane Grey Swisshelm as a young woman, ca. 1840. (Self-portrait, courtesy of the Library and Archives Division, Historical Society of Western Pennsylvania, Pittsburgh)

knowledge, and common sense rather than intellect to get him through life. He was a man for whom formal education had no importance. If he read anything, he read his Bible. His reserved manner was relieved by his hearty laugh. Jane was just the opposite. She was energetic and lively, contentious and self-righteous. Her emotional intensity was balanced by a splendid sense of humor. Blessed with an aesthetic sense and an inherent understanding of the power of language, she was talkative, artistic, and creative. She loved to read, to paint, and to write.

Their backgrounds did nothing to make them more compatible. James was the son of a soldier, John Swisshelm, who had spent the winter of 1778 at Valley Forge with George Washington. John married after the war, receiving a farm as a wedding present from his new father-in-law. After giving birth to three sons, his wife died. John married again, this time to a much younger woman; brought his new wife, Mary Elizabeth, to Pennsylvania; and bought the 162 acres and 19 perches that comprised what the locals called Nine Mile from William and Margaret Pollock in 1808 for the impressive sum of one thousand pounds. There the couple had six children—four sons (Samuel, James, William, and Henry) and two daughters, both of whom eventually married into the neighboring McKelvey family.[4] The Methodist community to which the Swisshelms belonged was evangelical and egalitarian. It welcomed anyone who was willing to choose Christ as his or her savior, had little regard for an educated ministry, and chose leaders from among those who could evoke an awakening of the Holy Spirit in others.[5]

The focus of Jane's world was that of urban commerce. When Jane was born in 1815, Pittsburgh was a town of about five thousand inhabitants.[6] The river system, which provided both transportation and power, and the rich coal deposits in the surrounding hills allowed business leaders to add an industrial component to the city's commercial base. Noted for its production of glass, textiles, and iron, Pittsburgh was on its way to becoming a bustling city.[7] Its streets, fanning out from the point where the Allegheny and Monongahela Rivers met and connected to each other by small alleys, were filled with the rumble of drays, carts, wagons, and carriages; cries of peddlers hawking their wares; the snorting of pigs foraging for garbage; the barking of dogs; and the laughter and screams of children playing in the street—when they were not working. Crossing the streets, pedestrians might have to dodge an auctioneer selling horses as he galloped by, taking bids from bystanders.[8]

Some of the streets were paved and lit, but most were not. According to a city directory, "unless it be in the dry time of mid-summer, a lady's slipper cannot be worn after more than one promenade in the streets, with any moderate deference to neatness and fashion. Even the more mire-defying, water proof boots of the gentlemen run great risk of having their polish so much sullied, by an attempt to cross one of the avenues, as to be utterly unfit for public exhibition before they have received another varnishing."[9]

The air was filled with smoke and a fine, dark soot that coated everything in sight. Only the most persistent of sunbeams could make their way through the grimy windows of the shops and homes that lined the streets. Laundry, hung inside or out, was soiled before it had time to dry. Carpets, walls, and furniture were impossible to keep clean. Anne Newport Royall, an American journalist who visited the city in 1828, wrote that no one in Pittsburgh wore much white. The ladies, she reported, "mostly dress in black" and the "cap or white ruff" that was "put on clean in the morning" was soiled and "tinged quite black by bed time."[10]

Jane Cannon and James Swisshelm grew up not far from one another, but to some degree they lived in different worlds. She claims that they met, quite literally, by accident. On her way to boarding school at Edgeworth, the wagon in which she was riding plunged off the road in the dark and into the stream that ran along side the Swisshelm farm. Hearing cries from the rushing water, James appeared on the bank to rescue the travelers. Jane described him as little more than an overgrown boy, "beardless, with a long swarthy face, black hair and keen black eyes." Laughing at their predicament, he jumped into the water, rescued the driver and passengers, and took them all home to dry off. They were met by his mother, Mary Elizabeth, who ushered them into the house and sat them down before a roaring fire. When they were ready to proceed on their journey, James accompanied them over the bridge that crossed the stream and sent them on their way.[11]

Jane met James again a few years later at a frolic held after a quilting bee. She instantly recognized him as the man who had saved her from drowning in the stream. "He was handsomely dressed," she remembered, "and his manner that of a grave and reverend seignor. A Russian count in a New York drawing room, then, when counts were few, could not have seemed more foreign than this man in that village parlor, less than two miles from the place of his birth." She next saw him on horseback. To her, he was impressive, "this man of giant strength in full suit of black, riding a large spirited black horse." Even in her old age, years after they were divorced, she still thought of him as her "black knight."

The approach James took to courtship was, to say the least, unusual. The night they were formally introduced at the quilting party, Jane says that he announced that he planned to make her his wife. His abrupt proposal must have come as something of a shock to such a conventionally reared young woman. Despite the fact that her suitor had informed her that she was to wed rather than asked for her hand in marriage, she appears to have been enchanted by James's dark good looks and flattered—perhaps even a bit overwhelmed—by his sense of purpose when it came to proposing marriage. "He had elected me as his wife some years before," she wrote, "and had not kept it secret; had been assured his choice was presumptuous, but came and took possession of his prospective property with the air of a man who understood his business." Jane found James's forthrightness extremely romantic. She appears to have been swept off her feet.

Despite James's determination to make Jane his wife, they did not marry right away. Jane's sister did not think as highly of James as Jane did. In fact, according to Jane, Elizabeth "hated him." And Jane's mother was not at all sure that she wanted her daughter to marry a Methodist. So the young couple courted for two years.[12]

Nineteenth-century courtship rituals were highly gendered affairs. While men were expected to initiate courtship, women set the parameters that controlled its conduct. Tentative is the word that best describes the progress of most romantic relationships between young men and women. Generally speaking, neither a man nor a woman was willing to be entirely candid about his or her feelings or intentions early on in their relationship. Part of the reason for this is that added to the fact that many courting couples did not know each other well, most had every reason to fear that they might be disappointed if not humiliated if they let their feelings be known. The thought of rejection was enough to make young men and women quite careful about expressing their true feelings toward one another.[13]

We know very little about James and Jane's courtship and nothing about their feelings for each other during that time. Over the objections of her family, however, they married on November 18, 1836.[14] The Reverend John Black officiated and probably preached a wedding sermon that followed the pattern of those preached by his western Pennsylvania colleagues. Like the Reverend Samuel Wilson of the Big Spring Presbyterian Church, Black no doubt pointed out that marriage was intended to prevent fornication and to produce "legitimate offspring, and a seed for the church." He would have admonished both husband and wife to love one another, be faithful to each other, keep each other's secrets, and tend to their children's spiritual and physical well-being. He would have ordered James to "be the head of the family" and to maintain the authority that God had given him but to resist the temptation to treat his new wife "in a tyrannical manner, much less as a slave." The minister would have told Jane to be her husband's frugal and industrious "helpmeet and a bosom companion" and to acknowledge his God-given authority over her. Should there be any disagreement between them, Black would have advised Jane to use persuasion and reason to convince James that he was wrong. But if she failed in her efforts, she would have been admonished to submit to her husband except when matters of conscience were at stake.[15]

Had the couple been married by a Methodist circuit rider, he would undoubtedly have told them much the same thing. Methodists, like Presbyterians, expected a wife to promote her husband's physical and emotional well-being, to encourage him to be a useful member of society, to satisfy his sexual needs, to spare him financial embarrassment, and to provide a home for him that would give him a peaceful sanctuary from the outside world. She was supposed to refrain from criticizing or contradicting him, was never to demand too much of his attention, and was to avoid at all costs any word or deed that would wound his vanity.[16] In return, a husband such as James was expected to responsibly carry out his own quite different and equally gendered set of obligations and responsibilities. As the head of the household, he was supposed to love, support, and protect his wife and children; judiciously to mete out whatever disciplinary measures were necessary to maintain order in the household; and to represent the family's interests in the public sphere through voting and holding office. In their marriage sermons, ministers simply reminded their congregations that sexual difference had social consequences and that marriage was one of the sites where gender distinctions were most obvious.

Marriage was central to the construction of gender in American life. Maturity in a man was measured in part by his willingness to embrace marriage, his success in convincing a woman to be his wife, and his ability to support a household. Single men were regarded as suspect, and women who for whatever reason remained single were considered by many of their contemporaries as somehow inadequate, as having failed on some fundamental level to fulfill their feminine destiny.[17]

One of the most troubling issues confronting ministers, lawyers, and social critics, however, was that ideals of marriage were in a state of transition in the early nineteenth century. During the seventeenth century and much of the eighteenth, marriage was an inherently unequal relationship in which men held most of the power. The ideal marriage may have been viewed as a partnership in the sense that men needed women as much as women needed men to survive and flourish economically, socially, and emotionally. But under the law, the husband was always the senior partner. As a married man and householder, he could claim the right to vote and hold office. And as the guardian of his wife, children, and servants, he could rule his home with an iron rod if he so chose. In return for a husband's support and protection, a woman gave up her legal identity. As far as the courts were concerned, a wife and her husband became one in the eyes of the law, and that "one" was "him." As a result, the price a woman paid for the prestige and respectability of being married was the loss of her legal existence under common law. Once married, she no longer had a right to her body, a right to her property, a right to her wages, or a right to custody of whatever children she might bear.[18] Getting married meant that a woman could expect to spend the rest of her life subordinating herself to her husband's power and authority.

Because of these circumstances, social critics with feminist sensibilities had long equated marriage with slavery. Mary Astell and Mary Wollstonecraft, both English writers, had used slavery as a metaphor to describe women's position in eighteenth-century British society. In the early nineteenth century, woman's rights advocates, many of whom were abolitionists, simply borrowed the metaphor.[19]

By the time that Jane and James married, however, this patriarchal model of marriage was being replaced by a new ideal that historians have called the companionate marriage. More egalitarian than hierarchical, this type of marriage was characterized by a mutual sense of understanding and sympathy between husband and wife that deemphasized a husband's power within the household. Jane was caught between the two models. Her Covenanter background prepared her to accept James as the head of the household—at least in theory. But Jane was strong willed, so it was a struggle for her to submit to the authority of anyone other than God. It is not surprising, then, that she found the idea of a companionate relationship more congenial. "A marriage union," she wrote, "should be on terms of perfect equality, and that arrogance and usurpation, that have taught man to expect slave like submission from his wife, have unfitted him to be the husband of a woman with a soul."[20]

Jane wrote that she cried while she was dressing for her wedding and then cried again the next day as she was preparing to visit James's parents, but she did not explain the reasons for her tears.[21] She may have anticipated being homesick. She may have been anxious about her ability to fulfill her obligations as a wife. There certainly was much about which any nineteenth-century woman could be anxious. For many women, choosing to marry was the only really important decision they had the opportunity to make, and the possibilities for making a mistake were endless.

In a stream of cautionary tales, domestic novelists outlined the various pitfalls inherent in choosing a husband, warning readers that after marrying, a woman who had spent her youth sheltered in her father's home was as likely as not to discover that her husband had misrepresented himself, drank too much, or had gambled away his income and her inheritance. He might be unloving or unlovable.[22] When the wedding was over, a woman who found that she had made a mistake in choosing her husband was largely without recourse. Until the mid–nineteenth century, the law in most states denied women control over whatever property they brought to their marriages as well as that which was subsequently inherited or earned. Running away was an unrealistic solution to the problem because it required women to find refuge elsewhere and be prepared to support themselves and their children. And seeking a divorce was not only difficult and expensive but also potentially socially humiliating and ruinous to a woman's reputation.

For middle- and upper-class women, choosing the wrong husband was easy. Relatively isolated in the home and prohibited from participating on an equal basis with men in public life, such women had little opportunity to observe their future husbands outside of the domestic environment, which was essentially controlled by women. Courtship may have become increasingly unsupervised as the century progressed, but it was still conducted in a location that clearly put the prospective bridegroom on display, demanded that he at least temporarily conform to female-dictated social conventions, and denied his future bride the opportunity to see him in alternative environments such as his place of work or the places where he and his male friends entertained themselves.[23]

Because courting men and women were on their best behavior, the courtship process was not likely to give a woman the type of information she needed to make a judicious and informed decision about whether to marry a particular man. She was not likely to have accurate information about his drinking habits and leisure pursuits. And while it was her father's responsibility to inquire into a prospective son-in-law's financial situation, she could easily marry with little or no understanding of the way her fiancé managed his money. In fact, she had very few reliable ways to assess the real nature of her future husband's character.

Of course, men faced essentially the same problem. They were unlikely to be subjected to displays of female temper, contempt for male authority, or indications of female independence during courtship. But while such knowledge might have been useful in helping them anticipate what marriage might really hold in store, there was some reason for them to ignore and discount such lack of knowledge. Their manhood was, after all, tied to their confidence in their ability to demand that their wives conform to their expectations. Underlying that confidence was the law, which acknowledged a householder's power to discipline his dependents.

When women married, their lives changed in fundamental ways. Even under the best of circumstances, marriage meant an end to the pleasures and relative freedom of girlhood. Married women had to assume primary responsibility for the physical, emotional, and moral well-being of others. Marriage was often accompanied by separation from family, anxiety about fulfilling the duties expected of a wife, and fear of the dangers inherent in childbearing. Marriage had the potential to enrich a woman's emotional life. In the best of all possible worlds, marriage could offer companionship, assurance of financial support, and physical intimacy. The best marriages were characterized by a mutual respect and reciprocity that led to a satisfying partnership full of love, kindness, and trust. But marriage also restricted women's freedom on a day-to-day basis.[24]

There is no way to know what James was thinking on the day he married Jane. In some ways, it must have been a day of triumph: he had waited patiently for two years to make her his bride. At the same time, however, it is possible that he also approached marriage with a certain degree of anxiety.

In some respects, a man entered marriage assuming that some aspects of his life would probably remain the same. In theory, marriage merely meant that he exchanged the practical services and nurturing love of his mother for those of a wife. Instead of resisting his mother's attempts to control his behavior, he now had to resist his wife's similar, if somewhat less direct, attempts to do the same thing. But marriage also changed a man's life in fundamental ways. It meant exchanging the casual companionship of male friends for that of an intimate confidant and sexual partner. The married state provided a man with new opportunities to exercise power. Wives and children were more easily dominated and controlled than were mothers, sisters, and friends. Marriage brought with it the practical need to prove his manhood by supporting a family and the psychological opportunity to use that support as a sign of commitment and love, an inevitable source of some concern in an economic climate characterized by boom-and-bust cycles. Marriage and the parenthood that usually accompanied it might restrict a man's freedom to do what he pleased with his time and his money, but they also held out the promise of a peaceful home as a haven from the rigorous competition of the business world and a wife and children whom he could expect to love and respect him.[25]

Being a married man clearly had its attractions. Social convention and the law granted a husband considerable power and authority over his wife and children, but it was not necessarily always easy to exert that authority. Wives might love and respect their husbands, but those women with a propensity to exert their independence were not always willing to obey. And when they did not, the married state could become a source of considerable frustration, humiliation, and public embarrassment for their husbands.

There is no reason to believe that James harbored anything other than very conventional ideas about how marriage might affect his life. When he married, he appears to have expected Jane to defer to his authority, get along with his mother, educate his brothers, bear his children, cook his meals, clean his house, and conserve his assets in whatever home he chose to provide for her. As it turned out, he was culturally, emotionally, and intellectually unprepared to deal with the woman he had chosen as his wife. He does not seem to have been either uncaring or unloving, but from Jane's point of view, he proved incapable of expressing his love in a way that she could understand, thus making it difficult for him to satisfy her emotional needs.

Their marriage got off to a rocky start. Jane wrote that James deeply resented the tears she shed at the time they wed. His refusal to move with his new wife to Allegheny as he had promised further strained their relationship. He may have had good reason for reneging on his pledge. His father was in his eighties. Samuel, the brother closest to James in age, had set up a business, and James's other brothers were still too young to run the farm. So, he argued, the time was not right for leaving Swissvale, and he assured Jane that his mother would welcome his wife into the Swisshelm home. Moving to Swissvale might have been accomplished with little trouble had he not accompanied his request that Jane share housekeeping with his mother with the demand that Jane become a Methodist. Shortly before their wedding, James experienced a religious conversion and became, according to Jane, "quite zealous" in his religious enthusiasm.[26]

Religious conversion experiences were common among Methodist evangelicals. Indeed, such an experience was necessary for church membership. The complicating factor in this case was that in choosing to accept God's grace, James accepted the obligation to convince others to do the same. To accomplish this task, no stone could remain unturned, no effort could be too onerous, no resistance could be too great. So one of the first tests of James's husbandly authority was to make Jane obey his demand that she convert to Methodism and join his church.

Given her background as a Covenanter, it is not surprising that Jane refused. "I was obstinate," she wrote. "I would not get religion, would not preach, would not live in the house with his mother, and stayed with my own." For her, it was a matter of conscience, and because it was a matter of conscience, she considered herself exempt from the injunction that she obey her husband's demands. So she remained in her mother's house. The two younger Swisshelm boys came there so that she could supervise their education, and James visited once or twice a week.[27]

During the next summer, Jane's mother took an extended trip and offered to let the newly married couple live in her house in Wilkinsburg while she was gone. James did not move in, however. Instead, he bought property in the village, sent a hired man to board with Jane, and continued to live with his mother, visiting Jane when he had the time and inclination. Jane's mother had previously refrained from interfering in her daughter's marital affairs, but when Mary Cannon returned from her travels to find James still living at Swissvale, she was indignant at what she considered her son-in-law's disgraceful behavior. She made it clear that Jane was welcome to stay and advised her daughter to refuse to see her husband.

Jane had been married for less than a year. Embarrassed about her unconventional living arrangements, she hoped she could redeem her relationship with James. So she left her mother's house and moved into the house James had just purchased in Wilkinsburg. For some reason, James did not join her there. He simply continued to visit her once a week, bringing supplies from his mother's larder for her use. Living alone left Jane with time on her hands. When an itinerate painter made his way through Wilkinsburg, she visited his temporary studio. Convinced that she had found her vocation, she began a portrait of her husband. Painting consumed her. When she held a paintbrush in her hand, she was oblivious to everything else. She forgot to fix dinner, forgot to stoke the fire, and let "the bread run over in the pans." Her obliviousness to her domestic responsibilities made her feel guilty. She had not yet accepted the idea that a woman had as much right to self-expression as a man, so, she wrote with some resentment, "I put away my brushes; resolutely crucified my divine gift, and while it hung writhing on the cross, spent my best years and powers cooking cabbage."[28]

She also claimed to have sacrificed her love of books on the altar of marriage. Jane was willing to acknowledge that manliness was tied to the belief that the wifely deference that a husband had the right to expect depended to some degree on his ability to demonstrate his superiority to her. But Jane seems to have believed that James was her intellectual inferior. "I knew from the first that his education had been limited," she wrote. Like many young wives, in love and optimistic about the future, she assumed that her husband's defects "would be easily remedied." She apparently misjudged the situation. Not only was James indifferent to her interest in art, but it became painfully obvious to her that "he had no love of books." Theirs was not to be a relationship based on shared intellectual interests. Jane seems to have concluded that for her to pursue her love of art and literature demeaned and embarrassed her husband. "An uncultivated husband could not be the superior of a cultivated wife," she wrote in her memoir, so she gave up reading all books except the Bible. "I must be the mate of the man I had chosen; and if he would not come to my level, I must go to his," she added.

Jane continued to live apart from her husband until the spring of 1838, when she convinced James to lease his mills at Swissvale and move downriver to Louisville, Kentucky, to work with his brother, Samuel. Moving to Louisville did not solve the couple's problems, however. The Swisshelms did not set up their own household, and James failed to flourish as a businessman. Arriving in Kentucky in the midst of a depression, they rented rooms in a boardinghouse. All over the country businesses were failing, and those in Louisville were not exempt. Victims of bad timing and an unsettled economy, Samuel and James went bankrupt.[29]

Bankruptcy posed a powerful challenge to a man's gendered identity. Conducting business honorably and profitably established the basis for the definition of what it meant to be a man. When a man failed in business, it was considered a personal failure. No one gave much thought to the larger economic forces that might be involved.[30] As a result, bankrupts such as James were, in a sense, stripped at least temporarily of their masculinity. To make things worse, James decided to sell the property he had purchased in Wilkinsburg to provide the capital for Jane to set up a corset- and dressmaking business so she could be the breadwinner.

Jane found this reversal of gender roles completely unacceptable. She had married expecting her husband to provide her a home and to support her. She had sacrificed both her art and her pleasure in reading to preserve what she felt to be the fiction of man's superiority to woman. After three years of marriage and the sacrifices she had made to keep herself in the kind of sphere considered proper for a wife, she found herself in circumstances that she felt degraded both of them. He was supposed to be the breadwinner, not she. "If it was my duty to keep his house," she wrote, "it must be his to find me a house to keep, and this life must end. I would go with him to the poorest cabin, but he must be the head of the matrimonial firm. He should not be my business assistant. I would not be captain with him for lieutenant."[31]

She was determined to "extricate" herself from the situation, but the opportunity to do so did not present itself until August 1839, when she received a letter calling her home to take care of her mother, who was dying of cancer. Much to Jane's amazement, James refused to give her permission to leave Louisville. An argument ensued, with James quoting a passage from Ephesians that said "Wives submit yourselves unto your own husbands as unto the Lord" and threatening to use his legal right to detain her. When it became apparent that nothing would dissuade her from leaving, he agreed to book her passage back to Pittsburgh. But when he failed to return from the ticket office, she bought her own ticket and left him in Louisville to fend for himself.[32]

James eventually joined Jane in Pittsburgh. After Mary Cannon's death in January 1840, however, he returned to Louisville to settle his affairs and then followed his brother to Little Rock, Arkansas. Left to her own devices, Jane was at loose ends and in need of employment. A distant relative, Isaiah Niblock, eventually invited her to live in his household and arranged for her to serve as headmistress and teacher at a girls' school in Butler, Pennsylvania, where she earned the "munificent" sum of twenty-five dollars a month.[33]

In the spring of 1842, James was back at Swissvale, and Jane finally agreed to move to the Swisshelm homestead. The transition from independent schoolteacher to compliant daughter-in-law was not easy. Both Jane and James's mother were exceptionally strong willed. So it was in some ways predictable that a power struggle would ensue as both women tried to work out their relationships to each other and to James. Jane wrote in her memoir that James and his mother expected her to do heavy farm work out of doors. She considered it to be man's work and refused. Mary Elizabeth found fault with Jane's housekeeping skills, and to demonstrate who was in charge of the garden and land surrounding the house, James's mother ordered Jane's favorite willow tree dug up and transplanted in the swamp. Jane challenged her mother-in-law's authority by planting another tree and then had to stand by and watch while it too was removed at Mary Elizabeth's insistence. Not one to give up easily, Jane planted some willow twigs in the ground. They were left alone.[34]

After Jane had moved into the Swisshelm homestead, the campaign to convince her to convert to Methodism resumed, and she continued to resist pleas that she give up her Covenanter beliefs. Jane's role in the removal of the meetinghouse, whether real or imagined, did nothing to endear her to her mother-in-law or her husband.

After the Methodists moved their church to Wilkinsburg, Jane escaped the increasingly unhappy household during the day by teaching school in the abandoned church on the Swisshelm farm. While Jane was working with her students, Mary Elizabeth complained constantly to her son about Jane's perceived failings as a daughter-in-law, wife, and house-keeper. James apparently decided that he had had enough, and one day, as Jane lay writing on the bed, he burst into their room and berated her for such things as spending the butter money without his permission, not keeping track of the pickles and preserves, failing to keep the house neat and tidy, and wasting her time gossiping. Her disrespect for his mother and her scandalous behavior were disgraceful, he told her. He accused her of humiliating him and so undermining his reputation that he was ashamed to show his face in public.[35]

Caught between his loyalty to his mother and his love for his wife, James found himself in an impossible position. His outburst that day clearly had as much to do with his sense of inadequacy as a husband as with Jane's alleged failures as a housewife. Wilkinsburg was a small community where everyone knew a great deal about their neighbors' business. James must have found the public interest in his domestic problems extremely embarrassing.

After their confrontation, Jane returned to school. But as the day progressed, she began to dread going home. She found refuge with neighbors and spent the night at their farm. She claimed that when she woke them with her sobs that night, they offered to take her in permanently. When James came to school the next day to look for her and apologize for his tirade, she burst into tears, dismissed her pupils, and fled to the woods. She spent that night at the home of another neighbor. Her brother-in-law appeared the next day to play the role of mediator and offered to take Mary Elizabeth to live with him. Jane returned to Swiss-vale after school the next evening but found her mother-in-law still ensconced in the house.[36]

Jane's desperately unhappy marriage, her inability to get along with her mother-in-law, and her sense of outrage at the way she was being treated prompted her to begin thinking in a systematic way about the general condition of married women in America. When she began editing the *Pittsburgh Saturday Visiter* in 1847, she found a platform from which she

could publicly demand changes in women's legal status and in gender
relations that would result in more opportunities for women to pursue
their own interests and assert their independence from men.

One of the ways that she explored the possibilities for changing the
gender conventions that helped to define what it meant to be a woman
was through fiction. Jane needed material to fill the literary columns of
her newspaper, but she lacked the money to pay others to write copy for
her. She clipped poems, stories, editorials, and articles out of the newspapers on her exchange list and republished them. But she also wrote and
then serialized her own stories, all of which can be classified as domestic
fiction in the sense that they explore issues facing women.

One of her first lengthy pieces of fiction was "The Locust's Song."
Published between July and December 1849, it tells the tale of a loveless
marriage and suggests strategies for dealing with its consequences.[37] The
heroine of Jane's story is Susan Morrow, a quiet and demure young
schoolmistress who marries Judge Horace Watson. Like James, Horace is
an attractive man—"unusually tall, with large muscular frame, swarthy
complexion, bushy black hair and whiskers, small black eyes, and nose of
the Roman form." But he is also "a stern, calculating, and matter-of-fact
moralist" who never "talked of love." Horace admires Susan immensely
but is determined never to praise her lest she become vain and conceited.
The new bride displeases her husband on the day of their wedding by
crying at the thought of leaving home.

Susan is willing to be the model subservient wife and to exhibit the
forbearance of a saint, but her good intentions are sorely tried by her
husband's sister, Matilda, who is determined to continue to control his
household. Together, Horace and Matilda conspire to cut Susan off from
her family and friends and exploit her labor while they demean and insult
her. Matilda refuses to give Susan the keys she needs to run the household and orders Susan's favorite honeysuckle cut down. Both Horace and
Matilda pressure Susan to give up her belief in Calvinism, "get religion,"
and join the Methodist Church. As she and her husband become increasingly estranged, Susan begins to feel herself "an unloved and unloving wife."

In desperation, Susan runs away from Horace and supports herself by
teaching school. Horace advertises in the area newspapers, summoning
her to appear before the court to "show cause why her husband should
not have a divorce." Susan does not contest the divorce. Indeed, she finds
exhilarating the idea of owning herself. As a divorced woman, Jane wrote,
Susan would be as "*free*, emancipated, disenthralled, as the American

slave when he touches British soil." Susan moves into her own home, opens an infant school, and lives happily as a divorced woman.

"The Locust's Song" is transparently autobiographical. Susan is clearly a mirror image of Jane—hardworking, sensible, romantic, loyal, willing to make sacrifices to preserve her marriage. James is portrayed as Horace Watson—loving but incapable of showing it, unwilling to transfer his primary loyalty from his family to his wife, critical of his wife but filled with admiration for her abilities, and jealous of her love for others. The suspicious, domineering, and manipulative Matilda represents Jane's mother-in-law, a woman willing to engage in an exaggerated form of passive-aggressive behavior to maintain her power.

Through these characters, Jane reviewed her marital history, explored her relationship with James and his mother, verbalized her deepest anxieties, and confessed her feelings of vulnerability in a milieu that distanced her from them and gave her some power to control them. Writing "The Locust's Song" allowed her to create a vocabulary and a social context for exploring her options. As an author, she could control the narrative and play out her fantasies of escape without having to accept real responsibility for the consequences of having done so. Social, religious, and legal conventions demanded that she martyr herself to her circumstances and suffer in silence whatever unhappiness she was experiencing. Literature gave her both a voice and protection from the consequences of using it. Through the publication of a piece of fiction, she could both express and displace her desire to declare her independence.

Jane published "The Locust's Song" at a time when the status of women in American society had become the subject of widespread public debate.[38] By suggesting that women had the right to remove themselves from the domination of their husbands—whether by desertion or by divorce—she helped to lay out a strategy of escape for women who found themselves trapped in loveless marriages. The issue of divorce had long been a topic of public discussion. During the period following the American Revolution, the consensus among intellectuals and social critics was that in a republic such as the United States, domestic relations should be egalitarian. In this view, marriage was analogous to any other civil contract, which could be broken if its terms had not been met. By the 1850s, however, attitudes had begun to change. Social critics, theologians, lawyers, and many novelists argued that stable marriages were critical for preserving social stability. As a result, these commentators opposed any attempt to liberalize divorce law. They also charged women with responsibility for maintaining the bonds of marriage. If a woman found herself married to a man with whom she was incompatible, she was advised to exhibit resignation and self-control to preserve domestic tranquility.[39]

Jane did not necessarily think that divorce was the ideal solution for resolving marital difficulties, and she held both husband and wife responsible for maintaining marital harmony. In "Matrimonial Difficulties," an 1849 essay, she wrote, "The nearest we may go toward real happiness in the married and social state is by practicing a system of marital forbearance and concession. If more of this were practiced, and less brooding over wrongs and neglects, too often imaginary, were indulged in, we should hear far less of troublesome divorce cases, and see much more of unalloyed enjoyment in families."[40]

In her opinion, however, there were limits to what anyone could expect from a woman whose relationship with her husband had deteriorated to the point where whatever affection they had once had for each other was gone. Responding to those who criticized her for her view of marriage and support of divorce in "The Locust's Song," she wrote, "As to the views of marriage which appear heretical, they are of our own matured convictions. We have not the slightest idea that God joined these people together whom the state or church joined and who live contriving ways and means to keep each other miserable. Whenever a couple habitually violate the obligation which binds them to love and cherish each other, they should take separate houses, neither do we think marrying again, advisable even when legally separated. It is a false view of life which makes marriage so essential. Marriage should be purely a matter of choice, and no rule should make it more respectable than virtuous and useful single life."[41]

She wrote in a subsequent editorial, "We do believe that all *well considered* requests for divorces should be granted; and do maintain that folks who are living together, per force, are not married—that mercenary matches are not marriage—that woman who *marries* for a living is no more virtuous at heart than she who lives illegally with a man for so much per annum—that all who are living as husband and wife without the bond of affection are living in a state of prostitution." She maintained that to avoid such deplorable situations, women should be educated so that they could support themselves in some employment or profession. When that was the case, there would be little reason to marry except for personal attachment. "People should not be allowed to separate for a quarrel, or for any cause that is removable by time and patience; but a fixed dislike, or as much aversion as would make a single life preferable to the society of one's companion, is no light matter, and where such feeling exists there can be no marriage. The idea of such an union is revolting, disgusting beyond measure, and if society cannot exist without such profanation— without compelling any of its members to submit to personal violation, then, we 'cannot perceive the necessity' for its existence."[42]

Some in the woman's rights movement—including Susan B. Anthony, Elizabeth Cady Stanton, and Ernestine Rose—agreed in principle with Jane on the subject of marriage and divorce, but others within those ranks did not. The issue of liberalizing divorce law was deeply divisive. As Norma Basch has pointed out, the gender identity of many woman's rights supporters was tied to being married. They wanted protection within marriage, not the ability to flee from it.[43] Jane, however, had made up her mind on the issue. From her point of view, when a woman's efforts to sustain the marriage relation failed, she should have the right to end it.

Jane's neighbors were probably aware of her domestic situation, but the publication of "The Locust's Song" exposed the Swisshelm family's private affairs to a much wider audience. Jane's willingness to air dirty laundry in public must have been painful if not humiliating to James and Mary Elizabeth Swisshelm. It is inconceivable that they would have remained ignorant of the story's publication, and it is equally inconceivable that if they read it, they would not have recognized themselves as the tale's main characters. It may have been partly for that reason that within a few weeks of the publication of the last chapter of the story, James's younger brother, William, became Jane's coeditor at the *Visiter*. A college graduate with no editorial experience, William explained in his letter of introduction to the paper's readers that he had no intention of taking over Jane's position as senior editor. His job, he told them, was to wield not the pen but the scissors.[44] With William looking over her shoulder, Jane stopped publicly embarrassing her husband and his family with tales told out of school, at least temporarily. But her silence about matters of private concern did nothing to improve her relationship with James.

Despite the problems that plagued her marriage, Jane gave birth to a daughter in the spring of 1852. She and James had waited a long time to become parents. They named the little girl Mary Henrietta and affectionately called her Nettie or Zo. Jane's views on motherhood remain unclear. She rarely mentioned the existence of her child in her public writing. Nowhere in her surviving personal documents did she mention when the child was born. And in the 363 pages of her memoir, published some twenty-eight years after her daughter's birth, she mentioned Zo only six times in passing and never called her by name.

Jane's relative silence on a matter that most of her contemporaries considered a woman's most important role does not mean, however, that she did not take seriously her maternal responsibilities. When Nettie was born, Jane found it increasingly difficult to carry on her public activities. Keeping for herself the title of editor, she eventually turned the *Visiter* over to Robert M. Riddle, the editor of the *Pittsburgh Daily Commercial Journal*. In May 1852, she told her readers that she found herself "quite unequal to the task of managing our Irish twins. So long as the Visiter was our only baby, we did not find the nursing and tending of it a very difficult matter . . . but since baby Nettie has come, with her multitudinous demands for attention, baby Visiter has been badly neglected." She admitted that she had enjoyed spending one or two days a week in Pittsburgh attending to newspaper business, but she was unwilling to leave Nettie with a nurse so that she could continue to do so. Jane said that she believed that a mother's first duty was to care for her child. So, with some reluctance, she decided to trade her public life for a private one, assuring her readers that she "gladly" exchanged "the big arm chair before the desk for the little rocking chair beside the cradle."[45] Her self-imposed retirement lasted for only three months, however. In August she was back at the helm of the *Visiter*, writing copy and supervising its weekly publication.

Parenthood did little to bridge the ever-increasing breach between husband and wife. By March 1857, Jane's unhappiness in her marriage had become unbearable. Eight years earlier, she had described her situation in "The Locust's Song," discussing the conditions under which desertion and divorce might be warranted. She had seriously contemplated the consequences of the dissolution of a marriage and had concluded that everyone involved might benefit. So she asked James for a legal separation. He adamantly refused.

His refusal is not surprising. First, there were no legal grounds for a separation: neither Jane nor James had committed adultery; he had not physically abused her; and remaining at Swissvale posed no danger either to her or to their daughter. The law did not recognize what would subsequently be called emotional incompatibility as grounds for breaking up a marriage. No matter which spouse had asked for a separation, no court would have granted it. Furthermore, going to court would have been humiliating, requiring James to admit publicly that despite his best efforts, he could not discipline his wife and carry out his responsibilities as the head of his household.[46]

Around the middle of April, Jane left Swissvale and rented a room in

Wilkinsburg. James sent a friend to her boardinghouse with a note beg-ging her to return home. She ignored his pleas.[47] After twenty years of marriage, she had finally declared her independence. Her liberty was ten-tative, however. Being separated did not mean that her legal status had changed. Theoretically, she was still bound to her husband. He was still obliged to support her, and she was still obliged to provide him with all of the services required of a wife.[48] Only a divorce could legally free them from one another.

After a struggle to regain possession of her belongings, she left James for good. On May 20, 1857, she boarded a steamer with five-year-old Zo and headed for Minnesota to join her sister's family and James's brother, Henry, all of whom had settled in St. Cloud. She had spent twenty years married to a man she no longer loved and almost fifteen years living unhappily in her mother-in-law's house. In her memoir, she wrote, "I must run away or die, and leave my child to a step-mother. So I ran away." She admitted that her marriage had been a mistake and felt that ending it would be good for both her and James. He was, she wrote, "a man in the prime of life, with unspotted reputation." She assumed that he could easily find another wife and felt that her desertion would leave him free to do so.

James took Jane to the wharf and, carrying Zo in his arms, escorted them both onto the boat. He was sure that Jane would return. He went home to Swissvale, improved the house, sent her letters, and waited for three years before running out of patience. By that time it was clear that Jane, now the editor of the *St. Cloud Democrat*, had no intention of return-ing to Swissvale to live and that there was little or nothing James could do to change the situation. She had demonstrated to everyone in Pittsburgh and St. Cloud how little control he had over the woman he called his wife. On June 9, 1860, having given up any hope of reconciliation, he peti-tioned Allegheny County's Court of Common Pleas to grant him a di-vorce. Among the various grounds the state of Pennsylvania recognized for divorcing a wife was desertion.[49]

James's divorce petition was very straightforward. He swore that he and Jane had legally married in November 1836, that they had cohab-ited until April 1857, and that "in all respects" he had "demeaned and conducted himself towards her as a kind and affectionate husband." He charged that in April 1857, "in violation of her marriage vow and in dis-regard of her duty in that behalf," Jane had "willfully and maliciously" deserted and absented herself from the home that he had provided for her. He asked that Jane be subpoenaed to appear at the next session of the court to answer his charges and that a divorce be granted subsequent to her appearance.[50]

The judge issued the subpoena, and Jane returned to Pittsburgh in July 1860. She told her readers in Minnesota that she had to tend to some legal matters and expressed the hope that she could get her "long standing [personal] difficulties satisfactorily and pleasantly settled."[51] They would eventually get settled, but the process would not be pleasant. After she arrived in Pittsburgh, Jane apparently decided that it was useless to try to defend herself in a court of law and that her only hope was to place her case before the court of public opinion. Toward that end, she gave a public lecture in Lafayette Hall on the subject of marriage. According to one of James's friends, she stood at the podium and defamed James, verbally "abused his friends, his mother, and various other members of his family, boasted of her desertion and subsequent life as an independent woman, and pledged that she would try to prevent him from divorcing her."[52]

Jane may have gotten some personal satisfaction from her ability to embarrass James and his family one more time, but there was very little she could do to stop the divorce proceedings. In the eyes of the law, she had indeed abandoned her home and deserted her husband. She was in Minnesota when the court held its fall session, so the judge issued an "alias subpoena," again requesting her appearance. After she failed to appear at the December session, the court ordered the sheriff to have the subpoena published in the *Pittsburgh Legal Journal* and authorized the taking of depositions.

They were given before a commissioner of the court on February 9, 1861. Both of the deponents, James McKelvey and William Shields, substantiated James's claim that Jane had deserted him in the spring of 1857. She never appeared to contest the charges, so the court granted James a divorce on April 6, 1861.[53]

Jane was in Minnesota when she heard that James had obtained the divorce. "Late in '60 or early in '61, I lectured in Mantorville, and was the guest of Mr. Bancroft, editor of the *Express*, when he handed me a copy of the New York *Tribune*, pointed to an item, and turned away," she wrote in her memoir. "It was a four line announcement that he who had been my husband had obtained a divorce on the ground of desertion. I laid down the paper, looked at my hands, and thought: 'Once more you are mine. True, the proceeds of your twenty years of brick-making are back there in Egypt with your lost patrimony, but we are over the Red Sea, out in the free desert; no pursuit is possible, and if bread fails, God will send manna.'" She sat down, and Mrs. Bancroft put her arms around Jane and tried to comfort her.[54]

Being divorced meant that Jane's custody of Zo became even more tenuous than it had previously been. Jane was painfully aware that a mother's claim to custody of her children had little legal value. In the *St. Cloud Democrat* she wrote that when a woman left her husband, she could expect to have trouble retaining control of her children: "This" was "one of the penalties of the legal crime of marriage, a penalty which the law inflicts upon any woman who runs her head into that noose." When a woman merely lived with a man without the benefit of marriage, she was free to take her children and leave at any time. "But the law punishes marriage in woman with a loss of her natural right to the custody of her children." Children belonged to their father in much the same way that slaves belonged to their masters, she concluded.[55]

Jane was right to be concerned about whether she would be allowed to continue to rear Zo. Even though confidence in women's superior child-rearing capacities was beginning to undermine men's claims to custody of their children, women who deserted their husbands were in no position to make strong legal claims to the right to keep their children. If a husband could convince a judge that he was not at fault—if he had not beaten his wife or committed adultery—he generally was assured that if he wanted custody, he could get it. The court considered any woman who voluntarily abdicated her position as a wife to be morally unworthy as a parent.[56]

Jane had no intention of giving up custody of Zo. Because they were living in Minnesota, it would have been difficult and expensive for James to have petitioned successfully for the right to bring his daughter back to Pennsylvania. In the end, James and Jane appear to have worked out a mutually satisfying shared-custody arrangement whereby Zo remained with her mother in St. Cloud and occasionally visited her father and grandmother. There is no evidence to indicate that, other than the times she came to visit, James spent much time with his daughter, nor does he seem to have contributed much to her support or concerned himself with her education. He knew that Jane was resourceful enough to do both. The informal custody arrangement that they worked out allowed him to continue to think of himself as a father. At the same time, it gave him the opportunity to abdicate many of the responsibilities that normally accompanied that role.

When James divorced her, Jane had to give up her role as a wife. In an

Jane Grey Swisshelm and her daughter, Zo, ca. 1860. (Courtesy of the Library and Archives Division, Historical Society of Western Pennsylvania, Pittsburgh)

age when true womanhood was usually defined in terms of being married, to do so had potentially serious social consequences. In respectable society, a woman whose husband had divorced her was a social pariah for various reasons, not the least of which was the fact that she had clearly been shown to have left unfulfilled her feminine responsibility to help preserve her marriage.

Jane was willing to accept responsibility for having failed as a wife. She had, she admitted, broken her marriage contract and was prepared to accept the consequences of having done so. However, the only consequence she felt compelled to identify specifically was that she felt it necessary to accept celibacy as the price of her freedom.[57] In retrospect, this seems a rather odd comment. The nineteenth century was not known for its forthrightness in discussing the issue of human sexuality. The commercial world of sex was a secret world, possibly a source of pleasure for some men but certainly a source of concern and anxiety for many others. Generally speaking, most people did not discuss their sex lives in their private papers and did not expect sex to be casually alluded to in public.

Because this reference to celibacy is isolated, we know virtually nothing about Jane's attitude toward sex. She had only one child in an age in which she might have been expected to have had many more. But lack of evidence makes it difficult to speculate about what caused her relative lack of fertility. Before the Civil War, birth control information was available, but those who were most likely to have access to such information lived in New York City and other large metropolitan areas.[58] Given Jane's domestic situation, it is not terribly surprising that she did not bear a large number of children.

For Jane to have even mentioned the subject of celibacy indicates the degree to which her identity as a divorced woman was circumscribed by public attitudes. A divorced woman was socially suspect. Her sexuality could no longer be controlled by either a father or a husband. If she wanted to express her sexual nature, she had to do so outside the bounds of marriage.

In the end, her life in Minnesota does not seem to have been greatly affected by the fact that she deserted and was subsequently divorced by her husband. There is no way of knowing what the good citizens of St. Cloud thought about the fact that she appeared in their midst with a child in hand but without a husband. Given the presence of James's brother in St. Cloud, she could hardly have pretended to be a widow, grieving or otherwise. Nor is there any reason to think she ever considered doing so. It was more her style to present herself as she was, to acknowledge that she had run away from her husband, and simply to ignore whatever stigma others might try to impose on her for having done so. That seems to have been the case. By the time James received the divorce, she had already spent two and a half years shocking the sensibilities of St. Cloud's inhabitants with her strong opinions and sometimes unorthodox behavior. She was known throughout Minnesota as a public lecturer, a staunch advocate of woman's rights, and a controversial newspaper editor. Whatever her reputation, there is no evidence to suggest that her divorce affected it one way or another.

By the time she began writing her autobiography in the late 1870s, Jane had become somewhat philosophical about her failed marriage and her contentious relationship with James. Despite the fact that her memoir contains a litany of complaints against the man to whom she had pledged undying love, she did not hold him totally responsible for their marital difficulties. She continued to think of him as her tall, dark, and handsome "black knight" and remembered him being loving and supportive in his own way. "There never was a time when my husband's strong right arm would not be tempered to infantile gentleness to tend me in illness, or when he hesitated to throw himself between me and danger. Over streams and other places impassible to me, he carried me," she wrote.[59]

She believed that in different circumstances, her marriage might have succeeded—if she and James had set up housekeeping in Allegheny as he had originally promised; if they had lived in a place where the laws governing the relationship between husband and wife were more equitable; if he had proposed that they move to Minnesota before she thought of going. But none of those things happened.

Jane clearly regretted that her marriage had failed and blamed social convention, the law, and temperamental incompatibility for its demise. Social convention accepted a husband's right to control and dominate his wife. The law gave him the power to do it. And she was obstinate enough to try to resist that power. Under those circumstances, she came to believe that marriage was akin to bondage and that a wife was no better than a slave.

She admitted that James had a right to the expectation that when she married she would be an obedient and deferential wife. He was no better than most men, she explained, who understood the power that derived from being a husband and tried to use it to their advantage. James "knew his rights," she wrote, "and knowing sought to maintain them against me."[60]

Not until the end of her life did the bitterness and acrimony that characterized her relationship with James begin to dissipate. By the time she published her memoir in 1880, she appears to have wanted him to think well of her and took comfort in a comment that he allegedly made to a neighbor long after she left him: "I believe she is the best woman God ever made."[61] By the time she died in 1884, it had become public knowledge that while she was not willing to reconcile with James, she no longer harbored any "enmity" toward him. According to a local reporter who wrote her obituary, after her return to Pennsylvania, "she had no objections to him visiting their daughter and when he came he was always courteously received." But the reporter conceded that "while there was no ill feeling or vindictiveness" between them, there also was no "friendship."[62]

His dominating mother. Her obstinacy. His demands. Her willfulness. His disloyalty. Her lack of deference. There was more than enough room for blame on both sides. All recriminations aside, the Swisshelm marriage was as much a casualty of larger economic and social forces as of the interference of outsiders or the personal failings of either Jane or James. As Jane and other women strove for more autonomy in their lives and some degree of economic independence, the men with whom these women were associated often felt compelled to do what they could to reinforce their patriarchal authority. Male identity was too strongly associated with the domination of women to allow most self-respecting men to permit their wives or the property they brought to marriage to escape masculine control without some sort of struggle.

CHAPTER THREE

THE

TROUBLESOME

MATTER

OF

PROPERTY

Mrs. Swisshelm's Watch

A case was tried in the District Court, commencing on Monday, and concluded yesterday, to decide the liability of Mr. James Swisshelm for the cost of a watch purchased by his wife, Mrs. Jane G. Swisshelm, now editing a newspaper in Minnesota, but well known as the editress of the Saturday Visitor, in this city. The purchase appears to have been made about the time that the lady, who is one of the strong-minded women of the country, concluded to go West and set up for herself. In the month of May, 1856 [1857],[1] Mrs. Swisshelm bought a gold watch, chain and key, for $130, at the jewelry store of Mr. Roberts, during his absence, and directed the person from whom she obtained the jewelry to charge it to her husband. She was accompanied by a lady who was an old customer of Roberts. Her husband, Mr. Swisshelm, disapproved of the purchase, on two grounds, namely, that it was made without authority, and that she was separated from him at the time. The plaintiff, without attempting to prove an express authority, grounds his claim on the alleged fact, that the articles were such as were befitting her circumstances and position in society, and that this, if proved, would raise an implied promise to pay for them. The defendant rebuts this implication by the alleged proof of a separation prior to the purchase, which was notoriously known among the business community; that the husband had always provided his wife with necessaries; and that there was a lack of care and diligence on the part of Mr. Roberts to ascertain the nature of the credit he was about to give. The case was one of considerable interest.

The jury, after a careful consideration of all the facts and circumstances of the case, returned a verdict for the defendant. Mr. Roberts will think twice before he sells another hundred and thirty dollar watch to a strong minded woman, and charges it to her husband without his consent.

Pittsburgh Post, *reprinted in the* Boston Daily Evening Traveller, *March 12, 1860, typescript, Minnesota Historical Society, St. Paul.*

When Jane wrote about her marriage in her memoir, she claimed that the conflicts between her and James were "all spiritual."[2] This claim was at the very least disingenuous. In fact, arguments over the distribution and control of income and property were at least as important as arguments over questions of conscience in both the Swisshelm and Cannon households.

The issue of property must have been the source of much anxiety, hostility, and concern in the Swisshelm family long before Jane became one of its members. Before he died at the age of eighty-six, John Swisshelm, James's father, disinherited the children of his first marriage and both of his daughters from his second. Family tradition had it that in his old age John "became blind and when the time came to make his will desired that all of the children should share and share alike in his estate." His wife, Mary Elizabeth, "had two wills prepared, one the way John desired and the second the way she desired. She had the first read to him and had him sign the second." The will that he signed on December 3, 1838, just before he died, left his farm of a little over 162 acres to his wife during her lifetime. At her death, the property was to be divided equally among the four sons that she had borne. It further provided that if any of those sons were to die without children, his share was to be equally divided among his brothers.[3]

James and his brothers lived in a world where possession of property was one of the measures of a man. It provided men with status and power within their communities and allowed them to demand deference from others and to exert social, political, and economic influence in their communities. With property, men could assert their independence in terms of both thought and action and could guarantee their physical comfort. Possessing property allowed them to fulfill their social and legal obligations to provide materially for their families and, at the same time, gave them a way of controlling and disciplining those who depended on them for support. The successful accumulation of property provided men a basis for evaluating their self-worth.[4]

John Swisshelm's will, therefore, had serious social and economic implications for his sons. It left them with a claim to valuable property but without direct access to it. They could not sell it, and any profits to be derived from it went directly to their mother, not to them. The only way James and his brothers could raise capital from the property was to sell their claims, pledge them as collateral for loans, or ask their mother for money. Their father's will meant that they might have to spend much of their adult lives as dependents in their mother's household, taking care of the farm for her in anticipation of their inheritance. When their mother died, they would become landowners. Until then, however, they were dependent sons and only potentially men of means.

Of the four boys, James appears to have had the most interest in running the farm. His three brothers sought their fortunes elsewhere. Samuel went to Louisville, Kentucky, and then migrated further west to Little Rock, Arkansas, where he died in 1840. John Swisshelm's estate was then divisible by three. William attended Allegheny College and in 1849 went to work for Jane as assistant editor and then business manager of the *Pittsburgh Saturday Visiter*. And Henry emigrated to St. Cloud, Minnesota, in 1856. Before he left, he signed over his share of Swissvale to James, giving him claim to two-thirds of the estate.[5]

Concern about money and control of property was also an issue in the Cannon household. When Jane was born in 1815, her father was a man of property. In the early nineteenth century, Pittsburgh was a boomtown. Between 1808 and 1818, the price of real estate in the city rose to increasingly high levels. Most city lots were not sold in fee simple but rather were let out on perpetual leases. As a result, people leased rather than bought the land on which their houses or businesses stood. The price of leases in the central business district, where both Hance Scott and Thomas Cannon had their homes and shops, ran from ten to twenty dollars a foot. The space above the shops on Market, Wood, and Water Streets rented for about $100 a year, with rent for the shops themselves running as high as $500.[6]

The desirability of the land that Cannon leased in the business district of Pittsburgh made it easy for him to sublease it for $450 per year to move with his family to the more healthful climate of Wilkinsburg in 1816.[7] There he bought property from Dunning McNair, built a home, and settled down to making his living as a storekeeper, unaware that the title to his Wilkinsburg property was not clear.[8]

Unfortunately, Cannon's timing was not good. A nationwide depression hit following the end of the War of 1812, and Pittsburgh was not immune from the depression's impact.[9] The value of his Pittsburgh property plummeted, and when McNair declared bankruptcy, his creditors claimed his land. As a result, Cannon's title to his Wilkinsburg house and store was worthless. Jane and her family found themselves in reduced circumstances and in the fall of 1821 moved back to Pittsburgh, where they took up residence in a house owned by her grandfather.[10] Cannon subsequently developed tuberculosis and died in 1827. He left his wife and children his debts, his shop, and a warehouse. He owed hundreds of dollars to Samuel Ewalt for the ground rent on his Pittsburgh real estate. So, according to Jane, her father's property "was in the hands of lawyers."[11]

After her husband's death, Mary Cannon and her three children continued to live in the house owned by her parents, but the executors of her father's estate required her to pay ground rent. Mary was enterprising and resourceful, so she borrowed some money, bought a lot in Wilkinsburg and a stock of goods, and opened a general store there.[12]

When she had set up her store, she hired a lawyer and began trying to straighten out her family's financial affairs. Shortly before Thomas Cannon's death, he had granted his wife power of attorney over matters relating to her father's estate, which meant that she was responsible for both her affairs and those of her mother.[13] According to Jane, Hance Scott's executors did not do a good job of looking after her grandmother's interests. So when Mary heard that the sheriff had advertised the sale of her father's estate, she "had the proceedings stayed, the executors dismissed, and took out letters of administration" for herself.[14]

When Jane married James in 1836, Mary looked to him for help in settling her affairs. But when she asked him to join her in a lawsuit to try to recover Thomas's Pittsburgh property, he refused. It is not clear why he did so. It may have been that the amount of money needed to pay off the past due ground rent plus interest was beyond his means. However, he did agree to sign a deed consigning to his mother-in-law any interest he might claim in the property through his wife.[15]

At about the same time that Jane and James moved to Louisville in 1838, Mary moved back to Pittsburgh, where she set up a dressmaking shop.[16] Sometime during the next year, she became ill with what appears to have been cancer, and she died on January 17, 1840. She bequeathed her property and her claims to property to her daughters in a separate estate, thus thwarting any attempt by James to gain access to it.[17]

In the absence of a separate estate, Jane's property would have been controlled by her husband. The law regulating married women's property was based on the idea of marital unity (the idea that husband and wife were one and that their economic interests were the same). Under English common law, which served as the basis for much of U.S. law, married women were in a state of coverture, which simply meant that they had no control over their property unless it was protected by a prenuptial agreement or separate estate. In the first case, the prospective bridegroom signed a legal document before the marriage guaranteeing that he would not claim his wife's property. In the second case, a person desiring to transfer property to a woman placed it in the hands of a trustee to prevent the woman's husband from controlling it. In either case, any wages she earned during her marriage were considered to be her husband's. Who actually owned her personal property, such as jewelry, clothes, and household goods, was not always entirely clear, and when conflicts over the ownership of such items could not be resolved privately, the courts had to intervene.[18]

Some states used equity courts, also known as chancery courts, to allow a woman to sue her husband or the trustees of her estate for misusing or misappropriating her property. And some states had laws that held that a husband could not sell his wife's property unless she assured a judge in the privacy of his chambers that she agreed to the sale. But Pennsylvania had no equity courts, and during most of the state's early history the law did not require women to be privately examined by judges. Even after the legislature guaranteed such protection for women in 1770, the courts showed no real enthusiasm for enforcing the law. Indeed, the legislature had so little regard for the requirement that in 1826 it passed a measure guaranteeing the validity of deed transfers from husbands and wives without proof that the wife consented or documentation that a private examination had taken place.[19]

The fact that Mary Cannon provided Jane with a separate estate suggests either that Mary did not believe that Jane and James had the same economic interests or that Mary had little faith James's willingness to represent Jane's interests when it came to the use and disposition of her property. Whatever the case, Mary cut off James's access to Jane's property and placed control of it in the hands of trustees. There are few things she could have done that would have been quite so publicly insulting to her son-in-law.

According to Jane, James was so furious about what he considered Mary's betrayal of his interests that he threatened to sue her estate for the money he had lost when Jane returned home to nurse her mother through the last days of her life. He argued that his wife had left him alone in Louisville to care for himself and that under the law he had a right to compensation for the loss of her domestic services. The law, he insisted, was on his side.[20]

There is no evidence that James carried through on his threat, but his anger is not very surprising. He was a married man whose property was controlled by his mother, and now his mother-in-law had cut off his access to his wife's property. Furthermore, in establishing a separate estate for Jane, Mary had provided her daughter with a kind of financial independence that had the potential to undermine not only James's self-esteem but also his domestic authority. With the help of her trustees, Jane could, for example, invest in real estate or establish a business without consulting him. Having access to her own money would allow her to avoid having to negotiate with him when she wanted to buy something. Depending on how and when she chose to spend her money, she could usurp his tenuous position as head of the household. It is in this context that conflicts over property between Jane and James need to be understood.

Mary's arrangement of a separate estate for her daughters did nothing to contribute to the sense of marital unity that was supposed to characterize Jane's marriage. Long before Mary died, Jane's propensity to see property in terms of "mine" and "theirs" had already begun to poison her relationship with her husband and his mother. Shortly after the couple married in 1836, James bought property in Wilkinsburg that included a wagon shop. He hired a wagon maker and sent him to board with Jane, who, having refused to move into the Swisshelm farmstead, was still living with her mother. To compensate Mary Cannon for the expense of keeping the workman, Mary Elizabeth Swisshelm sent over provisions to provide for his needs. Jane does not appear to have resented the fact that James expected her to feed and clean up after the wagon maker, but she was very clear about how she felt about her mother-in-law's attitude toward her stewardship of the supplies. Jane always felt, she wrote with some vehemence in her memoir, that when either Mary Elizabeth or one of her daughters came to visit, they were more interested in making sure Jane was not wasting the supplies they had sent than in expressing concern for her welfare or simply passing the time of day. She deeply resented their possessive attitude and eventually became so incensed that she claims to have returned the supplies they sent and refused to receive any more.[21]

Neither Jane's refusal to move to the Swisshelm farm after her mother's death nor the fact that James left her to her own devices to support herself while he sought his fortune in Arkansas did anything to make her feel that she was an integral part of an economic partnership. And the financial arrangements they worked out while she taught school in 1842 made her feel that she was being exploited. According to Jane, during that time James not only "collected all the income I then had from the unsettled estate left by my mother, and applied it to his own personal use" but also forced her to use her salary to buy her clothes and household goods. "During half that school term," she wrote, "I did the greater part of the housework, all the sewing in Mr. Swisshelm's house; and with . . . the money thus earned, bought material and made a bonnet which I wore seven Winters without altering. I permitted people to think I did so from eccentricity, when the facts were, that the demands of the family upon my purse, were so pressing I could not afford another."[22]

After her mother's death, Jane recovered the title to the house on Pittsburgh's Water Street where she had been born. Her lawyer, William Lowrie, arranged to have possession transferred to Jane and her sister on July 1, 1845. She expected the income from the property to amount to about eight hundred dollars a year. But on April 10, 1845, a washerwoman on Ferry Street built a fire in her yard, and high winds carried sparks into a nearby stable. From there, the fire spread from west to east, consuming everything in its path. Before it was extinguished, it had destroyed a third of the city. Estimates of the losses ran as high as eight hundred thousand dollars, and four Pittsburgh insurance companies went bankrupt. The Cannon house on Water Street was one of those consumed by the flames.[23]

Even though the house had been destroyed, Jane and her sister had to continue to pay ground rent on the lot. So when someone offered to buy their lease on the land, they were eager to sell. Unfortunately, to protect their title, the purchasers insisted that both James Swisshelm and Henry Z. Mitchell, Elizabeth's husband, sign the deed. According to Jane, James refused to sign unless her share of the purchase price was paid directly to him instead of into her separate estate because he wanted to use the money to make improvements on the farm. Jane knew enough about property law and the terms of John Swisshelm's will to know that if James died before his mother and before she and James had children, his interest in the farm would automatically go to his brothers. Traditionally, wives were entitled to up to one-third of their husbands' estates (in this case, James's interest in Swissvale). But John Swisshelm's will had cleverly short-circuited Jane's claim. "I had not even a dower right in the estate," she wrote bitterly in her memoir, "and already the proceeds of my labor and income from my separate estate" were to be used to benefit it.[24]

The struggle over money and property continued when, according to Jane, James ordered local merchants to keep separate accounts for him and his wife. On his account were his clothes, those of his mother and brothers, and ordinary groceries. To her account were charged her clothes, "all high-priced tea, white sugar, etc., all table-ware, fine cutlery, table linen, bedding, curtains and towels." He paid for his purchases with farm produce such as butter and eggs. She had to pay for hers in cash.[25]

Jane deeply resented what she considered to be the exploitation of her labor and James's apparent unwillingness to provide her with clothing and household supplies. So she borrowed some law books so that she could see exactly what constituted married women's property rights and husbands' financial obligations.[26] What she read in those law books could not have been very reassuring, but the law was about to change. The depression that had sent James into bankruptcy in Louisville helped to prompt a legal reform movement in the Northeast. Debtors and creditors as well as members of the legal community demanded codification and clarification of the status of married women's property. By 1847 the state of New York was considering the passage of a married women's property act that would protect inherited property, and Pennsylvania legislators were prepared to follow suit.

Determined to put as much pressure on the legislature as possible, Jane wrote a series of letters in support of the proposal to circumvent the law of coverture and to grant women more control over their property. She sent her correspondence to Robert M. Riddle, editor of the *Pittsburgh Daily Commercial Journal*, for publication. She pointed out that the courts were wrong to automatically assume that husbands and wives necessarily had the same interests where property was concerned. "So far from a husband endowing his wife with all his earthly goods, no single part of them becomes truly hers. All they both have and all they can acquire are his, and only his, to dispense of as he thinks fit," she wrote in the fall of 1847. She also argued that laws providing for separate estates were too complicated to effectively protect a woman's property interests and that the trustee system was subject to abuse. With tongue in cheek, she charged that "four lawyers, if they are smart, can usually draw up a simple deed between two men and get it right in a week—signed, sealed, and delivered—that is if no delay occurs. But if there is one of these trusteeships in the matter—one of those 'sole and separate use' affairs, there is no use of getting less than six legal gentlemen, or giving them less than six months, and the next six who examine it will pronounce it all wrong, and one chance against fifty but you have to begin where you started. There are that matter of quirks, quibbles and turns in the laws which relate to married women, and there is not one lawyer out of fifty who understands them or is fit to conduct any business which concerns them."[27]

While Jane carried on the campaign for the reform of married women's property law in western Pennsylvania, Lucretia Mott, Mary Grew, and Sarah Pugh of Philadelphia spearheaded a similar crusade in the east. These efforts paid off. Pro-reform legislators incorporated provisions for protecting married women's property into an omnibus bill that the leg-islature passed amid considerable wrangling. The governor of Pennsyl-vania signed the measure on April 11, 1848.[28]

The law provided that "every species and description of property . . . which may be owned by or belong to any single woman, shall continue to be the property of such woman, as fully after her marriage as before." The measure provided that her property could not be claimed as a means of settling her husband's debts and that her husband could not sell, convey, or transfer her property without her written consent or agreement under private examination. Furthermore, she could dispose of her property in a will; if her husband had no property, she could be held liable for "debts" that might "be contracted for necessaries for the support and mainte-nance of the family"; and if she died without a will, her husband and children would share her property equally.[29]

The passage of the law did not represent a great victory for married women's property advocates such as Jane Swisshelm, however. Unenthu-siastic about enforcing the law's provisions, the Supreme Court of Penn-sylvania decided in 1852 that a deed by a married woman without the signature of her husband was void. A year later, the same court held that the "earnings of married women were not property within the meaning of the Act of April 11, 1848" and that such earnings belonged to their husbands. In 1854, another Pennsylvania Supreme Court decision de-clared that granting "dependent" married women the right to control their property might be "an injury instead of a benefit to her." Married women in Pennsylvania would have to wait until 1887 for the passage of a stronger law.[30] And Jane would have to continue her campaign to assure that courts would respect women's property rights.

Just a few months before the Pennsylvania state legislature finally passed the 1848 married women's property act, Jane decided to use the money from her separate estate to begin publishing the *Pittsburgh Satur-day Visiter*. James supported her in this effort. He thought of himself as an entrepreneur, he supported the cause of antislavery, and he had some reason to believe that his wife had talent in the area of journalism because other editors had demonstrated a willingness to publish her poems, sto-ries, and letters. He may also have had an ulterior motive for supporting the idea of publishing a paper. James had no direct access to Jane's inheri-tance, but he did have legal claim to money she earned. Whatever his motivations, he encouraged her to proceed on what at the time was an extremely unconventional business venture for a woman.[31]

Unfortunately, the *Visiter* was not a financial success, and its publication placed a great strain on Jane's resources. In January 1849, a year after the newspaper's inauguration, she needed more capital. So she transferred a half interest in the paper to Robert Riddle, who in return for his investment became partner and coeditor.[32] Some time later, Riddle offered to buy her out and to give her a job writing for him. She was tempted to accept his offer, but James's brother, William, who by this time had been made the paper's business manager, assured her that the paper was making money. William suggested that rather than selling out, Jane lend him the money from her separate estate to buy Riddle's share, thus keeping the paper in the family. Jane was worried about risking any more of her capital but eventually agreed to the plan on the condition that William guarantee that the value of her share be maintained. He agreed, and she lent him the money to buy out Riddle in late 1849.[33]

Jane assumed that the paper was doing well until 1854, when she learned that she was essentially bankrupt. To avoid a sheriff's sale, she and William sold the paper to Riddle and paid off their creditors. She was now free of debt, but her separate estate was gone, and William still owed her the money she had loaned him. While trying to sort out her financial affairs, she discovered that William had cosigned notes for his friends and that one of his creditors had already "entered a lien against his [one-third] interest" in Swissvale.

Jane decided to seek legal counsel. Her lawyer, William Shinn, advised her that since William's only asset was his claim to his third of his father's estate, the only way she could protect herself was to get a deed to William's share of the family farm. Shinn prepared the deed, and she took it back to the newspaper office and informed William that if he refused to sign it, she "would sue him for a settlement." He signed. Thus, on February 22, 1856, William deeded his share of his father's estate to Jane as security for the two thousand dollars he owed her.[34] Because the money William had borrowed had come out of her separate estate, his third went to her, and James had no legal claim to it. A little over a week later, Thomas Mellon, who was also James's lawyer, obtained a judgment against William for bad debts.[35]

By 1857, therefore, her newspaper was in Riddle's hands, and the money in her separate estate was gone. Since her claim to Swissvale did nothing to enhance her cash flow, she demanded that her husband support her and their daughter as he was obliged by law and custom to do. "When the property inherited from my parents had so far melted away that I had not sufficient income to supply me with the common necessaries of life, and when my health was so broken that I was no longer able to support myself by sewing or trading, I notified Mr. Swisshelm that if I remained with him I should require him to support me," she wrote. "To this he replied that if I attempted anything of the kind he would convey all his property to his mother, and would like to see where the support would come from." He hired a lawyer. She did the same. She purchased some household items and some clothing for herself and Zo. James paid the bills but notified the merchants not to extend any further credit to her on his account.[36]

In April 1857, she left her husband, abandoned her home at Swissvale, rented rooms in Wilkinsburg in anticipation of leaving for Minnesota, and set about trying to recover what she considered to be her personal property. Her lawyer arranged for her to gain possession of her piano and bookcases by posting a writ of replevin—a bond to guarantee that if she failed to prove ownership in court, she would return them to James. But she had no legal grounds for claiming the trunks full of clothing, books, china, silver plate, pictures, and bedding that she had left behind. It appears that while she had purchased all of these items with the money from her separate estate, she had failed to have the bills of sale made out in the name of her trustee. Therefore, as far as the law was concerned, her personal property belonged to her husband. This was not good news. In desperation, she convinced some of her neighbors to help her break into the house and take what she wanted. Even so, she was forced to leave behind her parlor furniture as well as her buggy and harness.[37]

The time for her departure drew near. But before she left town, she went on a shopping spree. She marched into a milliner's shop and bought two dresses made of black silk, a shawl priced at $30, a dozen pairs of black kid gloves, and some stockings. She then proceeded to the dry goods store, where she purchased some flannel, a beautiful piece of fine linen, and six yards of elegant Brussels lace. In both cases, she ordered the shopkeepers to send the bills to her estranged husband. Then, accompanied by a friend, she went to a jewelry store. J. M. Roberts, the owner, was not there, so with the help of his clerk she perused the merchandise, selected a gold watch, key, and chain costing $130, and asked that her husband be charged for this purchase as well. The clerk hesitated. He may or may not have known who she was. She was well known in Pittsburgh business circles for having been a newspaper editor. Whether or not he recognized her, she certainly looked respectable, and the woman with her was an old customer. So in the absence of his employer, he handed over the watch and thanked the ladies for their patronage. When Jane returned to her boardinghouse, the contents of her bundles represented an expenditure of about $700.[38] On May 20, 1857, she left for Minnesota.

Presumably she took her new purchases with her, leaving James behind to pay for them.

Jane said that she thought nothing about those purchases until about three years later, when, living in Minnesota, she read that the jeweler had brought suit against James in District Court in Pittsburgh, demanding that he pay for the watch. Arguing before a jury, James's attorney claimed that he had not authorized the purchase and that since he and Jane had been separated at the time, he should not be held responsible for payment. The jeweler's lawyer claimed that there were three reasons why James should pay for the watch. First, at the time of the purchase, Jane and James were still married. Second, the law held a woman's husband responsible for supporting her and paying any debts that she incurred. And third, the watch fell under the law applying to "necessaries" because James was a propertied man and might be expected to support his wife in a manner "befitting their circumstances and position in society." James's attorney rebutted with the argument that it was common knowledge in Pittsburgh at the time that James and his wife were separated and that it was Roberts's responsibility to make sure that James was willing to pay the bill before selling Jane the watch.[39]

James's liability depended on two legal issues. The first involved the assumption that since a wife was supposed to play an active role in managing the household's resources, she acted as her husband's agent when she went shopping and was therefore entitled to use his credit with local merchants. Informal separation did not in any way limit her right to do so because she legally remained his wife.[40] The second depended on the judicial interpretation of what was commonly known as the law of necessaries. According to this principle, a husband was obliged to provide his wife with food, clothing, and shelter according to his means and commensurate with her status in society as his wife. What was at stake was defining what goods were necessary to do so, pinpointing what social status James was obliged to demonstrate in his support of his wife, and assessing his ability to pay.[41]

Jane's memoir stated the judge's charge to the jury as follows: "If a wife have no dress and her husband refuse to provide one, she may purchase one—a plain dress—not silk, or lace, or any extravagance; if she have no shoes, she may get a pair; if she be sick and he refuse to employ a physician, she may send for one, and get the medicine he may prescribe; and for these necessaries the husband is liable, but here his liability ceases."[42] Following the judge's instructions, the jury—composed entirely of men— found for the defendant, James. They could agree that he was obliged to clothe his wife, but in their minds, he did not have to provide her with an expensive gold watch. Roberts, the jeweler, lost the case and had to absorb the loss of the jewelry as well as the cost of the lawsuit. Stories about the lawsuit appeared in newspapers as far away as Boston and New York.[43]

When Jane read of the suit in the *New York Tribune* in 1860, she wrote to the paper to defend her reputation and clarify her position on the matter. After she left James, she said, she "asked nothing of him, but exception from his presence." She claimed that James refused to let her have about two hundred dollars' worth of her personal possessions and that her lawyer could devise no legal way for her to retrieve that property, so she simply bought the watch instead. She also suggested that she intended to use her purchases as a way to publicly expose James's refusal to support her and to demonstrate to the world that the law was powerless to force him to do so. Her dispute with James, she claimed, proved that "there is no process in our laws by which a wife can enforce her claim of support. It establishes beyond question, so far as that Court is concerned, that while a woman, by marriage, resigns all claim to the proceeds of her own indus-try, and the custody of the children she may bear, she acquires no valid claim on her husband for even the common necessaries of life. She be-comes a servant for life without the power to collect wages, while her husband acquires that right in her stead, and when collected, may make such use of them as he sees proper, may provide for her, or may not, just as he pleases."[44]

By 1857, when Jane deserted her husband and left Pittsburgh for St. Cloud, she had spent more than twenty years wrangling over money and property with him and her in-laws. Until her death, Jane was convinced that James had used his legal status as her husband to deprive her of her rightful property and that he had used the proceeds from her labor and separate estate to build mills and improve the land at Swissvale. In the end, she believed that her inheritance had ended up in her mother-in-law's hands. She wrote in her memoir, "All my husband's labor for all his life, and mine for twenty years, with a large part of my separate estate, had gone to swell his mother's estate, on the proceeds of which she kept her carriage and servants until she died, aged ninety-four, while I earned a living for myself and his only child."[45]

After James divorced her in 1861, any money Jane earned was hers to keep. But her property war with James had not ended; indeed, in some ways it had only just begun. Before leaving Pennsylvania, Jane and James agreed to sell twenty acres of Swissvale land to R. H. Palmer.[46] That James consulted his wife was significant because it laid the groundwork for her to allege that he acknowledged that she had a legitimate claim to Swissvale and that the deed that William had signed over to her to settle his debt was legal. That claim meant that James could not sell parts of Swissvale without her approval. After she left Pittsburgh, however, she was not inclined to cooperate in any scheme to sell off more land. So when James sent her sales agreements, she simply refused to sign them, assuming that since she had legal claim to one-third of Swissvale, he could not sell any part of the farm without her permission.[47]

While Jane was living in Minnesota, however, James and his mother sold two parcels of farmland without her knowledge or signature. During the same period, Mellon, James's lawyer, bought William's creditors' claims against him—the same claims against which Jane had tried to protect herself by forcing William to turn over his portion of the estate to her. Now holding both his original claim against William and the ones that he had purchased and knowing that Jane was not around to protect her interest in Swissvale, Mellon demanded that William's third be sold by the sheriff and the money from the sale be used to satisfy both his claim and the ones he had purchased.

James appears to have colluded in Mellon's efforts. James went to his lawyer's office and conferred with him about the purchase price, and the two agreed that James would buy William's third at the sale for the amount of Mellon's claim. The sale was held on December 28, 1857, and the sheriff's deed was acknowledged on January 2, 1858. James ignored his wife's claim to William's share, bought the property for $580, gave Mellon the money, and accepted title to the land. Between 1858 and 1866, James and his mother, Mary Elizabeth, sold seven more pieces of Swissvale. In none of these cases did they notify or consult Jane.[48]

Jane apparently found out about the sales when Dr. James King, one of the purchasers, wrote to her shortly after the Civil War to ask if she would sell her interest in ten acres of Swissvale. He confessed that he and his wife had purchased the land from James, only to discover that Jane owned an interest in it.[49] At the time, she was in Washington, D.C., and had just been fired from her job as a clerk in the quartermaster general's office. She needed money to support herself and her daughter, and the only property to which she had access was land deeded to Zo in 1852 by Robert Mitchell, an abolitionist from Indiana County, Pennsylvania.[50] Jane consulted with her friend, Edwin Stanton, a lawyer as well as the U.S. secretary of war, and returned to Pennsylvania to try to settle her affairs. At issue was her claim to Swissvale and her right to the proceeds from the sale of the land.

On January 4, 1867, Jane filed suit against her former husband in the

Allegheny County Court of Common Pleas. In essence, she charged him with fraud. She alleged that despite his knowledge of her claim to William's share of Swissvale, James had conspired with his lawyer, Mellon, to get control of her share of the property. She charged that James encouraged Mellon to purchase notes signed by William Swisshelm, conspired with Mellon in demanding a sheriff's sale of the property, and colluded to set the price at an amount that would allow Mellon to settle his claims—$580. She asked the court to acknowledge her legal claim to one-third of Swissvale and to one-third of the profits from the land that had been sold, and she asked that James be prohibited from selling any part of the land she had left.

The court found in favor of Jane and declared that she was entitled to one-third of Swissvale except for those portions previously sold by James and his mother. The court forbade James from selling any more land and allowed Jane to sue James for one-third of the value of the land that had already been sold. Both parties appealed. The Pennsylvania Supreme Court handed down its decision on February 4, 1868, affirming the lower court's decision that Jane had a valid claim to one-third of the land in question, that she was entitled to one-third of the remaining estate, and that she could sue to receive one-third of the proceeds from the land that James had sold without her knowledge. In the decision, the justices wrote,

> Taking the evidence in the most favorable point of view for the defendant, it would appear that he intended originally to strip his brother, but on discovering his wife's title, it became necessary to strip her when she was absent, and without deigning to inform her of his intention to become the owner of her property. James and Jane Swisshelm were part owners of the same property, they were also husband and wife, occupying towards each other a fiduciary relation of the most confidential character, requiring the utmost degree of good faith between the parties. The husband, without notice to the wife and under the cover of another's name, virtually possesses himself of the control and practical ownership of three judgments of small amounts, sells out his wife's property, and for the pitiful sum of $580 becomes the owner of a very valuable interest in an improving tract of land. He is practically the vendor and the vendee, the seller and purchaser, both characters are united in him. No court of law or equity could ever permit so gross an abuse of the marriage relation.[51]

Having won her case, Jane arranged to take possession of the old log house that had been the Swisshelm homestead for more than fifty years.

The Swisshelm homestead, Swissvale, ca. 1880. (Courtesy of the Library and Archives Division, Historical Society of Western Pennsylvania, Pittsburgh)

James and his mother moved out, and Jane and Zo moved in. James built another house, where he and his mother lived while Jane made improvements on the one that had been his home for so many years. She added a room so that Zo could have a place to practice the piano and set aside space for herself so that she could continue to write. When Jane was not visiting her sister in Minnesota, living temporarily in Chicago, or spending time at her cottage, Zozonia, in Indiana County, Pennsylvania, she lived at Swissvale.[52] She died there in 1884.

The struggle between Jane and James over control of property and distribution of income illustrates the degree to which ideas about gender, class, and property were intertwined. It is true that men such as James were expected to "support" their families, but it is also true that women such as Jane were expected to contribute to that effort. Even if women did not bring property to the marriage or work for wages, their duties as a part of their domestic role had considerable economic value. They cooked meals, cleaned the house, made clothing, raised poultry and vegetables, and milked cows. What they did not use could be bartered with neighbors or sold on the open market. Their frugality, their management skills, the comfort they provided their husbands and children, and the "egg money" and "butter money" they saved for family emergencies or personal indulgences were valuable.[53]

While women were expected to practice "domestic economy," however, neither the law nor custom expected them to manage large amounts of money or any real estate brought to their marriage or subsequently acquired. The management of family finances and property was considered men's business. Indeed, public evidence of business acumen and the pursuit of mercenary interests had the potential to cast doubt on a married woman's femininity and her claim to respectability. Qualities such as greed and love of competition were proscribed for any woman who wanted to be regarded as a lady.

At the same time, however, knowledge of finance and the ability to earn a living could be great assets to a woman. Widowhood could force a woman into the role of breadwinner, and the economic depressions that plagued the U.S. economy in the nineteenth century often forced otherwise respectable men of substance into unemployment or bankruptcy. When that happened, they and their wives and children were likely to find themselves in severely reduced if not desperate economic straits. Because few community resources were available to tide families over during such times of crisis, it became increasingly clear that women needed to be trained to perform wage labor and be prepared to manage their families' financial affairs if doing so became necessary.

Jane's bitter struggle with James over control of money and property led her to conclude that women could easily be victimized by the law as well as by prevailing gender conventions and relationships that discouraged women from asserting economic independence when their circumstances seemed to warrant it. She idealized marriages in which husbands adequately supported their wives and regretted that hers had not turned out to be that kind of marriage. Experience taught her that women were naive and foolish to assume that when they married, their husbands would support them for the rest of their lives. It is no surprise, then, that she not only campaigned for reform of married women's property law but also supported efforts to provide women with the training they needed to earn a decent living.[54]

I went to the Journal *office, found Mr. Riddle in his sanctum, and told him the* Albatross *was dead; the Liberty Party [was] without an organ, and that I was going to start the* Pittsburg Saturday Visiter; *the first copy must be issued Saturday week, so that abolitionists would not have time to be discouraged, and that I wanted him to print my paper.*

He had pushed his chair back from his desk, and sat regarding me in utter amazement while I stated the case, then said: "What do you mean? Are you insane? What does your husband say?"

I said my husband approved, the matter was all arranged, I would use my own estate, and if I lost it, it was nobody's affair.

He begged me to take time to think, to send my husband to him, to consult my friends. Told me my project was ruinous, that I would lose every dollar I put into it, and begged, entreated me to take time; but all to no purpose, when a bright idea came to him.

"You would have to furnish a desk for yourself, you see there is but one in this room, and there is no other place for you. You could not conduct a paper and stay at home, but must spend a good deal of time here!" . . .

Then I suddenly saw the appalling prospect thus politely presented. . . . Here was I, looking not more than twenty, proposing to come into the office of the handsome stranger who sat bending over his desk that he might not see me blush for the unwomanly intent. . . .

"I will get a desk, shall be sorry to be in your way, but there is plenty of room and I can be quiet," [I replied].

He seemed greatly relieved, and said cheerfully: "Oh yes, there is plenty of room, I can have my desk moved forward and take down the shutters, when there will be plenty of light. Heretofore you have been Jove thundering from a cloud, but if you will come down to dwell with mortals we must make a place for you."

Jane Grey Swisshelm, Half a Century, *106–8.*

Light, of course, was not the only issue. By all accounts, the office where Robert M. Riddle edited the *Pittsburgh Daily Commercial Journal* was grungy and cluttered. But in the late fall of 1847, when he offered to take down the shutters and allow Jane Grey Swisshelm to publish her newspaper in his pressroom, Riddle acknowledged implicitly that her presence would fundamentally change both the working environment in his office and the way in which the business of journalism was conducted in Pittsburgh.[1] With the shutters open, the interior of his office would be exposed to public view. Passersby, curious about what was going on inside, could peer in and confirm that only public business was being conducted within and that the behavior of Jane and the men with whom she worked was beyond reproach.

Neither Jane nor Riddle had ever worked as an equal in an office with a member of the opposite sex. And they knew only one other man and woman in Pittsburgh who had done so.[2] They had no precedent to follow in creating a working environment that would serve the business interests of each yet preserve their claims to respectability. Knowing that in working together they would be transgressing prevailing gender boundaries in the city's business district, they found it necessary to establish a professional relationship that would both allow them to do their work and protect their personal reputations.

Jane's collaboration with Robert Riddle was the first of her three opportunities to work in male-dominated environments that were in the process of shifting to include the presence of women. (The second and third occurred during the Civil War, when she worked in Washington, D.C., as a clerk in the quartermaster general's office and as a nurse in Campbell Military Hospital.) Her intrusion into the male world of work, her efforts to secure a place there for herself and for other financially needy women, and her concern about establishing standards of deportment and demeanor for male and female coworkers exposed anxieties and concerns about the meaning of masculinity and femininity, about the gendered dimensions of economic opportunity, and about social relations between men and women in the workplace in nineteenth-century America.

Shortly after the American Revolution, the U.S. economy was transformed by what historians have called a market revolution. Trade increased, and towns began to grow into cities. The invention of the cotton gin and the development of the textile industry in New England assured the prevalence of slave labor in the South and the encouragement of industry in the Northeast, thus expanding economic opportunity for workingmen and -women.[3] These changes profoundly influenced the development of class consciousness, the kinds of work men and women were expected to perform, their ideas about that work, and their relation to each other in the workplace.

Merchants and shopkeepers with capital to invest took advantage of the opportunities offered by these economic changes to accumulate enough wealth to make a place for themselves in the middle class. But ordinary men who farmed the land or worked as artisans increasingly found themselves subject to forces beyond their control. As available land became scarce in the East and machines replaced skilled hand labor, those without land or capital turned to towns and cities to find jobs as wage laborers. Men with education might find employment as clerks. Men with skills might transfer them to work in factories. Men who were unskilled and uneducated might make their living as day laborers, accepting temporary jobs wherever they could find them. Whatever they did to support themselves and their families, they typically worked in environments that were decidedly masculine.

It is impossible to overestimate how important those environments were to establishing and maintaining male identity and how determined men were to exclude women from or marginalize them in that work space.[4] The shop floor, the countinghouse, and the newspaper office were not considered appropriate places for respectable women who aspired to middle-class status to spend their time. Even mercantile establishments were off-limits to women except as customers.

Gender shaped the nature of work, the physical space in which that work took place, the way workers behaved, and the way they related to one another. Male employers and their male employees set standards for acceptable behavior in their work spaces, and those standards did not necessarily qualify as either genteel or refined. In some workplaces, men might swear, spit tobacco onto the floor or into spittoons, drink alcohol, or openly express their ambivalent attitudes toward women by making crude, unflattering remarks about them.[5] Businessmen conducted their affairs in all sorts of places—offices, taverns, private clubs, stag dinner parties, the parlors of men's boardinghouses, and hotel lobbies.[6] And whether talking politics or haggling over the terms of a contract in a quiet office or in a noisy tavern, men did not need to concern themselves with women, their "female sensibilities," or their aesthetic tastes. Nor did men necessarily try to conform to behavior patterns that would have been seen as appropriate in polite society. They could be as coarse and vulgar as they liked, or they could behave like gentlemen and demand similar behavior from their business associates. Offices, workshops, or factories could be clean or dirty, messy or tidy as the situation warranted or as concern about the appearance of the working environment dictated. In their work spaces, men set the standards. Women might have a great deal of influence over the appearance of their homes and the behavior of people within those dwellings, but in the workplace masculinity was defined partly in terms of men's power to relate to each other any way they wished and to work in whatever physical environment suited them.

The intrusion of women such as Jane into male work spaces forced many men to accept changes in definitions of masculinity and femininity that were sometimes extremely unwelcome. Men not only found it necessary to contemplate competing with women instead of with other men but also were forced to acknowledge that breadwinning was not an exclusively male enterprise and that femininity might be defined in terms that had little to do with physical weakness or economic dependence. The presence of women also compelled men on occasion to modify their behavior and the way they related to each other as men.

The rise in the market economy during the early nineteenth century also brought changes in women's lives. Women who lived on farms and plantations continued to contribute to their families' economic well-being by producing goods for consumption as well as for the marketplace.[7] But women in towns and cities had more options. Many women began to work for wages and became part of the working class. Some worked for and with other women as domestic servants. Those who worked in shops and factories found themselves in working environments that were more often than not controlled by men who trained the women, paid their salaries, and/or supervised their work.[8] While female wage laborers developed their own subcultures, dependence on the goodwill of male supervisors and employers left these women with little influence over the behavior patterns of the men around them or the physical characteristics of the places where they all worked. Those circumstances meant that no matter how modestly these women dressed, no matter how reserved their demeanor, and no matter how morally upright their behavior, their gender and their working-class status meant that on the job and on the streets, they were relatively powerless to protect themselves from whatever insults and indignities men might subject them to.

Women whose male relatives were able to support them were in some ways more fortunate in this regard. They established and maintained their families' middle-class status by remaining in their homes, where they managed household resources and reared children.[9] Their work was arduous and time-consuming and required great skill and managerial competence, but it was largely invisible to those who were not family members.[10] Visitors did not usually see housewives beating rugs, scrubbing floors, or bending over washtubs. In the sitting room, a hostess might tat or embroider while her guests drank tea, but she would not normally fit a dress in their presence. Her parlor was in essence her domestic showroom. Kept neat and clean, with tables covered with knickknacks and decorative lace doilies adorning the stuffed furniture, the parlor was a space set aside to display a housewife's domestic skills and aesthetic taste as well as where women had the power to demand that people conform to behavior patterns characterized by moral uprightness and civility.

The respectability and gentility of middle-class women to some extent depended on the degree to which they could remain out of the public eye and avoid attracting attention to themselves. Even when they ventured forth during the day for an afternoon of shopping, paying calls, or charity work, they were supposed to do so as inconspicuously as possible. Women's public appearances were dictated to some degree by the belief that they needed the protection of appropriate dress and modest demeanor to avoid being subjected to rude glances, verbal insults, or even physical injury.[11]

Women who considered themselves middle class but were forced to work for wages struggled to preserve whatever claims to respectability could be salvaged. In some cases, this problem was solved by charging for performing jobs in their homes that were extensions of their domestic roles, such as teaching, dressmaking, or taking in boarders. Those with literary talent could support themselves by writing. Others made tentative attempts to claim jobs traditionally performed by men. Whatever such women chose, they tried to preserve the value system and behavior patterns that signified their claim to membership in the middle class despite their financial embarrassment. Thus, for both men and women, attitudes toward work and the realities of the workplace were inextricably intertwined with ideas about gender and class. No matter the personal circumstances or the motives for trying to earn money, all women from respectable families who worked for a living helped to some degree to undermine prevailing middle-class gender conventions that held women to be unassertive, economically dependent, lacking in physical strength and stamina, and in need of male protection and deference.

Jane was determined to do what she could to assure that women's claims to an equal place working beside men were respected and that

women were fairly paid for their labor. "It is not only in shutting her out
from employments, some of which are peculiarly appropriate, and for all
of which she is amply qualified, that society is unjust to woman," she
complained. "It is unjust in the remuneration which she awards her labor."[12] She also appreciated the need to protect workingwomen from the
indignities and disrespect that they commonly endured. While working
as a dressmaker in Louisville, Kentucky, she had been mistaken for a
prostitute as she walked back and forth in front of her boardinghouse to
get some exercise after a long day of cutting and fitting dresses. When she
wrote her autobiography many years later, she was still indignant about
the incident.[13]

Jane was not the only person to bemoan the fact that the list of vocations for women was short. Nor was she the only one to demand that
working-class women be freed from harassment on public sidewalks. But
as a newspaper editor and employer, Jane was in a position to provide
women with job opportunities and to promote the idea that workingwomen were worthy of respect.

Jane held a wide variety of jobs during her lifetime, but despite the fact
that she was a female wage earner, she was hardly typical. She never
thought of herself as working class and refused to submit to the indignities that such women often endured. Her family was part of Pittsburgh's
propertied, entrepreneurial artisan class. Her father and maternal grandfather had worked for profit rather than for wages and employed others to
work with them. Blessed with education and some access to capital, she
was more often self-employed than not. And finally, no matter in what
kind of work she engaged and no matter in what unconventional situation she found herself, she always thought of herself as a lady, presented
herself as a lady, and expected to be treated as such. The fact that she
worked for wages before and during her marriage combined with her need
to support herself after her divorce may have strained her claim to middle-
class respectability, but the claim nevertheless remained. Self-assured and
supremely confident in her ability either to do a job or to learn how to do
it, she carried into male work spaces no sense of deference based on
gender. She respected those with skills, those who learned quickly, and
those who did their jobs well, and in return she expected them to respect
her. She tended to think of herself as working *with* men rather than *for*
them. Those circumstances combined with her role as a journalist interested in reform encouraged her to argue that women had the right to
a place in conventionally masculine vocations such as journalism and
printing. And she did what she could to establish standards of compe-

tence for judging women's work and to create a work etiquette that would enable men and women comfortably to work together.

Jane was fortunate in finding men with both power and prestige to serve as colleagues and mentors. Sometimes ambivalent about transforming the workplace into the kind of space that would accommodate both men and women, these men were willing to make those accommodations as a matter of expediency. The man who sponsored Jane's entry into the world of journalism was Robert Riddle, the urbane and politically influential editor of the *Pittsburgh Daily Commercial Journal*. A four-page, eight-column newspaper published six days a week, Riddle's *Journal* provided Pittsburgh businessmen with commodity prices, steamboat schedules, and advertisements as well as local, state, and national news. On Saturdays Riddle published a weekly edition that contained a summary of the week's business and political news.[14]

It is unclear why he was so receptive to the idea of collaborating with a woman in the publication of a newspaper. He obviously had an economic motive. Jane paid him from her separate estate for space in his office and for the right to use his pressmen, presses, ink, and paper. But he may have had an ideological motive as well. Riddle intended his paper to serve the needs of Pittsburgh's business community. He was willing to relinquish space that might otherwise be devoted to advertising and market prices and to publish discussion of such issues as abolition, temperance, and woman's rights, but that space was limited. So the publication of Jane's *Pittsburgh Saturday Visiter* allowed him to encourage the discussion of social and political issues without sacrificing space in his paper. He did not always agree with Jane's reform positions, but he supported her efforts enough to continue to publish her letters to the editor in the *Commercial Journal* after she began publishing her paper, to provide her with free advertising for the *Visiter* in the *Commercial Journal*, to coedit the *Visiter* between January 20, 1849, and January 12, 1850, and to take over her editorial duties while she cared for her baby during the summer of 1852.[15]

Whatever Riddle's motives, neither he nor Jane was so naive as to have believed that their business arrangement would not pique public interest and provoke comment in drawing room and countinghouse alike. The Pittsburgh business district was most decidedly male territory, and Riddle was apparently considered both handsome and charming. Jane described him as "one of the most elegant and polished gentlemen in the city, with fine physique and fascinating manners. He was a man of the world." He was socially prominent and active in local politics. His civic activities made him "the target for many an evil report in the bitter personal conflicts" that characterized political life.[16] Jane was a lively, attractive, and personable woman of thirty-two with no editorial experience whose husband was not in a position to supervise her business activities.

Riddle seems to have been more sensitive than Jane to the potential for their working relationship to be a source of gossip. She wrote years later that when she proposed editing her newspaper in his office, she "did not reflect that he was in the prime of life, a man of commanding address . . . that he had the reputation of having fallen into some of the sins, which public opinion scarce considers blamable in one of his sex; and that the relations we thus ran into, could scarce fail to awake the voice of scandal."[17] To avoid potential scandal, she and Riddle adopted strategies designed to allow them as much personal freedom as possible yet minimize public anxiety about their relationship. Riddle, for example, absented himself whenever possible when it was necessary for Jane to work in the office. If he had to remain to do his own work, he took down the shutters on the street-side windows, ostensibly to let in light. And he never escorted her anywhere without his wife as chaperon.[18] During their business association, he carefully avoided placing either of them in any kind of compromising situation.

Riddle's father even collaborated in efforts to preserve Jane's reputation and by extension that of his son. According to Jane, James Riddle often stopped by the *Journal* office, rarely leaving without reminding the printers that Jane was there to keep an eye on them and to make sure they behaved themselves. With great diplomacy as well as "with the nicest unspoken appreciation of the difficulties of our position, he installed us into the office as guardian, as it were, to all about the premises, and made it generally understood that we were quite an old acquaintance with both himself and his wife, and as such were entitled to all deference in an establishment where his son was proprietor," she wrote.[19]

Jane, in turn, did what she could to assure that her relationship with Riddle remained purely professional. A little more than a month after she began her editorial duties, she wrote in the *Visiter* that she had been warned not to speak well of Robert Riddle in public lest her comments be misinterpreted by people anxious to destroy her reputation. She understood that her friends were only trying to protect her, but she refused to be circumspect in this regard. Her eighteen-month acquaintance with Riddle had served, she said, only "to increase [her] respect" for him, and she was not ashamed of their close relationship. She admitted that she spent "a considerable portion of [her] time at his office" but insisted that while there she felt as if she were "under the protection of his honor." She assured her readers that she had always found Riddle to be "a perfect gentleman" and an "affectionate, fond, and true" son, husband, father, brother, and friend. She maintained both the highest respect for him and "the most implicit confidence in his honor." And, with her usual forthrightness, she insisted on reserving the right to "say so whensoever and wheresoever [I] happen to take the notion."[20]

Despite her protests, she was aware of the risks that she took. She admitted that she worked "in a city where no woman had ever been employed in a newspaper office in any capacity" and that her need to "have intimate business relations with gentlemen almost entire strangers" to her was a cause of some concern. Under such circumstances, she realized that she "might expect to become the subject of all manner of gossip" and that her actions posed a threat to her reputation. Consequently, she did as much of her work at home as she could and frequently asked William Swisshelm to escort her home so that she "never might need the escort of a stranger if detained after dark."[21]

She seems to have understood that in working where she did, she discouraged contact with other women who, while interested in promoting various reform movements, were also concerned about protecting their respectability. "Some ladies sent us word," she wrote, "they would call at the office on Thursday forenoon about temperance business." She waited patiently for them to arrive, but they never came. Suspecting that they were unprepared to be so forward as to enter space so clearly defined as male, she assured them, "Ladies need have no scruples about calling at the office. We are always here on the forenoon of Wednesday, Thursday, and Friday and if they come in at the door next to Wood St., they avoid the public office, and the other is *ours* at those times."[22]

Another matter that concerned her was her appearance. She apparently made a quite self-conscious effort to present herself in such a way as to deemphasize her physical attractiveness and femininity by wearing a particularly unattractive net scarf tied underneath her chin when she worked with Riddle in the office. In her memoir, she wrote that about three years into their partnership, he turned to her and said, "Why do you wear those hideous caps? You seem to have good hair. Mrs. Riddle says she knows you have, and she and some ladies were wondering only yesterday, why you do make yourself such a fright." Taken aback, she responded that she was "subject to quinsy" and that she wore the cap to protect her tonsils. She observed retrospectively that Riddle seemed totally unaware of the fact that her tonsils did not need "such protection outside the office."[23]

This unease about appearance and clothes reflected Jane's attempt to balance her need to preserve her femininity with her need to establish herself as a professional. She was not alone. During the nineteenth and early twentieth centuries, women who gradually made a place for themselves as students in coeducational schools or became doctors, lawyers, social workers, or insurance agents often expressed some anxiety about what constituted the proper attire for professional women. Generally speaking, these pioneers resolved the problem by wearing tailored suits, simple dresses made of dark fabric, or black skirts with shirtwaist blouses. Whatever they chose, they hoped their clothing would make them as inconspicuous as possible yet testify to the seriousness with which they took their work.[24]

Jane felt very strongly that women should not use any aspect of their femininity to advance their job opportunities and was always aware of the precedent that she was setting. "Any attempt to aid business by any feminine attraction was to my mind revolting in the extreme, and certain to bring final defeat," she wrote. "When a woman starts out in the world on a mission, secular or religious, she should leave her feminine charms at home. Had I made capital of my prettiness, I should have closed the doors of public employment to women for many a year."[25] She clearly appreciated the fact that for women to earn acceptance in the male world of work, they would have to separate their identities as workers from their identities as women. It was important for them to understand, she felt, that women's advancement would be determined more by competency than by physical appearance and that the use of so-called feminine wiles would in the end be self-defeating.

Robert Riddle may have welcomed Jane as a colleague, but her presence forced him to confront gender issues that he had previously ignored. Besides working to preserve Jane's reputation and claims to respectability, he took steps publicly to validate her claim to authority, to express confidence in her competence, and to grant her the space to demonstrate her self-reliance.

Jane's presence in Riddle's office was unsettling to the men he employed. They had no way to frame their understanding of her status and their relationship to her. The protocols for proper behavior were unclear, and they consequently were confused about how to treat her. When they saw before them was an outwardly respectable woman hard at work putting out a newspaper. But in their experience ladies belonged beside the tea table in the drawing room, not in a newspaper office bending over a proof sheet. And while ladies might be seen walking the streets during the

Jane Grey Swisshelm, ca. 1850. (Photo by Eugene S. Hill, courtesy of the
Minnesota Historical Society, St. Paul)

daytime, they certainly did not do so unaccompanied at night. Yet here was what appeared to be a lady working at night in an office full of men—a lady who at some point had to go home.

On the evening on which the first edition of the *Visiter* was published, one of Riddle's employees, Reese Fleeson, the former editor of the *Spirit of Liberty*, a reform newspaper, criticized Riddle for neglecting to offer to escort Jane home from the office.[26] As Jane remembered it, while a boisterous crowd of men waited impatiently outside to snap up the first copies of a newspaper edited by a woman, Riddle informed Fleeson that it should be "distinctly understood that Mrs. Swisshelm's relations in this office are purely those of business. If she wants anything of any man in it, she will command him and her orders shall be obeyed. She has not ordered my attendance, but has kept her servant here all the evening to see her to her friends' house, and this should be sufficient notice to any gentleman that she does not want him."[27]

Fleeson's concern for Jane's safety exposed the fact that he found it impossible to separate her economic function from her social role. He was clearly afraid that because she was a woman, her safety and her reputation would be at risk if she walked home alone along Pittsburgh's darkened streets. He also assumed that she needed a man to accompany and protect her. Riddle's directive provided his employees with permission to reconceptualize what it meant to be simultaneously a respectable woman and a female worker. First, he essentially separated her womanhood from her right to male deference. He ordered his clerks and pressmen to respect her authority and carry out her instructions not because she was a woman but because she was the editor of a newspaper being published in that office. In that sense, she was as much their employer as he was. At the same time, he confirmed her claim to femininity by confirming the legitimacy of concern for her safety. But by pointing out that she had already arranged to be accompanied and thereby had protected herself from any danger, insult, or blemish, he suggested that she was capable of taking care of herself.

Riddle also seems to have been sensitive to the fact that the male work environment might be aesthetically offensive to Jane. In an early issue of the *Visiter*, Jane commented on the appearance of Riddle's office, describing it as "festooned with black cobwebs and furnished with flour barrels and files of dirty newspapers." Riddle was offended; like his father, Riddle made gendered assumptions about women's presumed influence on the physical space that they occupied and on the people in that space. In response to those assumptions, he had attempted to domesticate his office in deference to what he assumed to be her feminine sensibilities. Responding to her criticism, he wrote in the *Commercial Journal*, "When Mrs. S. is expected to honor our office with her presence, all the boys and men are at work from early in the morning until about nine o'clock, 'making things look decent' as possible. The editorial rooms are swept out," and the floor is scrubbed until it is as "white and clean as Mrs. S's own fair hands."[28] He did not discuss how the printers and compositors felt about being asked to do what all the world recognized as domestic work. Not only did Riddle make it clear that they were no longer in the position to unilaterally dictate what their office would look like, but he may have inadvertently humiliated them by announcing to the general public that, like women, they had spent hours dusting the furniture and scrubbing the floor.

Despite their unconventional relationship, Robert Riddle and Jane Swisshelm appear to have allayed the kind of gossip and innuendo that might have been expected under the circumstances. Their business relationship was well established when Robert Watson, a wealthy lawyer whose office was nearby, stopped to chat with Riddle. Watson said that he had been watching them from his office window for years and wanted to congratulate both of them "on the relations [that they had] for so long maintained."[29] In the end, the two editors worked together for almost ten years and emerged from their partnership with reputations unsullied. They provided a model for transforming the male workplace not only to accommodate the presence of women but also to enable both men and women to preserve their claims to social respectability.

Having established a secure place for herself in the male world of Pittsburgh journalism, Jane used her position as editor to open up newspaper jobs to other women. The circumstances surrounding an 1853 union printers' strike provided her with her first opportunity. The strike was in part a response to the fact that the printing trade was in a state of transition. In the late eighteenth and early nineteenth centuries, master printers, who owned presses, chose what to print and then apprenticed young men who were literate, had some knowledge of spelling and grammar as well as good eye-hand coordination, and exhibited some sense of aesthetics. In small printing shops, young men learned to prepare books, pamphlets, broadsides, and newspapers for publication by selecting appropriate typefaces, setting up pages, and justifying lines so that the page was pleasing to the eye and easy to read. After proofreading the carefully prepared text, the apprentices sent it to the printer or learned to print it themselves. Successful completion of an apprenticeship in the printing industry provided young men with a rite of passage into manhood. Male typesetters and printers commanded wages high enough to allow them to marry and support families, and their skill and income served as a measure of their competence and their ability to fulfill their manly obligations.

But by the 1850s, the apprenticeship system had begun to decline in some parts of the country. The rise of the so-called penny press in the Northeast meant that entrepreneurial journalists with access to capital could buy presses and hire fully trained master compositors to set the type and equally well trained printers to print it. Small-town printers lacked the capital to follow this example and continued to rely on apprentices as a source of cheap labor. But instead of apprenticing young men, they tapped into a ready supply of willing, dependable, and sober young women interested in learning to support themselves as typesetters and printers. When the training was finished, however, country printers could not afford to pay the salaries that these women had a right to command. Female compositors and printers who had completed apprenticeships in small towns consequently began to flock to cities, where as itinerants they competed with men for whatever jobs were available. This competition threatened not only the financial competence of male compositors and printers but also the integrity of the masculine nature of their occupational culture.[30]

When Pittsburgh's male printers went on strike for higher wages in 1853, Jane and Riddle advertised for replacements.[31] They were deluged with applications from women. Some of them were qualified, and others were not.[32] Riddle was more disposed than Jane to evaluate female applicants in terms of their need for the job rather than their qualifications. At one point, for example, he recommended that they hire a woman who had previously been employed as a vest maker. Jane was very sympathetic toward women who needed employment, but she was willing to sponsor only those whom she thought qualified and was deeply suspicious of women who got what they wanted by exploiting their femininity and by taking advantage of male deference to serve their interests. Thus, she adamantly objected to Riddle's proposal. "A woman who cannot make a living at one good trade already learned, will not mend matters by learning another. I do not propose to turn this office into an eelemosynary [sic] establishment. I want the women whom the work wants, not those who want the work. How long could that weak woman maintain her respectability among all these men? Would it be any kindness to put her in a place she is incapable of fulfilling, and where she must inflict incalculable injury on herself, and the general cause of woman's right to labor? Do not let your generosity run away with your judgment," she scolded Riddle.[33] Jane was convinced that to earn or maintain men's high regard in the workplace, women would have to be as skilled and as conscientious as their male coworkers. As she put it, she intended to hire only those with "heads, not hat pins on their shoulders."[34]

Fortunately, she and Riddle found women who were more qualified than the former vest maker, and the female printers incorporated themselves easily into the office culture. Jane attributed their success to a number of factors. Realizing that they would have difficulty "until the men in the various rooms were familiar with the sight of women in the dominions hitherto exclusively occupied by the other sex," she worked with the male printers for two weeks before the first women began working in the office. Much to her relief, the women she and Riddle employed proved their competence and skill. But she acknowledged that their success also resulted from Riddle's appreciation "of what was suited to their circumstances; and the tact with which his own conduct towards them enabled them to command the respect of his employees and the public. Young girls, some beautiful, some educated, and pretty and sentimental, did their regular days work in the office, where there were dozens of men and boys employed, without meeting word or look to wound their self-respect."[35]

Other Pittsburgh editors also hired female printers as strikebreakers, but Jane felt that some of these editors were extremely patronizing toward their new employees. She reported that the editor of the *Pittsburgh Chronicle*, for example, could not resist referring to his female compositors as "engaging" and "charming creatures." Exasperated by his attitude, Jane wrote, "With all its good intentions and praiseworthy actions on this head, the *Chronicle* is doing very wrong to treat this matter in a jocular vein." Referring to female workers in such a way, she argued, "is not the way to induce women of refinement to seek the situations it offers. Please, Mr. Burr, just talk in a straight forward business way as you would to one of your *equals*. Do not spoil the justice of your arrangements by bespattering them with gallant speeches. Women who have brains enough to learn to set type will never stand to be called 'charming creatures.' And to keep up the idea of their presence in printing offices making 'a flutter' any where than amongst the cobwebs, is to prevent their coming there."[36] Female printers, she assured her readers, were not dilettantes but could be highly skilled, thoroughly dependable, sober, and as dedicated to the work as any man.[37]

Jane was fortunate to have found in Riddle a man who not only tolerated her presence in his newsroom but welcomed and respected her. Her good fortune in finding that kind of sponsorship continued during her sojourn in Washington, D.C., during the Civil War. Jane arrived in the capital city in January 1863. In need of employment and well connected politically because of her support of the Republican Party in Minnesota, she prevailed on fifteen members of Congress to sponsor her application for a job in the War Department's quartermaster general's office. Testifying to her "intelligence, ability, patriotism and effective service for the public good," these congressmen sent their collective recommendation to Secretary of War Edwin M. Stanton.[38]

Stanton, a lawyer who had begun his career in Pittsburgh, was well acquainted with Jane Swisshelm.[39] Interested in her efforts to change Pennsylvania's laws governing women's right to own property, he had called on her to express his sympathy with her efforts and to offer his support shortly after his arrival in the city.[40] Stanton made a reputation for himself in Pittsburgh defending business interests against labor before moving on to Washington. A Republican and Lincoln supporter, Stanton replaced Simon Cameron as secretary of war in 1862.[41] Shortly after arriving in Washington, Jane met Stanton in a White House anteroom, and they renewed their acquaintance.[42] Not surprisingly, Stanton gave her the job she wanted.

She found the government bureaucracy to be as male dominated as the newspaper business. Government offices were full of white, middle-class men, many of whom had formerly been employed as teachers, clerks, businessmen, or professionals.[43] Not until 1861 did U.S. Treasurer Francis Spinner convince Secretary of the Treasury Salmon P. Chase to begin hiring women to trim new bank notes. The experiment was a great success. Not only was there a large pool of respectable, well-educated, middle-class women in desperate need of employment, but they were willing to work for less money than their male counterparts.[44] As the war continued and more men joined the military, the government expanded opportunities for the employment of women. Jane benefited from that policy.

Like the newspapermen in Pittsburgh, the male clerks in Washington found the presence of women in offices disconcerting. Training in drawing-room etiquette made it difficult if not impossible to view these female interlopers as colleagues. These men's view of themselves as protectors of women was no doubt to some degree exaggerated in the sense that, unlike many of their friends, they were not out on the battlefield helping to preserve the Union. Safely ensconced in government offices while other men fought for their lives, these workers may have felt the need to overcompensate. "Of the [male] clerks employed here," Jane wrote in a letter to the *St. Cloud Democrat*, "there is not one in twenty who can go into a room where women are employed, and transact any business with any one of them without in some way reminding her of her womanhood. They are 'sorry to trouble the ladies,' or they 'hope the ladies are quite well.' . . . In some way the ladies are to be deferred to or encouraged, and their shortcomings excused because they *are* ladies. The idea of treating them as copyists and clerks, simply this and nothing more, is beyond the mental caliber of almost any man with whom they are brought into personal relations."[45] While the behavior and deference of the male clerks in her office may have been appropriate in a strictly social context, she believed it to be unsuitable and demeaning in a professional setting. Deference based on gender, Jane was convinced, would surely undermine women's ability to earn the respect they would need to obtain a permanent place in the civil service and thus assure their ability to support themselves.

But while she criticized men for patronizing and flirting with their female colleagues, she was also concerned about the demeanor of the women with whom she worked. In general, she agreed with the sentiments contained in an unsigned letter to the *Washington Chronicle* that was reprinted in the *New York Times*. The author complained that because women insisted on "carrying the drawing-room to the office," the experiment in hiring them as government clerks was doomed to fail. "A fixed rule of good breeding excludes the shop from the parlor. A man who lugs his business, habitually, into his social hours is always a bore; and what should we think of one who went to his counting or consulting room in the ball-dress of the previous evening?" The same was true of women, according to the *Chronicle*'s correspondent. In dressing inappropriately, "they fail to see the distinction between business and social life, and so drag the drawing-room with them, with its coquetries, on to and into the office."[46] She reiterated these feelings a little more than a month later in *The Reconstructionist*, a paper she had begun to publish in December 1865. "It is not airs and graces which will bring business success," she wrote. "A woman will not become independent by sticking a feather in her hair and making eyes at the unfortunate man compelled to do business with her. Business relations and business hours must be kept separate and distinct from social hours or women must retire to private life."[47]

Jane was convinced that women's success as government clerks depended on their ability to strike a delicate balance between maintaining their womanliness and sense of propriety and giving up their claim to dependence and to the kind of deference that gentlemen usually directed toward ladies. At least subliminally aware of the sexual tension that characterized any work space occupied by both men and women, she believed that both male and female clerks had to modify the rules of social etiquette that governed their relations to accommodate the fact that the office was not the parlor and that office relationships were not primarily social.

Jane was also concerned about the competence of female clerks. She knew that many of them had been appointed to clerkships not because they possessed the necessary qualifications for their posts but because they needed jobs and had influential friends. As a result, she feared, such women could not be counted on to take pride in their work or to refine what few skills they had. "To expect that all women or even a majority, are fitted for this advance post on the picket line of civilization, is expecting superhuman perfection of the feminine half of humanity," she warned.[48] To become permanent fixtures in federal government offices, it was imperative, she believed, that women take their work seriously and set the tone in establishing personal relationships with their male colleagues. As moral guardians of society, women were responsible for ensuring that men had no reason to misinterpret the behavior of female employees.[49]

Because she was a clerk, Jane was no position to unilaterally establish the parameters of the duties to be performed by women in the quartermaster general's office, and only by example could she help to establish rules of deportment for female clerks and the men with whom they worked. Instead, she had to persuade her superiors to approve any innovations that she might hope to institute in order to establish a satisfactory working relationship with her male colleagues. Her approach to doing so is illustrated in a letter she wrote to General Charles Thomas in the early spring of 1865 in which she requested permission to make and serve tea to two of her male colleagues during working hours. "In the room of Mr. Parsons, who has charge of officer's accounts, is a young man, E. A. Perkins, who boards with me," she wrote. She informed Thomas that despite the fact that Perkins was "a very rapid writer and laborious clerk," he was in poor health and invariably returned home at the end of the day in a state of exhaustion. "His habits are strictly temperate & he can take no stimulant but tea. Being accustomed to the best, he cannot drink that which is sold in the hall," she continued. Since she was in the habit of making a pot of tea for herself, she saw no reason why she should not share it with both Parsons and Perkins and assured her superior that she "would be careful to lose no time about it." Concerned about the propriety of her request, she assured Thomas that there was a precedent for her benevolence. "In the comptroller of the currency's bureau, in the Treasury," she reported, "a lady, who is an intimate friend of Secretary [William Pitt] Fessenden makes coffee for all the gentlemen & and so takes away the temptation which exhaustion brings, to use alcoholic drinks."[50]

Jane's request is an example of the fine line that a respectable woman walked in an effort both to retain her feminine sensibilities and to establish a professional persona. Jane offered to expand her duties as a clerk to perform what was essentially a domestic service for her male colleagues in an office environment. Her letter is couched in terms that indicate her sensitivity to issues of gender and class. First, she took care to assure her employer that although the young men were not members of her family, at least one of them boarded with her. He was, therefore, something more than a casual acquaintance. She testified to Perkins's gentility by indicating that he was used to drinking tea of the highest quality. And, finally, she accepted as her feminine duty the need to safeguard his health and to do what she could to discourage her male coworkers from consuming liquor.

It is not surprising that Jane should have been sensitive to her male colleagues' needs and eager to do whatever was possible to establish a comfortable and supportive relationship with them. When she first received her appointment from Stanton, she had been forced to wait until office space became available before she could begin work.[51] Never one to remain unoccupied for long, she volunteered as a nurse at Campbell Military Hospital in Washington, D.C. Once more she found sponsors who placed her in a position to try to establish an environment that would accommodate the presence of respectable women who needed employment. This time Jedediah H. Baxter and F. W. Kelly, both surgeons employed by the military, made a place for her in their wards.[52]

Most of what is known about Jane's stint as a Civil War nurse comes from her memoir. Indeed, she devoted almost one-third of her autobiography to her nursing experiences. Humility was not one of Jane's virtues, so it is not entirely surprising that she tended to ignore or dismiss the work of other women who spent their days and nights in the wards of the military hospitals around Washington. In her book, she always placed herself at center stage.[53] However self-serving her words might have been, her description of the conditions that prevailed in those hospitals provides insight into the tensions and anxieties that arose when women began to intrude into the vocational space in which military medicine was practiced.

Jane wrote that she became interested in nursing at the end of April 1863, when she was working as a freelance journalist for Horace Greeley, editor of the *New York Daily Tribune*. She visited Campbell Hospital following the Battle of Chancellorsville to collect material to use in a letter she planned to send to the *Tribune* for publication.[54] She found that despite the best efforts of those in charge, the medical services available to men wounded on the battlefield were fragmented and poorly administered. Neither the North nor the South was prepared to deal with the high casualties of war. The result for the Union was that nurses were provided through the cooperation of government and civilian agencies. Dorothea Dix, whom the War Department had appointed as superintendent of nurses, and the U.S. Sanitary Commission, a civilian agency, worked to recruit, assign, and supervise nurses working in government hospitals, transport boats, and trains.[55] Supplies not provided by the Sanitary Commission were controlled by the stewards working for the quartermaster general's office. Military protocol and hospital regulations made it difficult and sometimes impossible to assure regular delivery of supplies. And, theoretically at least, none were obtainable through normal channels without the proper requisitions.[56]

Jane was outraged by what she saw and heard during her visit. Men who had been willing to give their lives to preserve the Union were lying on cots in crowded wards pleading for such basics as something to quench their thirst. She immediately wrote a letter to the *Tribune* asking the newspaper's readers to send supplies directly to her for distribution. As soon as she received them, she began to deliver these materials to the wounded soldiers. And as she made her rounds, she occasionally stopped to assist the male nurses who were tending to the needs of their patients.[57]

Jane wrote that Baxter did not at first welcome her. He had found Dix difficult to deal with and was willing to do without nurses rather than accept the women she sent. Consequently, by the time Jane arrived, he had banned women from his ward.[58] But he apparently could not help but appreciate the fact that she used her reputation as a journalist to cut through the government bureaucracy by appealing to civilian patriotism and benevolence. Shortly after her first letter to the *New York Tribune* was published, she fired off a second one. Gangrene had appeared in Campbell Hospital, she reported: "The doctors have committed to my special care wounded feet and ankles. . . . I want whiskey—barrels of whiskey—to wash feet, and thus keep up circulation in wounded knees, legs, thighs, hips. I want a lot of pickles, pickles, pickles, lemons, lemons, lemons, oranges. No well man or woman has a right to a glass of lemonade. We want it all in the hospitals to prevent gangrene."[59] The response so overwhelmed Jane that she solicited the help of twenty women to distribute lemons to various area hospitals.[60]

Jane believed that her ability to provide Baxter's patients with necessities and her willingness to serve without being obtrusive and interfering led the army surgeon to reevaluate his prejudice against female nurses. In any case, he asked her to stay. Army regulations prevented him from appointing her to nurse on his own authority, but there were ways of circumventing army regulations. According to Jane, Baxter simply welcomed her to his ward as a "guest," instructed her that she was free to employ her time as she wished, and had a room in the hospital prepared for her to occupy so she would not have to return at night to her boardinghouse.[61] She also gained entree to Kelly's ward and worked at Campbell Hospital for seven weeks during the summer of 1863.[62]

Most middle-class women were familiar with the work of female nurses in military hospitals since it was in many ways an extension of women's domestic duties. Like well-organized housewives, nurses were expected to arrange clothes, supplies, and equipment and to supervise other hospital staff members to promote order, efficiency, and cleanliness.[63] Thus, Jane occupied her time as Baxter's guest quietly weaving among the cots lined up on the floor, serving drinks, changing dressings, bathing and feeding the convalescing soldiers, entertaining her bored patients with conversation, and soothing them with occasional prayers.[64]

Because she was a volunteer, she was not subject to hospital discipline and could ignore or cut through rules of protocol that interfered with her ability to comfort her patients. In her memoir, she claimed that she soon noticed that her patients were suffering from the removal of dressings that were hard, stuck to wounds, and encrusted with blood and pus. She wrote that when she asked the male nurses why they did not soften dressings with warm water before removing them, she was told that the only hot water in the hospital was in the kitchen and that nurses were not allowed on the premises. Further inquiry revealed that at night the kitchen was locked to prevent pilfering and that even the surgeons did not have keys to it. Neither a nurse nor a doctor, Jane simply marched into the kitchen, asked the cooks to give her some hot water, carried it over to a patient, and tenderly began to soak his dressing.[65] She claims both that the cooks eventually presented her with a key to the kitchen so that she could heat water, blankets, or whiskey punch for the patients any time she wanted and that she ultimately received free access to the dispensary and storerooms as well.[66]

Jane was pleased with her relationship with Baxter and Kelley. Both needed all of the help they could get, and she tried to defer to their medical expertise and to avoid challenging their authority despite the fact that as a "guest" she did not have to follow their orders. "I kept no secrets from any of them," she wrote in her memoir, "told each one just what I had done in his ward; thankfully received his approval and directions, asked about things I did not understand, and was careful that my nursing was in harmony with his surgery."[67]

From her point of view, there was no room in Campbell Hospital for misplaced modesty on the part of female nurses. The issue came up when a male nurse insisted on changing a dressing covering a groin wound without her help because he felt that she should be shielded from exposure to that part of the male anatomy. She berated the nurse for his willingness to cause a patient to suffer in order to protect what he assumed to be her feminine sensibilities.[68]

Jane also criticized other volunteers. She was particularly concerned that some women were unwilling to forgo wearing fashionable clothing while tending to the patients in the crowded wards. Despite the volunteers' patriotism and sympathy for the wounded, she complained, "not one in a hundred" of the women "would dress so as not to be an object of terror to men whose life depended on quiet." She focused most of her attention on and directed most of her criticism at women who insisted on wearing hoops underneath their skirts while working. She considered these undergarments a danger to the patients, whose cots lay close together and whose recovery often depended on keeping very still. Her outrage at the degree to which female thoughtlessness combined with slavery to fashion placed her patients at risk was expressed in a story of a young soldier with a history of hemorrhage. One day, she reported, two women insisted on entering the ward, and "one of them caught her hoops on the iron cot of the dying man." As she pulled to release the hoop, she jerked the bed. The young man again began bleeding, and, as Jane melodramatically put it, his "young, strong life ebbed steadily away in a crimson current which spread over the floor."[69]

But Jane also censured women who sacrificed their hoops and donned bloomers in order to do their work. This choice of clothing was objectionable because in wearing bloomers, she believed, they "gave offense by their airs of independence." Instead, she preferred that they wear dresses "entirely destitute of steel, starch, whale-bone, flounces, and ornaments" that flowed from the waist to the ankle loosely and did not inhibit the ability to breathe freely.[70] Her ideal nurse's dress resembled the religious habits worn by Roman Catholic nursing sisters.

Jane's advocacy of such a costume testifies to her continuing appreciation of the need for women to be circumspect in their self-presentation. Physical attractiveness combined with circumstances that placed women in potentially compromising situations posed a potential threat to respectable women's reputations and could very well place them in physical danger. Some women, like the seven female volunteers she caught embracing officers in her cabin on a transport ship, were clearly more interested in enjoying a romantic interlude than in serving the needs of the wounded. But others had honorable intentions that both placed their reputations at risk and jeopardized their physical safety.[71]

Such was the case with Georgie Willets of Jersey City, New Jersey, a woman whom Jane described as "not merely handsome" but "grand" and "queenly" and whose respectability and social position were unquestionable.[72] Working with Jane as a nurse in Fredericksburg following the Battle of Spotsylvania Court House, Willets was called out one night to the residence of an officer who was reported to be in great pain and in desperate need of her services. Willets refused to visit the officer's quarters unless Jane went along. The reputedly "distressed" patient turned out to be a "colonel in uniform, seated in an easy chair, smoking, while his orderly sat in another chair, on the other side of the room." Surprised at seeing two quite healthy men, the two women did not immediately realize that the surgeon who had been sent to fetch Willets was essentially acting as a procurer. This incident convinced Jane that although she often disagreed with Dix, the director of army nurses was right to be concerned about employing young, attractive women as nurses. Jane was shocked by the ease with which women could be "led into traps of this kind, when it would have been well for them had they died there."[73]

Jane believed that women who needed to support themselves should have greater vocational opportunities and that they should be paid fairly for their work, but she understood the risks that came with transgressing gender boundaries in the workplace. She realized that such transgressions produced tensions in the relationship between men and women and understood that women would have to quite self-consciously negotiate with men to establish a permanent and respected place in male-dominated work environments. Women, she believed, should adopt strategies that would allow them to present themselves as strong, competent, rational, responsible, and self-reliant without totally sacrificing their claims to femininity. She would find such strategies equally valuable in her efforts to make a place for herself in the male world of politics.

There, in the ladies' gallery, is a woman who will not flinch under my pencil—or anybody's. Mrs. Jane G. Swisshelm, of Minnesota, one of the sharpest politicians among American women I think, and, for all that, a good housekeeper I know, for I have eaten her biscuits. She has a very large head, high over firmness and self-esteem, wide at combativeness, massive in the intellectual-moral regions, and a forehead as square as a marble block—causality jutting out in the most defiant manner. Added to this, a face full of self-assertion, a controversial mouth, which plainly says, "No compromise"—an inquisitive nose, sharp almost to fierceness and eyes four times as sharp as her nose. Fifteen years ago she was editor of the Pittsburgh Saturday Visitor, *and the most widely read and popular female writer in this country. Her recent miscellaneous articles show the same warm-heartedness and genial style, but party warfare has wearied and worried her, and on political topics, the ink flows acrid from her pen. As an opponent she is disagreeably witty, and in debate as unrelenting as Parson Brownlow. She leads off the applause in the ladies' gallery to-day, and when the mild Copperhead Clerk utters his mild reproof, she looks as if she would delight in tweaking his nose. In religion, she maintains the doctrines of the Old Scotch Covenanters, and as she makes a zealous champion, I am certain she would make an admirable martyr—for she would risk the stake any time for the privilege of the last word. She is positive, progressive and aggressive, and usually on "the other side." Her decision, courage, and self-reliance, the availability of her knowledge and the power of her personal magnetism, endow her with the qualities of a leader; and if she, with five hundred other American women, should be wrecked some fine morning, on any desolate island in the Pacific, Mrs. Swisshelm would be elected Queen in fifteen minutes, and have a provisional government organized before dinner.*

"Pen Portraits on the Floor of the House," Chicago Tribune, *December 23, 1863, p. 3.*

Given Jane Grey Swisshelm's background and particular sense of mission, it is not entirely surprising that she should have taken an interest in politics. "We learned our politics at our mother's knee, with the 23rd Psalm and Shorter Catechism," she wrote in 1853. She justified her participation in politics on that grounds that her religion demanded it. The Covenanter Church, she explained to her readers, required "all [its] members to 'meddle' in politics." She pointed out that gender considerations did not prevent Scottish women from standing beside their fathers and husbands when they challenged the political power of the English Crown in defense of the Scottish Church. And she reminded readers that during the Scottish rebellion against English authority, "Women enjoyed 'equal rights' to be shot, to be hunted as wild beasts, to be driven into 'dens and caves of the earth.' Tyrants," she declared, "never dispute woman's right to the martyr's crown." But male Covenanters did not consider women's willingness to sacrifice themselves for the Covenanter cause a political act. Only when men had made a mess of things, she said, were women allowed to intervene in the male world of politics: "When men have once got the politics of the world into such a fix that the good can no longer get leave to live in it, women may die on gibbets . . . or . . . strain every nerve to remedy the evil; but until matters arrive at this crisis, it is quite out of woman's sphere to 'meddle.'"[1] At the beginning of what was to become a long career in journalism, she clearly believed that the world was in just such a "fix" and that it was up to her to follow the example of her female forebears and martyr herself in an effort to remedy all the evils she could identify.

When she began her foray into politics in the 1840s, Jane did not expect a warm welcome. Some men were more involved in public life than others, but most would have agreed that the right to define political issues, debate them in public, choose candidates to run for office, and do what was necessary to get them elected was men's business. Generally speaking, political parties provided men with gender-specific rituals and institutions around which they could build their manhood.[2]

That did not mean, however, that women had no voice or role in politics. By the 1840s, competing political parties welcomed women at their rallies and solicited their moral support.[3] From 1831 to 1854, Anne Newport Royall edited a weekly political newspaper in Washington, D.C. In the columns of *Paul Pry* and then *The Huntress*, she supported states' rights, promoted the building of roads and canals, demanded tolerance for Catholics, and exposed graft and corruption among politicians.[4] And by the mid-1850s, large numbers of women were speaking out on and writing about such politically sensitive subjects as temperance, slavery, and woman suffrage and were exerting political power by lobbying, writing letters, holding conventions, and presenting petitions to state legislatures and the U.S. Congress.[5]

Isolated on the Swisshelm farm, Jane seems to have been largely unaware of the political activities of other women. With no role models at hand and no local network of like-minded female political activists to provide her with moral support, she at first pursued her interest in partisan politics tentatively, believing that she was a pioneer and alone. During the 1844 presidential campaign, Reese Fleeson, publisher of the reform newspaper *Spirit of Liberty*, printed her letters in support of James G. Birney and the antislavery Liberty Party. Abolitionists at the time were divided on two issues: whether to welcome women into their ranks and whether to organize politically to promote the cause of the slave. However much she admired slavery's opponents, she believed them to be contentious "men of sharp angles." "Organizing them," she wrote, "was like binding crooked sticks" together. Unwilling to expose herself to public criticism or notoriety and fearing that she might embarrass the Liberty Party with the "sex question," she insisted that Fleeson use her initials rather than her full name.[6]

When the *Spirit of Liberty* went bankrupt and Fleeson went to work for Robert M. Riddle at the *Pittsburgh Commercial Journal*, Jane simply began sending her letters to the *Journal*, and Riddle published them. When the United States declared war against Mexico in 1846, Jane, like other abolitionists, opposed the conflict and sent a series of letters to the *Journal* that accused southerners of using the Texas question to promote the expansion of slavery.[7] In 1847, Charles P. Shiras started a Pittsburgh antislavery newspaper, the *Albatross*, intending it to serve as the official organ of the Liberty Party. According to Jane, because he knew that she supported abolition and thought that the publication of her letters might appeal to his readers, he asked her to contribute to his columns. But the *Journal's* circulation exceeded that of the *Albatross*, so she declined and continued to write for Riddle. By the end of the year, the *Albatross* had followed the *Spirit of Liberty* into bankruptcy.[8]

The demise of the *Albatross* left Pittsburgh without an abolitionist newspaper, so Jane decided to begin publishing one of her own. Doing so carried with it a certain degree of risk. She had no experience editing a newspaper. But she had been writing newspaper copy in the form of letters for about three years. As long as she had exchange agreements with other editors, she could clip stories from their newspapers and republish them to fill her column space. She had enough start-up capital from her separate estate to pay Riddle for the use of his ink, paper, presses, compositors, and pressmen until her paper began to turn a profit. She knew something about how to run a business from her mother and from her experience as a dressmaker and corset maker in Louisville in the late 1830s. She had access to Shiras's subscription lists, and Riddle was willing to allow her to republish as many articles as she wanted from the *Journal*.[9]

Having made the necessary arrangements, she issued the first edition of the *Pittsburgh Saturday Visiter* on December 20, 1847, from the office of the *Pittsburgh Commercial Journal*.[10] With six columns on each of its four pages, the paper sold for five cents a copy. Those willing to buy a subscription paid two cents less. Within weeks, local cabinetmakers, cobblers, carpenters, grocers, bakers, confectioners, and dry goods dealers as well as doctors and lawyers had purchased advertising space.[11] To ensure her paper's success, Jane needed to appeal to the widest possible audience. Thus, in addition to political news and commentary, she published market reports as well as literary or general interest articles clipped from the papers on her exchange list.

Despite her determination to see slavery abolished, she hesitated to assume sole responsibility for the political commentary that she printed. It was not that she felt that women were unable or unqualified to speak out on political issues. "So long as life, liberty, and happiness of woman depends on the policy of her own country," she wrote, women had a right to discuss politics.[12] But she found herself in something of a quandary. She had no experience working in partisan politics and had no confidence that either the Democrats or the Whigs could be counted on to take a strong stand against slavery. There was always the Liberty Party, of course, but she was sure that its supporters wanted nothing to do with women. There was "division enough" among them without her causing further "contention" in their ranks, she wrote.[13] Convinced, however, that "the only proper mode of abolishing slavery" was "direct political action," she encouraged her readers to vote for the Liberty Party candidate, John P. Hale of New Hampshire, for president and offered her political column to "anti-slavery men."[14]

Jane was sensitive to the degree to which she transgressed gender boundaries by intruding into the male world of political journalism. In the first edition of the *Visiter* she wrote, "The point has not been generally decided, whether we wear a hat or bonnet—wrap ourself in a shawl or great coat, so that few can tell whether bowing or curtseying would suit us best, but a nod is seldom out of place to anyone."[15] However, her willingness to be recognized by a gender-neutral "nod" did not stave off the criticism that she had overstepped the bounds that defined "true womanhood." "Democratic roosters straightened out their necks and ran screaming in terror," while "Whig coons scampered up trees and barked furiously," she wrote in her memoir. When George D. Prentiss of the *Louisville Journal* charged that she was "a man all but the pantaloons," she decided that his disparaging comment was simply too much to bear. So she wrote and published a poem intended to put him in his place and to promote the cause of abolition:

> Perhaps you have been busy
> Horsewhipping Sal or Lizzie,
> Stealing some poor man's baby,
> Selling its mother, may be.
> You say—and you are witty—That I—and tis a pity—Of manhood lack
>   but dress;
> But you lack manliness,
> A body clean and new,
> A soul within it, too.
> Nature must change her plan
> Ere you can be a man.

Her response appears to have done the trick. She noted that the "tide of battle" turned, and she heard no more about pantaloons.[16]

During the first months of her editorship, Jane did what she could to promote the Liberty Party's interests. Knowing that access to the voters through newspapers was critical to politicians, she published the party's reports, accepted articles written by its leaders, discussed its activities, and ran the names of its candidates on her editorial page.[17] But she did not always agree with party members' decisions and was very much aware that despite her support, party supporters kept her at arm's length. Determined to promote the cause of abolition and any politician who was willing to take a strong position in opposition to slavery and its expansion, she gave up her editorial position in July 1848, reserving for herself the title of corresponding editor, and hired William E. Stevenson and J. E. Errett to edit and print the paper. She explained to her readers that both of these men supported "Free Speech, Free Land, Free Labor, and a Free World" and that she believed they might be more effective in promoting the cause of abolition because they were men and their influence was likely to be greater than hers.[18]

On August 9 and 10, Free-Soil Democrats, antislavery Whigs, and Liberty Party supporters joined together in an uneasy alliance and organized the Free Soil Party in Buffalo, New York.[19] Jane could not contain her enthusiasm. Despite the fact that Stevenson and Errett were presumably running her paper, she published an editorial endorsing the new party: "The Campaign is now fairly opened—the candidates are in the field—the principles for which we contend have gone forth to the world endorsed by the unanimous approval of our representatives, assembled in convention from all parts of the country." Those who espoused the cause of liberty had a "sacred duty" to perform, she told her readers. The cause of freedom would "triumph" only if her readers voted for "FREE TERRITORY, FREE STATES, FREE LABOR, FREE MEN."[20] By September 1, Stephenson and Errett were gone, and Jane was back at her editorial post with her pen poised for action. Both she and her subscribers, she claimed, were dissatisfied with the way the two men had run the paper. She was unhappy that they had published advertising that she considered "immoral and indecent." And she claimed that her readers were disappointed because they wanted to see "the experiment fairly tried of a political paper solely conducted by a woman."[21]

Despite the fact that she claimed to have more than six thousand subscribers, she continued to have difficulty meeting her expenses.[22] By the end of her first year of publication, she had lost between four hundred and five hundred dollars from her private estate.[23] In January 1849, therefore, she asked Riddle to become her partner and reluctantly turned her paper into a literary sheet dedicated to "solid instruction, entertainment, and amusement." "We enlarged, got new type, lost one-fourth of our subscribers, and set seriously to work to become refined, polished, literary, and all that sort of thing," she wrote. Her new partnership made it difficult if not impossible to continue relentlessly attacking those who disagreed with her position on the moral, social, and political issues of the day. As long as she was sole proprietor of the newspaper, she had free rein over editorial policy. But Riddle was now her partner, and she felt that he was more likely than she was to be prosecuted for libel. So instead of publishing bold, politically oriented editorials, she resigned herself to elevating and empowering her readers morally and intellectually by publishing short stories, poetry, and serialized novels on the front page of the *Visiter*.[24]

Her partnership with Riddle did nothing to solve her financial problems. Riddle withdrew in January 1850 and was replaced by Jane's brother-in-law, William Swisshelm.[25] By the end of 1850, she published notices explaining that she was going to cut her exchange list by half and asking her readers to help her recruit new subscribers. "Our circulation, though it has nearly doubled within the last year, is not yet sufficient to sustain a paper such as we want to make the Visiter," she wrote. She needed her subscribers to assist her because there was a limit to what a woman could do to solicit support. As she pointed out, unlike male editors, she could not "by means of flaming hand bills advertise ourselves in barrooms and street corners."[26] The need to expand her readership continued to plague her. She eventually hired agents to sell subscriptions, but their market was local. Pittsburgh had no wholesale dealers who could represent her in larger cities. So in early 1851, she hired agents in such places as Boston, New York, and Cincinnati.[27]

Her temporary retirement in the summer of 1852 after Nettie's birth caused male editors to note their opposition to her participation in public life. In a story headlined "Woman's Rights versus Babies," the *Boston Daily Journal* commented, "Mrs. Swisshelm, who conducts the *Pittsburgh Saturday Visiter*, is a staunch friend of 'women's rights,' but she recently, in her own person, illustrated the inconvenience which would attend the assumption of miscellaneous duties by females. . . . She naively says: 'The late 'afflictive dispensation' which has placed a crowing baby in our hitherto quiet home, appeared like a 'call' to deliver the pen editorial into other hands.' And consequently, like a sensible woman, Mrs. Swisshelm promptly determined that woman's first, best place is *home*."[28] The editor of *Western Reserve Transcript* noted that maternity was the primary reason why women should not be admitted to the professions and should be excluded from politics. Never one to ignore a challenge or criticism, Jane responded that just because she was about to give up her role in public life did not mean that she had abandoned her position that women had a right to participate in public affairs. "We do not believe in the best regulated state of society any large proportion of its women would be found in public life," she wrote, "but there should always be some there . . . simply to wipe off the brand of inferiority which has been arbitrarily stamped on them, and the mass of their avocations."[29]

The demands of motherhood neither kept her away from her editorial duties for long nor diminished her interest in politics. By the middle of August, Riddle had resigned as editor, and Jane returned to the office to continue her support of abolition with renewed energy and commitment. We make our paper "political once more," she told her readers. She was determined to support Pennsylvania's "Free Democracy" so that slavery could be "destroyed" through political action. She had met with the Free Democrat delegation at the state convention in Harrisburg, she reported, and had suggested that the party engage someone to take over as senior editor of her paper. But the delegation had voted to leave her in charge and gave the *Visiter* "their most cordial support." Having been endorsed as the official party organ, the *Visiter* would support the cause of Free Democracy and promote the agenda of antislavery politicians.[30]

The Free Soil Party nominated John Hale for president in 1852. But many Democrats deserted the new party, returned to the fold, and helped elect Franklin Pierce as president.[31] The *Visiter*'s fate remained unclear. "We have received several letters of inquiry about the future course of the *Visiter*, by persons who look upon its present political character as a merely temporary arrangement," she wrote to her readers after the November election. "This is a mistake," she assured them. "The Visiter is a Free Democratic paper," she declared, and would "remain so until Hale is elected president. The Visiter can only fail to sustain Free Democratic principles by a most unlooked-for failure in Free Democrats to sustain it."[32] In December, she assured her readers that her miscellany and literary columns would continue "to improve the mind, ennoble the affections and render agreeable the hours passed by the domestic hearth." But she warned that her paper would also have "opinions to avow, principles and measures to advocate, and the general good of the r[a]ce to promote." She intended, she wrote, to help "eradicate the evils that infest" society and to help abolish such evils as slavery and land monopoly, "which threaten to engulph our whole political fabric in irreparable ruin." To that end, she pledged to support "the ascendancy of that party which has inscribed on its banner, Free Men and Free Homes, without which there can be no national safety and prosperity."[33]

True to her word, Jane promoted the interests of Free Democracy in Pennsylvania by arguing that the party was pledged to "no more slave states, no slave territory, no nationalized slavery and no national legislation for the extradition of slaves." She denounced the Democrats and Whigs who had deserted the antislavery cause as "hopelessly corrupt and utterly unworthy of confidence."[34] And she called on the men of the state to support the platform of the Free Democrats, to appoint or elect delegates to represent them at the state convention in Harrisburg, or to attend the convention themselves.[35] During the summer she promoted the candidacy of Free Democratic office seekers, including her friends Robert Mitchell and Edward Allen as well as her husband, James, who was running for county auditor.[36] At the same time, she recruited her friends and political allies to provide more financial support. She attended a Fourth of July picnic in nearby Indiana County, where she made a speech attacking slavery and hobnobbed with party leaders. Much to her satisfaction, party members gathered under a grove of white pines, passed a resolution of support, and formed a committee of five to solicit their friends and neighbors to subscribe to the *Visiter*.[37]

Whether the paper could survive until an antislavery man was elected president remained to be seen, however. By January 1854, the *Visiter* was in serious financial difficulty. She had chided her subscribers for not paying for their subscriptions and tried to bully Free Democrats into ordering more copies of her paper. To save money, she decided to raise the subscription rate and adopt a cash principle in her financial dealings.[38] In desperation, she approached the leaders of the Free Democratic Party of Pennsylvania and asked them to buy her paper and hire her as correspondent or to underwrite her for a year. But they failed to respond. Her disappointment was clear when she wrote that she had devoted the *Visiter* to the interests of the party for three years without any financial support at all.[39]

Unable to continue bearing the financial burden, she turned the paper over to Riddle, who changed its name to the *Family Journal and Saturday Visiter*. She told her readers that the new paper would contain news but would not engage in partisan debate. She continued to oversee the editorial page until March 1857.[40]

The year before, in 1856, the newly organized Republican Party had nominated John C. Frémont as its presidential candidate.[41] While she had loyally supported abolition and opposed the expansion of slavery in the columns of her newspaper since its inception in 1847, the leaders of the Pittsburgh wing of the new party had no reason to welcome her into its inner circles. She was no longer a newspaper editor, she could do nothing to promote Frémont's election, and the Republicans were not willing to complicate their situation by embracing the cause of women. So Jane found herself on the outside looking in. "It seemed that it might injure rather than aid the party to have a woman take a prominent position in it," she wrote in her memoir.[42] For all intents and purposes, she had no political future in Pittsburgh.

With no paper to edit, she retired, at least temporarily, from public life and turned her attention to resolving her deteriorating relationship with her husband. In the spring of 1857, convinced that her marriage had been a mistake, she and Zo moved to St. Cloud, Minnesota, to live with her sister, Elizabeth, and brother-in-law, Henry Z. Mitchell.[43] With little to occupy her time and desperately needing money, she negotiated a deal with George Brott, a real estate developer, to take over the editorship of his *Minnesota Advertiser*. On December 10, 1857, having changed the name of the paper, she issued the first edition of her *St. Cloud Visiter* and began to try to carve out a place for herself in the world of Minnesota partisan politics.[44]

Like many other women, Jane found that the frontier provided fertile ground for attempts to expand the scope of women's activities. The movement of settlers westward led to a blurring of gender distinctions as well as to the opportunity to challenge gender conventions and expand women's roles in society.[45] Women's opportunities to participate in public life expanded because frontier communities needed services. In places such as St. Cloud, expediency rather than convention determined the degree to which women could exert economic and political power. Political life in Minnesota was no less dominated by men than Pittsburgh politics, however. So Jane's efforts to become involved simply magnified the tensions inherent in attempts to define gender roles in emerging frontier communities. Thus, her attempts provide some insight into the techniques that citizens of those communities used to resolve those tensions.

Minnesotans who were deeply committed to abolition were few and far between in the early stages of territorial development. As a result, antislavery advocates could not afford to discriminate on the basis of gender in soliciting support for their cause. But while frontier expediency may have provided Jane with an entrée into politics, she discovered that winning acceptance in the inner circles of male-dominated political life was not easy.

Jane began her editorship of the *St. Cloud Visiter* by attending to a practical matter. To survive as a frontier newspaper editor, she needed the financial support of the community's businessmen. Publishing a newspaper in Minnesota in 1858 was both difficult and expensive. Printing was done on hand presses that were often valued at more than eight hundred dollars. And supplies of paper, ink, and type had to be purchased in bulk and brought to Minnesota in the summer because overland transportation costs in the winter were prohibitive.[46] To succeed, she needed access to considerable capital or to an equally considerable amount of credit. Assuring the members of the business community that she would recommend St. Cloud, Minnesota, as an ideal place for emigrants, she asked them to provide her the means to pay her printers and buy her supplies. Most businessmen responded enthusiastically, but the most prominent figure in the community, Sylvanus Lowry, the leader of the Stearns County Democratic Party, held out.[47]

As the only newspaper editor in town, Jane had the potential to exert enormous influence on St. Cloud's social and political life. Her paper would provide her with a public voice that could not be ignored. As long as she controlled the press, she could determine what was news and what was not. She had the power to define or ignore political issues and to report (or not report) and interpret (or misinterpret) political events. She understood the implications of her position and took seriously her responsibilities. She claimed that editors had at least as much if not more public influence than ministers and, therefore, had a responsibility to their communities to expose corruption and the abuse of power by what she called "political hucksters and wire-pullers" who pursued their self-interests while pretending to represent the interests of the people. In her view, the press in general and her newspaper in particular should be the arbiter of both political and social affairs in the community.[48]

Beginning with the first edition of the *St. Cloud Visiter*, Jane acted on those principles and in the process imposed herself on male-dominated political life. Her intrusion began when she published her "prospectus," which announced that she would be independent in her editorial policy and that her paper would "not be the organ of any party or sect."[49] And she put her readers on notice that she would not be intimidated by the political authority of any man. Noting that she generally had a low regard for most men's pretensions to superiority, she claimed to be in "mutual antagonism" to many of them and warned that she did not intend to mince words in discussing the activities of those who failed to represent the public interest. "When any of our public men appear to require notice of us, or the public good to require that we should call attention to them, we shall say exactly what we believe to be true," she wrote.[50]

In St. Cloud, the political life into which she thrust herself revolved around a struggle over economic power based on land development and political power in a territory that was just becoming a state. Jane's presence as the editor of the local newspaper added a complicating gender dimension to an existing struggle between the male Democratic leadership of the county under Lowry and politically ambitious newcomers such as Stephen Miller.[51] Her intrusion complicated this struggle and intensified and made more immediate the problem of defining the role of women in community life.

Like many politicians, Lowry controlled political life in Stearns County based on his personal reputation for delivering votes for the Democratic Party, managing political appointments, granting other favors, and persuading the railroads to lay their tracks along routes that would serve the interests of Stearns County businessmen and farmers. Lowry's continuing political influence depended on his ability to reach out to newcomers and incorporate them into the political process by soliciting their membership in his party. By definition, he and his cronies were the "wirepullers" of whose machinations Swisshelm was suspicious and determined to expose. The existence of an independent press was not in their best interests. They needed a local newspaper that depended on their patronage and would enhance their political reputations and promote their political and economic agendas rather than a publication that had an unpredictable editorial policy, that held them accountable to high standards of public service, and that provided citizens with alternative leadership.

Lowry and those like him ignored and thus discounted the political opinions of most of the community's women, but Jane's position as editor of the local newspaper meant that she could not be ignored and, therefore, needed to be controlled. To preserve the political sphere as the exclusive domain of men and to confirm the private role of women that made them dependent and thus politically invisible, Lowry and his clique needed to minimize and, if possible, destroy her power to impose her personal political opinions on her readers. So after three issues of the *St. Cloud Visiter* had appeared, Lowry and his friends offered to support her paper in return for the right to dictate what she printed in it. According to Jane, Lowry sent her a note telling her that, in essence, he wanted to cut a deal. He agreed to support her paper if she would agree to support James Buchanan's presidential administration in her editorials.[52]

As an abolitionist, Jane looked with jaundiced eye on Lowry, who had been born in the South and whose family owned slaves.[53] And she was not predisposed to support the Democratic Party, most of whose members she believed supported both slavery and its expansion. But she saw in Lowry's offer an opportunity to attack the Democrats and slavery, so she agreed to the arrangement.

Her acquiescence to Lowry's demands must have been very reassuring to the local Democrats. By agreeing to support Buchanan and the Democratic Party, Jane ostensibly sacrificed her editorial independence. If they had not completely silenced her, they at least assured themselves that her political opinions would be subordinated to theirs. Public evidence of her dependence and deference would at the very least confirm male dominance over the community's political life. The members of Lowry's group no doubt believed that they would again be able to define political issues and control the debate that surrounded those issues and that they had reduced Jane to the traditional political role for women, that of little more than an observer of partisan struggles.

Jane was poor and politically disfranchised, and her marital status was ambiguous, but she was not without resources. She was surrounded by family and friends from Pennsylvania. She was bright, ambitious, self-assured, self-righteous, energetic, and an experienced journalist who was a master of sarcasm and satire. She was also a member of a community whose members had brought with them views about the character of women and men and their place in society. While those views ordinarily denied women direct access to political power, they could be manipulated to serve her interests. For example, she could reasonably assume that because she was a woman, many in her community would be inclined to view her as morally superior to men, untainted by the kind of self-interest that characterized the struggle for money and power among male politicians and businessmen. Therefore, when she took the moral high ground in any controversy, she would have more credibility than her male opponents even though she must have been aware that in the process her moral authority might be tainted by her political activity. She could hope that if her willingness to sacrifice herself to protect the interests and preserve the civic virtue of the citizenry of St. Cloud placed her in danger, some people would have a sense of male honor that would combine with kinship obligations to compel them to try to protect her. And finally, she could anticipate that male arrogance would lead her opponents to underestimate her intelligence and political savvy.

She could safely make other assumptions as well. She could be relatively sure that there were some men in her community—such as her two brothers-in-law and their friends, who had political aspirations and were shut out of the Lowry clique—who would be willing to take advantage of any opportunity to challenge Lowry's control of Stearns County politics. Similarly, she could count on those people to support the idea of freedom of the press, especially when it could be used for their personal economic and political gain.

Whatever the Democrats might have thought, Jane had no intention of giving up her agency as a politically independent newspaper editor. In the name of public service, she was determined to maintain her public presence, to force the county's Democratic leaders to acknowledge and defer to her political influence, and to subvert Lowry's attempt to control her editorial policy. So to fulfill her side of her bargain with Lowry, she published a four-column editorial on the front page of the February 18, 1858, edition of the *Visiter*, pledging her support to the Democrats in general and the Buchanan administration in particular. She wrote that Buchanan and his party sought to guarantee that every working person in the United States was offered the opportunity to become a slave and thus to enjoy the benefits of that condition. With a heavy dose of sarcasm, she invited Minnesota's farmers and workers to embrace slavery and vote themselves "a pair of handcuffs."[54] Lowry was outraged because he had been outwitted, but Jane continued to uphold her part of the bargain by expressing her support of Buchanan and the opportunities for servitude that he offered to voters.[55]

Having been publicly humiliated by a five foot, two inch, blue-eyed, middle-aged woman, the Democratic leadership no longer had any reason to deal privately with Jane, and the struggle that ensued took on a more public dimension. On March 10, 1858, James Shepley, Lowry's lawyer, gave a public lecture on "Woman," in which he played to an audience already plagued by anxiety about the role of women not just on the frontier but in American society as a whole.[56] His speech described four classes of objectionable women—"Coquettes, flirts, old maids," and "utterly depraved" woman's rights advocates. To anyone who had been following the struggle between Jane and Sylvanus Lowry, there could have been no doubt that Shepley was suggesting that Jane belonged in the last category. In an attempt to discredit, humiliate, and intimidate the pesky editor of the *St. Cloud Visiter*, Shepley turned to the gendered anxieties of his friends and neighbors. He alleged that she was no lady and that her presence was a public nuisance as a way of undermining her moral authority and thus rendering her socially and politically impotent and undercutting and trivializing her role in community life. His public action testifies to the degree to which he and Lowry perceived Jane to be a threat. By responding so dramatically to her challenge, he inadvertently acknowledged her influence and publicly incorporated her into the political process.

In choosing this particular line of attack, Lowry and Shepley chose well. At the time she moved to St. Cloud, Jane's claim to feminine respectability was at best fragile, although she conformed to many of the social conventions by which women were judged. Her friends and neighbors knew her to be a delicately featured woman who dressed modestly; a responsible, self-reliant woman who worked hard to support herself and her only child despite her scant resources; a woman whose strong voice could be counted on to uphold the moral imperatives of justice, equality, and fair play—all characteristics of conventional precepts of femininity.

But she was also known to have deserted her husband, and she was a social reformer with "advanced" views about the role of women in American society. She did not hesitate to advocate more rights for women and was determined to expand women's role in public life.

Jane attended Shepley's lecture but said not a word on the subject. Instead, she published a review of it in the March 18 edition of her paper. After she summarized the lecture's content, she calculatedly suggested that he had overlooked a fifth kind of woman—"the large, thick-skinned, coarse, sensual featured, loud-mouthed double-fisted dames, whose entrance into a room appears to take one's breath, whose conversational tones are audible at the furthest side of the next square, whose guffahs resound across a mile wide river, and who talk with an energy which makes the saliva fly like showers of melted pearls." Such women, she continued, "deck their portly persons in coarse prints, of bed-spread patterns and rainbow hues . . . as they stand to perform their office as high priestess at the shrine of Euchre." Not even the need to nurse their children could keep these women from making themselves "agreeable to companies of unmarried gentlemen and the husbands of other women" at the card table.[57] It was now Shepley's turn to express outrage: Jane's description apparently evoked images of his wife.

The little we know about Mary Shepley comes from census data. Born in Maine, like her husband, she was in her late twenties in 1857 and the mother of a two-year-old daughter.[58] From James Shepley's response to Jane's review, it seems likely that Mary spent at least some of her time playing cards, had somewhat eccentric taste in clothes, and did not quite meet the standards of social refinement that were held in high regard in the urban East.

As a journalist, Jane was reluctant to separate politicians' public and private lives. She wrote in an editorial that she looked "upon all politicians, whether in office or out, as fair subjects of editorial comment in all of their political relations—we do not recognize any man's right to privacy in any attempt to govern the people."[59] She was willing to subject the women with whom male politicians were associated to the same scrutiny. She was not the first to do so. Andrew Jackson's political enemies had not hesitated to use the marital history of his wife, Rachel, as a political bludgeon before he was elected president in 1828 and had subsequently impugned the reputation of Peggy Eaton, the wife of his friend and secretary of war, John Eaton.[60]

Association with public figures stripped women such as Rachel Jackson and Peggy Eaton of the right to privacy that their gender should have

assured. For male politicians and for women whose personal relationships imposed them into the world of politics, no clear line existed between what was public and what was private. But there was a difference
based on gender. A politician's enemies did not view his female associates
as political actors but rather as passive conduits to him.

Jane had done the same thing eight years earlier while serving as a
Washington correspondent for Horace Greeley. Angry that Daniel Webster had come out in support of the Compromise of 1850, which included
a new fugitive slave law, she sent a letter to the *Pittsburgh Saturday Visiter*
alleging that Webster kept mulatto women as his mistresses. Despite the
fact that she provided no evidence to substantiate the charge, the story
was clipped and reprinted by other editors.[61] Given the fact that Jane was
not above using the bigotry and racism of the reading public to advance
the cause of abolition in 1850, it is not surprising that a few years later she
was willing use Mary Shepley's behavior and appearance to discredit her
husband and by extension Sylvanus Lowry.

Whatever Mary's habits and attributes, Jane's description of Shepley's wife as much as Jane's intrusion into the male world of politics
prompted Lowry and his supporters to take further action against her.
On the night of March 24–25, 1858, a trio of vigilantes, allegedly including
Lowry, Shepley, and Lowry's doctor, Benjamin R. Palmer, broke into the
printing office of the *St. Cloud Visiter*. They destroyed the press, threw the
type into the Mississippi River and onto the road, and left Jane a note
referring to her paper as a nuisance and to her as little better than a
prostitute. They warned that if she persisted in challenging the power of
the Stearns County Democratic Party, she would pay an even "more serious penalty."[62]

The destruction of Jane's press was meant to render her politically and
socially impotent and to force her back into what Lowry and his cronies
considered her proper place in St. Cloud society. First, the break-in took
away the means by which she supported herself and her daughter and
made her dependent on her male friends and relatives. By destroying her
press, Lowry and his friends cut her off from access to public life, deprived her of her public voice, and destroyed her usefulness as a community booster. She could no longer serve the economic or political interests
of her friends and neighbors through the press.

Jane's relatives, friends, and supporters—both male and female—were
horrified by the attack and called for a public meeting, which was held at
the Stearns House the following evening. Unintimidated by the threatening note left in her office and determined to defend herself, she says that

she drew up her will, arranged for a friend from Pennsylvania to serve as her bodyguard, and then went to the hotel and delivered a lecture in which she named Lowry and Shepley as the men who had destroyed her press.[63]

At that meeting, twenty-nine of her supporters, including brothers-in-law from both sides of her family, formed the St. Cloud Printing Company to reestablish her newspaper and sent to Chicago for a new press and type. Despite renewed threats from Lowry and his friends, she resumed publication of the *Visiter* on May 13, 1858. The first issue was filled with her indignant descriptions of the attack on her press as well as accounts clipped and reprinted from other newspapers.[64] Infuriated, James and Mary Shepley instituted a libel suit against the printing company, claiming damages of ten thousand dollars.[65]

This suit had a number of gender implications. When Shepley filed suit over the libel of his wife, he virtually discounted Jane's responsibility for the affair. Instead of suing the editor who wrote and then published the libel, he sued the male investors in the printing company. He named Jane's actions but not her person in the suit. Shepley sued Jane's supporters for obvious economic reasons. It had to have been clear to everyone in St. Cloud, as well as anyone who read her paper, that Jane had little or no property. She had been living with her sister and brother-in-law. She frequently did not have the wherewithal to publish her paper regularly. Notices that appeared in her paper indicated that she would be willing to be paid in kind for subscriptions because she needed such necessities as firewood.[66] And she did not initially own the office where her paper was published or the press that printed it. Her supporters, however, owned not only the press and type but also substantial amounts of property— some liquid, some not.[67] Shepley was lawyer enough to know that to gain a moral victory and collect damages in the process, he had to sue people who had assets. But there was another dimension to his actions. By suggesting that Jane's supporters could be held morally and financially responsible for her behavior, he figuratively made them surrogate husbands, reaffirming the traditional, common-law principles on which the doctrine of femme covert was based and denying Jane the right to independent action necessary to support her claims to political prerogatives.

Jane responded to the Shepley suit by publishing a disclaimer in the June 17 edition of her paper. Without referring directly to Mary Shepley, James Shepley's public lecture, or the lawsuit, she explained to her readers that her previous description of card-playing women was based on incidents that had occurred before she had come to St. Cloud. Referring to her sojourn in Louisville in the early years of her marriage, she told her readers that she had first seen women playing cards in a "fashionable" boardinghouse. "We had never, up to this time, seen a pack of cards," she wrote. But "night after night," she watched as a "little wife" and an "older widow" sat at the card table with two gentleman boarders, each woman holding a "dainty little cigar in [her] teeth." Always at the table was "the mother" of a young child "who might wail or wake or sleep as suited him best" while his mother flirted with her two male companions. Her second encounter with card playing, she continued, occurred on a steamboat, where "two coarse, sensual-faced women bedizened with vulgar finery sat in the cabin, sometimes with their vulgar husbands, sometimes with other male passengers," playing cards and drinking. One, she reported "had an infant wandering about the boat in the arms of his nurse." The other was in the last stage of pregnancy. "These are the only women we ever saw play," she wrote, "and in our mind, cards, coquetry and coarseness are a trinity, odious and inseparable." Card playing, she warned her readers, threatened the town's moral and social fabric, and she called on the women of the community to lead a campaign against this evil.[68]

Jane's explanation seems to have had little influence on the Shepleys, and the judge who would have heard the libel suit was a friend of Lowry.[69] So Jane's investors settled out of court, guaranteeing under bond that she would publish a statement assuring her readers that the attack on the *Visiter* was not politically motivated and agreeing "never again to discuss or refer to the destruction" of her office in the *Visiter*.[70]

To protect her supporters' property, Jane agreed, and the bond was executed. She published the statement without comment and then closed down the *Visiter*. Her investors dissolved the printing company and turned its assets over to her.[71] On August 5, she began publishing the *St. Cloud Democrat* as the editor and sole proprietor. "Into the first editorial column I copied verbatim, with a prominent heading, the article from the *Visiter* on which the libel suit was founded, and gave notice that I alone was pecuniarily responsible for all the injury that could possibly be done to the characters of all the men who might feel themselves aggrieved thereby." "It seems strange," she wrote in her memoir, "that those lawyers should have been so stupid, or should have accredited me with such amazing stupidity when they drew up that bond; but so it was, and the tables were completely turned."[72]

One of the more interesting aspects of the statement that she was forced to publish to settle the libel dispute was the declaration that the attack on her press had not been politically motivated. This statement provoked a public debate over the nature of the conflict between Jane and her supporters and Lowry and his. Early on in the controversy, Shepley had sent a letter to the editors of the *St. Paul Pioneer and Democrat* in which he argued that the affair that had ended in the destruction of Swisshelm's press was strictly personal.[73] Stephen Miller, one of Jane's supporters, countered by publishing a letter arguing that such was not the case.[74]

It is unclear why the involved parties felt it necessary to debate this question. One explanation is that by this time there was no way to ignore the fact that Jane could not be excluded from public participation in politics. By arguing that the conflict between Jane and the leaders of the Stearns County Democratic Party was a personal quarrel, Lowry and his political supporters could reduce it (and her) to public insignificance, something unworthy of attention and discussion, and thus deny the legitimacy of her political voice and reclaim their exclusive right to define what was political and what was not.

Jane's supporters were not willing to grant that the conflict between her and the Lowry faction was merely a personal matter. It was in their interest to emphasize the political dimensions of the quarrel and to argue that Jane had the right to a public voice. That voice gave balance to political life in a community that before her arrival had been charac-terized by what they considered to be Lowry's demagoguery. Her voice helped them to challenge Lowry's political power and to compete with him on a level playing field for political leadership in the county. As in other aspects of frontier life, people were willing to support Jane in a nontraditional role because it was expedient to do so.

Now sole owner of her newspaper, Jane immersed herself even more deeply in politics. In anticipation of the fall election, she endorsed the Re-publican ticket.[75] And she used the destruction of her press as a bludgeon to discredit the Democrats politically: "Those citizens of St. Cloud who wish to have their place known abroad, as the town where destroying printing presses, is popular, need only vote for the ticket put into the field by his Lordship of Upper Town [Lowry]," she wrote just before the fall elections in 1858.[76] When antislavery Democrats collaborated with Repub-licans to defeat Lowry's ticket, she gave herself credit for having helped to bring about his political demise: "The issue of no press-breaking, entered largely into the canvass," she told her readers, "and the District has glori-ously redeemed itself from that reproach. The Dictator is fallen, fallen. His poor little laqueys are crushed; and the freedom of the press is a fixed fact in Northern Minnesota."[77]

Jane may have reveled in her victory over the Democrats, but she was not yet willing to proclaim herself a Republican. She had been present at the Pittsburgh convention of the Free Democrats, she had long supported the party's platform, she had made the *Pittsburgh Saturday Visiter* the party's official organ, and she had not been welcomed by the Republican leadership in Pittsburgh. So, at least for the present, she was determined to maintain her loyalty to the principles of "Free Democracy." "We say frankly to our Republican friends that we never were a Republican," she wrote in October 1858. And she called on Republican partisans to unite permanently "under the broad banner of [Free] Democracy and drive the Moccasin [Lowry] clique into everlasting imbecility."[78]

Even as late as May 1859, she was still wary of allying herself with the new party and seemed determined to maintain her editorial independence. It did not matter, she told her readers, "under what name the principle of Freedom may triumph." It was "principles" rather than "men or political names" that were important. She pledged to endorse any candidate, no matter what his party affiliation, who opposed slavery. "Whoever will assist in freeing the oppressed . . . shall receive our hearty cooperation and undivided support. We regard a Liberty-loving Democrat as better than a tyrannical Republican and *vice versa*."[79]

At the same time, however, she took note of Republican activities in her paper, chided party members when they fought with each other, and offered unsolicited advice on the conduct of party affairs.[80] When party leader Alexander Ramsey refused to support her friend Stephen Miller for the district's congressional seat, she wrote to Ramsey that she objected to having her preferences ignored: "No doubt you regard me as a maniac, but I have 'method' in my 'madness,'" she assured him. She then summarized the scope of her antislavery journalism in Pittsburgh and claimed that when she attacked those who opposed her, she rarely missed her mark, implying that it was better to have her on his side than against him. Her attacks on Democratic politicians, she argued, were motivated by her desire to see slavery abolished: "My plan of action, from the first, has been to create a public sentiment averse to slavery by all the arguments at my command, thus, to weaken the enemies' forces by shooting their officers." Her strategy, she reported, was to provoke enemies such as Lowry into attacking her first so that when she "killed" them it was seen to be an act of self-defense. "God has particularly fitted me for this and my instincts have never failed. I have all the force which fanaticism gives to scotch caution and in the twelve years of editorial fighting I have passed through, I have never made a statement which could require a retraction or one I was not ready to prove." She admitted her loyalty to the Free Democrats but was willing to work with the Republicans, she said. "If the Republicans throughout the state fail to recognize the merits of our case we must either run an independent state ticket or let our men go back into the Moccasin [Democratic] ranks. The numbers we can bring to the aid of Republicans in the next election may not be very important in a state contest, but this is the beginning of the end." She pointed out that settlers were pouring into Minnesota and that the potential for a Republican electoral victory rose as the population grew. "If we can make a fair gain . . . in the next election, we will be ready to sweep Northern Minnesota in the Presidential campaign with a very large broom. To this end I hope to contribute *more than any other person can do.*" She claimed to be the only editor of any significance above the falls at St. Anthony and demanded that Ramsey endorse Miller as a Republican candidate for Congress. She had laid the groundwork, she assured Ramsey. The voters in her area were ready to desert the Democrats and vote Republican. They were concerned about the Homestead and Land Bills being considered by Congress and were determined to have a representative on whom they felt they could depend. They knew and trusted Miller, she assured Ramsey. To promote his candidacy, she privately acknowledged a willingness to make a deal. If Ramsey would support Miller in this election, she would support Ramsey's candidate in the next. Should he refuse, she warned that she and other Miller supporters would feel that they had been "sold out" by the Republicans. "Don't," she admonished him, "drive our redeemed Democrats back into the ranks of the enemy."[81]

When Ramsey failed to come around, Jane endorsed Miller anyway.[82] And when Miller withdrew from the race, she accused him of imperiling "the cause of Freedom" in the state.[83] Disappointed but not deterred, she published a complete report of the Republican state convention held in St. Paul and endorsed the party's nominees for governor (Ramsey) and lieutenant governor (Ignatius Donnelly).[84]

That fall she contacted the head of the Republican Party's Central Committee to plan strategy for the coming election. She had heard that one of the Democratic candidates had once been a member of an anti-Catholic Know-Nothing Lodge and was determined to use that information to defeat him. Many of the citizens of St. Cloud were German-speaking Catholics, and this was the weapon she needed to force them into the Republican camp. "If you can get that evidence in this district soon," she wrote, "we will most likely carry our legislative ticket. If not we may as well give up now. We want documentary evidence or affidavits that the Democracy have nominated Know Nothings. . . . This District will be carried by one party on that issue *alone*." She also requested that the Central Committee send money to its Stearns County supporters to help them run the campaign. "It is said here that in St. Paul the Central Committee is expending thousands . . . while here in this old stronghold of democracy a handful of us are giving *all* our time and means, and are likely to lose the District for want of money," she complained.[85]

Jane found herself deeply engaged in Republican affairs, corresponding with the party's most prominent leaders and socializing with them when possible.[86] But she continued to pursue an independent road when it came to trying to secure the nominations of antislavery politicians. From the beginning of March to the middle of May 1860, she promoted William H. Seward for U.S. president and Cassius M. Clay as vice president, noting that her selection was "Subject to the Decision of *Nobody's* Convention."[87] When the Republicans nominated Lincoln that summer, however, she approved. Lincoln, she wrote, was just "as much of an anti-Slavery man" as Seward and suited her "admirably."[88]

Southern threats to secede from the Union if Lincoln were elected did not bother her in the least. "Living as we do, so far from the sources of such threats, we could not be expected to be very strongly exercised upon the subject. Indeed, we are of that number at the North, who do not think that a dissolution of the Union would work such fearful consequences. . . . The union between the North and South," she maintained, had "degenerated" to the point where it was nothing more that "a political sentimentality."[89]

She continued on this tack after Lincoln was elected. She could not understand, she told her readers, why anyone would object to the secession of either South Carolina or Georgia. "To our mind, it appears like perfect despotism to compel a State to stay in the Union when she wants to get out." She considered membership in the Union optional, a simple "business partnership" that could easily be "dissolved by mutual consent."[90] "The idea of getting up a civil war in order to compel the weaker States to remain in the Union, appears to us, horrible in the last degree," she wrote at the end of November. "We can see no good reason why the two confederacies should not live in as much harmony, at least as that which has existed for some time past or is likely to do in the future, as members of the same nation."[91] And she opposed spending money to try to reclaim federal property in the South. "Let the South keep the property in their hands, and go in peace," she wrote.[92]

During the early war years, she promoted Donnelly's political career, writing to him about the political situation in Stearns County; complaining about wheeling, dealing, and rascality over which she had no control; and suggesting strategies designed to win elections for the Republicans.[93] In August 1862 she wrote to warn him that he should not consider his election to the U.S. House of Representatives to be a "pregone conclusion." "There is so much dissatisfaction with the course of the National Administration—it so utterly fails to touch the heart of the people, that the masses are seized with apathy." But she wasn't just writing to give him the lay of the land. She was writing to point out that he needed her support and that she was not willing to give it to him for free. "If you are elected it will be after one of the hardest campaigns you have ever been through," she wrote. She assured him that she had "disregarded" her own "pecuniary interests in time[s] past, [had] served the Republican Party without money and without price, because there was a principle involved," but principle did not help to pay the bills. "You need the [*St. Cloud*] *Democrat*," she told him. "To it you owe most of your popularity in this region, for it has persistently kept you before the people. . . . I will do the best I can to further your election *if you pay me fair living wages* or guarantee me in case you are elected some sufficient remuneration in the form of such public printing as I am justly entitled to." She did not intend to entirely desert him if he did not comply with her request. But unless he and the Republican Party helped to sustain her paper, the most she was willing to offer was to continue to place his "name at the head of [her] columns." Donnelly responded by assuring her that when he was elected, he would gladly do what he could to help her but contended that until then, he lacked the means to do so.[94]

She also stayed in touch with Ramsey during the war, providing him information about the strength of the Republican Party in Stearns County and assuring him that she did "not want to work at cross purposes" with his "friends in other parts of the state." She was willing, she assured him, to keep quiet and let his friends work privately to do his bidding. She was also determined to have him lead the party. "We need you," she wrote, "and you are duty bound to give us your best since we will send you delegates if we can but you can get the nomination without them and I think I can wager that there will be no falling off of the vote."[95]

A week later, she wrote, "I do not recognize your right to decline serving Minnesota to the extent of your ability. . . . I have talked face to face with [U.S. Senator Cyrus] Aldrich and [U.S. Senator Merton S.] Wilkinson and cannot decide whether A[ldrich] is [Congressman Henry] Rice's dupe or his willing tool but incline to think both seek Rice's re-election."

As conspiratorial and manipulative as her male counterparts, Jane mistrusted the loyalty of Ramsey's associates and tried to warn him about their potential for betraying his interests and those of the party.[96]

Between 1861 and 1863, she supported Republican efforts to control the state, provided her readers with news about the war, and continued to campaign for the emancipation of the slaves.[97] Her view of Lincoln was influenced as much by his position on slavery as by his skills as commander in chief, and she did not hesitate to criticize him when she thought he deserved it. The matter of freeing the slaves in Missouri stands as a case in point. When General John C. Frémont invaded Missouri, he declared the slaves owned by those who lived in the state to be contraband, which in effect freed them. Afraid of the political implications of that order, Lincoln countermanded Frémont's order. When she heard the news, Jane banded her newspaper in black as a sign of her disapproval. "News comes this morning, that President Lincoln has filled the measure of his imbecility, or treachery, by countermanding Frémont's proclamation. We place our columns in mourning for this, the most terrible calamity that has ever befallen our nation."[98] Her faith in Lincoln was redeemed in April 1862, when he freed the slaves in the District of Columbia and issued his preliminary Emancipation Proclamation in September.[99]

Jane worked hard to make a place for herself in the inner circles of Minnesota's Republican Party. Even the advent of the Dakota Rebellion in Minnesota in the late summer and fall of 1862 did not distract her from her determination to promote the cause of the Republicans in Stearns County. Throughout the Dakota conflict, she never lost sight of the rebellion's political implications. In her columns she defended Republican officeholders' efforts to protect the settlers and continued to provide news concerning Republican political activities.[100]

By December the Dakota War was over. Dissatisfied with Lincoln's response to the uprising and determined to seek vengeance for the hundreds of white settlers who had been killed, Jane temporarily turned her editorship of the *St. Cloud Democrat* over to her nephew, William B. Mitchell. In January 1863, she left St. Cloud and traveled to Washington, hoping to convince Lincoln to take a stronger stand against the Indians.[101] Sometime that summer, she decided to give up her editorship of the *Democrat* and remain in Washington, so she returned to St. Cloud in September to sell to her nephew her press, type, accounts, and subscription list.[102] She continued to send letters filled with political news, commentary, and gossip from Washington to the *Democrat* for publication, but she ceased to have any real influence on Minnesota politics.[103]

Jane Grey Swisshelm's home and office in St. Cloud, Minnesota, ca. 1860.
(Courtesy of the Minnesota Historical Society, St. Paul)

That did not mean, however, that she was willing to leave her public life behind. Like other so-called Radical Republicans, Jane was convinced that the South needed to be punished for its part in the war. Lincoln was assassinated in April 1865, before he could establish a firm policy on the issue of Reconstruction. Vice President Andrew Johnson, a former Democrat and a southerner by birth, took Lincoln's place. With Congress in recess, Johnson struggled throughout the summer and fall to balance the interests of the federal government with those of the Republican Party, which needed southern votes to remain in power.[104] As Johnson used his authority to pardon to facilitate the creation of new state governments in the former Confederacy, Jane became distraught over what she perceived to be his predisposition to coddle the South and his betrayal of the freed slaves, southern Unionists, and the Republican cause. Using the money she earned as a government clerk and what was left of the six hundred dollars she had received from the sale of the *St. Cloud Democrat*, she rented two floors of a building on Tenth Street between N and O and began publishing *The Reconstructionist* on December 14, 1865. "Believing that Liberty is in danger of betrayal," she wrote in her prospectus, "we will publish

THE RECONSTRUCTIONIST," a newspaper "devoted to Equality before the Law—to Honesty, as the best Policy; and Christianity, as the best Statesmanship."[105]

Jane was well acquainted with such Radical Republican leaders as Charles Sumner of Massachusetts and George Julian of Indiana and sympathized with their determination to secure the rights of former slaves and to punish the South for having attempted to destroy the Union and for continuing to flout federal authority.[106] But there is no evidence to suggest that she approached these leaders for support or offered to serve as their official mouthpiece. That does not mean, however, that she did not promote their cause. In her paper, she argued that the federal government should make every effort to guarantee that freed slaves were treated fairly, that they be given the means to support themselves and their families, that they be educated so that they could carry out their obligations as citizens, and that they be given the right to vote.[107] Toward that end, she publicly supported legislation such as Julian's Land Bill, which pledged to give public land in Arkansas, Mississippi, Louisiana, Alabama, and Florida to poor whites and blacks under the Homestead Act.[108] To give her readers up-to-date information on southern recalcitrance, she solicited dispatches from Union supporters in the former Confederacy.[109] And she printed reviews and synopses of speeches made by Washington politicians and southern loyalists.[110]

In the first edition of her paper, she announced that she thought that President Johnson's plan to reconstruct the South was too lenient. "We have hoped against hope and tried to believe against evidence that President Johnson's reconstruction policy was an experiment and that he would frankly acknowledge it a failure," she wrote. But since he continued to pursue his plan, she felt compelled to oppose it. She did not do so with any sense of personal rancor, she assured her readers. Indeed, she claimed to have a very high personal regard for Johnson.[111]

As the weeks passed, however, she became increasingly critical of the president. She ultimately became convinced that he was nothing more than an unredeemed slaveholder who had no intention of punishing the South for its rebelliousness: "He appoints men he knows to be bitter rebels to positions of power, clothes them with such honors as he can, and treats them with distinguished consideration. . . . His ambition was and is, to be the hero of Southern chivalry, to restore to slaveholders their lost dominion over their slaves, and to do this he will risk all."[112] Like an Old Testament prophet, she warned that the God who had blessed the Union with victory was also a God of retribution. Unless the Republicans distanced themselves from traitors such as Johnson, unless the party saved "the country from the impending peril of the wicked coming into high places," the Republicans would "go down with the President, and God will raise up other instruments to do His will," she wrote.[113]

She had been publishing *The Reconstructionist* for a little over two months when she was dismissed from her job at the quartermaster general's office.[114] Ever one to equate misfortune with martyrdom, she claimed that she had been fired because of her criticism of Johnson. Although it is possible that her public stance played a role in her dismissal, it is also true that the war had ended and hundreds of federal employees were being dismissed from their jobs. After she was no longer working for the federal government, her charges against Johnson began to verge on the hysterical. In the March 10, 1866, edition of her paper, she charged that Johnson planned to use his power as president "to arrest the members of Congress as rebels and proclaim the members elect from the eleven [former Confederate] states, and his Copperhead allies *the* Congress of the United States."[115]

Jane's editorials added fuel to the fire that eventually led to Johnson's impeachment. In February 1868, the House of Representatives, dominated by the Radical Republicans, brought charges against him. In May the Senate failed by one vote to convict him.[116] But by that time, Jane's career as an editor was over, and she had left Washington. On March 24, 1866, around eleven o'clock in the evening, a servant opened the door to the pressroom to discover that someone had set a fire near the presses. It had not yet spread, so the servant doused the fire with two buckets of water. But further investigation showed paper drenched in kerosene oil lying near where the fire had begun and puddles of kerosene on the floor. Jane and her compositors lived above the pressroom, along with a number of other tenants, including some children.[117]

The next day, Jane wrote to Greeley of the *New York Tribune* asking to be permitted to say through the columns in his paper that she was discontinuing publication of *The Reconstructionist*. She said that she did not know whether the fire had been started by someone who objected to her editorial policy or someone who objected to the fact that she employed female compositors. Whatever the case, she simply did not have the strength to continue. Anyone who was so reckless as to set fire to a building that housed women and children had to be taken seriously, she continued: "What I may do in the future cannot now be decided upon, but, for the present, I ask 'a suspension of hostilities.'"[118]

With that, her editorial career ended. Her life in the midst of what she later called "the great political maelstrom" was over.[119] Her interest in political matters did not fade. But from that time on, her only access to the public was through the columns of other newspapers, such as the *Chicago Tribune*.[120]

Jane had spent almost twenty years as a newspaperwoman, trying to hold politicians to account for their actions and promoting what she considered to be the interests of social justice. She was convinced that women had an important role to play in American politics. Some might consider her a "fanatic," she admitted, but "the Lord is on our side." "No conviction could be stronger in our mind," she continued, "than the feeling that the Lord.has prepared us by a long course of discipline to stand publicly as the advocate of the oppressed of our own sex, as a representative of woman's right, under God, to choose her own sphere of action."[121]

To hear Jane tell the story, she was alone in such efforts. But as Rebecca Edwards and others have pointed out, a number of abolitionist women were drawn into Republican politics. Both Clarina Gove Nichols and Lydia Maria Child supported the Republican platform and Frémont's candidacy in 1856, Nichols by undertaking a stump speaking tour of Kansas in support of the cause and Child by publishing a pro-Republican, antislavery story in Greeley's *Tribune* just before the election. Seven years later, Anna Dickinson publicly campaigned for the Republicans in the Northeast.[122]

When it served their political interests, male politicians at least tolerated, if they did not necessarily welcome, women of influence. But how enthusiastically they "welcomed" Jane and how much influence she had is unclear. She certainly spent a great deal of time, money, and energy trying to defeat the Democrats, to promote the antislavery cause, to make a place for herself in the inner circles of the Republican Party, and to influence the course of Reconstruction. There is no doubt that she was an active participant in Minnesota's political life between 1857 and 1863. It is also clear that she desperately wanted to believe that she had political power and was a part of the small cadre of politicians who ran Republican Party affairs in Minnesota.

But her insistence on preserving her editorial independence and criticizing Republican leaders when she felt they deserved it made her a somewhat undependable ally. She could be gracious, charming, persuasive, and politically astute—when she wanted to be. But she could also be as prickly as a porcupine. When it came to writing about politics, she was much more likely to dip her pen in vinegar than to coat it with sugar. She often lashed out at those politicians who she believed, for whatever reason, were not toeing the line she had drawn or upholding the public trust as she defined it. The support she offered to antislavery politicians from the 1840s through the 1860s often had strings attached. And it is not clear whether or to what degree male political activists were willing to pay the price she demanded. The Free Democratic remnant of friends and relatives who emigrated from Pittsburgh to St. Cloud no doubt appreciated the attention and support she gave to their political aspirations and activities. But there is no evidence to suggest that Minnesota Republicans solicited either her advice or her endorsement: she simply offered both. Accepting her support cost these politicians nothing except the prospect of being held to account when she disapproved of their actions.

Some historians have argued that Jane's political influence in Minnesota was wide ranging, giving her credit for securing Minnesota for the Republicans, for assuring Ramsey's gubernatorial victory, and for helping to insure that when the state legislature established the University of Minnesota, it was coeducational.[123] Be that as it may, the vigilante attacks on her papers in both St. Cloud and Washington testify to the degree to which she was considered potentially powerful. Neither Lowry nor the Washington arsonist would have gone to the trouble of trying to destroy her press if she was politically impotent. Beyond that, however, there is no way to measure her precise impact on the conduct of political life, on the outcome of elections, or on the passage of specific pieces of legislation.

When Jane and others like her entered the realm of partisan politics, they confirmed that women had a vested interest in political affairs that could no longer be ignored and demonstrated that women could develop a competence that justified giving them political influence. Doing what they could to promote partisan interests, politically active women established a rhetorical and strategic legacy that other women could draw on both in efforts to make a place for themselves within the post–Civil War Republican and Democratic Parties and in efforts to win the ultimate political prize, the right to vote and hold office. During the antebellum and Civil War periods, female politicos discovered that women could not expect to negotiate a significant place for themselves in male-dominated partisan politics without persuading those in power that women had something to offer. It might be editorial support. It might be oratorical, organizational, or fund-raising skills. Or it might be literary expertise. Whatever it was, it had to be something that male politicians valued and believed they could not do without.

CHAPTER SIX

A

WORLD

IN

NEED

OF

IMPROVEMENT

"I remember Mrs. Jane Swisshelm well," said Mrs. P. Lorton, of 231 Market Street [in Louisville, Kentucky], to a reporter yesterday. "I was a young girl when she first came here. It was somewhere about 1840. They rented a house next door to ours on Second street, and Mr. Swisshelm went into some kind of business. As I remember her then, she was a delicate woman, with bright, piercing eyes. She was very nervous, and had a quick, sharp way of talking. . . .

She came down here from the North somewhere, and brought the Northern abolition idea with her. Abolition wasn't very popular down here then. An Abolitionist was regarded much as we would regard a man who made it his business to spread a deadly disease. They were accused of stirring up the slaves to mutiny, and whether they did or not, they got the blame for it.

Mrs. Swisshelm began by going around to her neighbors and talking down slavery. She was an enthusiast in everything; and she seemed to set her whole soul to freeing slaves. . . .

Her husband fell sick and she found herself in a strange and hostile community with neither money nor friends. She opened up a little corset store on Market Street, but nobody would patronize her. Then it was noised about that she was going to lecture through the State in favor of abolition.

This created intense excitement. There were talks of a mob and tar and feathers. I was only a girl at the time; but I was deeply prejudiced against this Northern woman. I was standing at our gate one summer evening watching some children at play. Mrs. Swisshelm was coming home from her shop, her face pale, and big rings under her sorrowful eyes. She stopped when she reached the children and patted a curly-headed darling softly while she beamed down on him the gentlest of looks. The young savage looked up and saw who it was. With a scream he dashed away, calling to the rest of his companions to follow him and leave the 'nigger lover' alone. The great eyes of the sad-faced woman filled with tears, and she wearily turned toward home.

It was a desperate fight she was making, a weak woman fighting single-handed against a people and a civilization for the mighty cause of right; and she was at last forced to give in."

"A Brave Woman: Jane Grey Swisshelm's Battle for What She Thought Right in the Old Abolition Days," Louisville Courier Journal, July 25, 1884, p. 8.[1]

Lorton was wrong. When Jane left Louisville to return to Pittsburgh to care for her dying mother, she left knowing that despite her efforts, she had not persuaded many Kentuckians that slavery should be abolished. But as tenacious and stubborn as her Covenanter ancestors, she was certainly not willing to "give in."

In her pursuit of social justice, Jane was determined to continue her fight against slavery, and as she did so she took comfort in the thought that she was part of a larger movement of intensely committed reformers determined to fundamentally change American society. In the 1830s, 1840s, and 1850s, reform movements were associated with almost every conceivable social problem. Thousands of well-meaning men and women organized to end poverty, to promote literacy, to save prostitutes, to end slavery, to promote peace, to end drunkenness, to promote gender equality, to outlaw capital punishment, and to spread Christianity. These civic-minded people donated money to support orphanages and maternity hospitals, while their tax money paid for prisons and asylums for the mentally ill.[2]

Like Jane, these reformers found the business of social engineering to be difficult. Benevolence and reform work could be satisfying, even exhilarating activities, but they were also exhausting and often lonely enterprises. While charity work was generally regarded as admirable, reform activities could cause considerable social disruption. Trying to change society demanded a great deal of emotional and physical energy as well as courage, self-sacrifice, dogged perseverance, and a self-assurance that sometimes bordered on arrogance and self-righteousness. Reformers were rarely popular people. They reminded the timid of their moral failings and the smugly complacent of their unfulfilled social responsibilities.

Despite the fact that the changes that reformers hoped to bring about typically came slowly and in increments so small that they were often hard to recognize and even harder to measure, peace advocates, temperance advocates, abolitionists, and woman's rights advocates persisted in their efforts. Their willingness to champion the cause of the weak, the poor, and the disadvantaged derived from a variety of sources, among them the conviction that reform efforts were a way of carrying out God's work on earth. This belief gave many of them the physical stamina and self-confidence needed to take a stand against sin, injustice, and inhumanity and inspired them to seek the fellowship and cooperation of other like-minded individuals in the effort to eradicate human suffering and improve society. Proponents of reform held national conventions and banded together in associations designed to promote particular causes and to pool energy and resources to make a mark on the world. As members of groups, these men and women found strength, solace, and comfort.

Jane Grey Swisshelm dedicated her life to trying to improve society, but she was never a part of the inner circle of reformers. Residing in Pittsburgh and then in St. Cloud, Minnesota, separated her geographically from such centers of reform activism as Philadelphia, New York, and Boston. And her editorial duties and family responsibilities left her little time to attend meetings and conventions. Opinionated, domineering, impatient, and contentious, she was not temperamentally suited to the kind of collaboration and cooperation that belonging to a reform or philanthropic organization demanded. She was not willing to let personal loyalty or feelings of affection stand between her and what she considered to be her duty to monitor and if necessary publicly criticize other reformers' ideas and activities. Moreover, she had little tolerance for the endless discussions that seemed to occupy much of reformers' time and energy. Therefore, she worked throughout most of her career in relative isolation and without the strong support networks that characterized the lives of other reformers, finding reassurance in the thought that God did not intend to make the road she trod smooth and that the crosses she had to bear stood as testimony to her covenant with the Lord.[3]

Jane was interested in a wide variety of reforms. Her crusade against capital punishment began when she was teaching in Butler, Pennsylvania, and wrote a series of letters to the local newspaper opposing the practice. She continued her opposition to the death penalty as editor of the *Pittsburgh Saturday Visiter*.[4] Her commentary was part of a debate conducted both in Pennsylvania and in the country as a whole. Influenced by the rise in evangelical religion, which emphasized repentance and forgiveness rather than punitive vengeance, many humanitarian reformers hoped to convince state legislatures to impose sentences of life in prison on people convicted of capital crimes. Death penalty opponents argued that execution cut off all chance of real repentance, that there was no evidence that capital punishment deterred crime, and that many jurors were unwilling to convict in cases that carried the death penalty.[5] Believing that making an effort to rehabilitate criminals was preferable to executing them, Jane wrote in the *Visiter* in 1849 that the job of "a christian magistrate" was to preserve the peace, "protect the innocent—and reform the guilty." "Nobody," she pointed out, "ever was reformed by being hanged," and she argued that incarceration was a better policy than execution.[6] In general agreement with her were some of the most prominent social reformers of the day, including Theodore Parker, Horace Greeley, Henry Wadsworth Longfellow, Gerrit Smith, Samuel J. May, Thomas Wentworth Higginson, and William Lloyd Garrison.[7]

But the cause to which she was most devoted was the cause of woman's rights. Her efforts to promote the interests of women took a variety of forms, including support for the temperance movement. Interest in temperance arose when drinking patterns in the United States began to change. During the colonial period, alcoholic beverages were widely available, and people drank liquor in one form or another in small amounts throughout the day. Some people, of course, drank too much. But communities were small, drunkenness was considered a personal rather than a social problem, and local authorities did what they could to keep local drunks from becoming public nuisances. By the 1830s, however, prejudice against Irish and German immigrants; the growth of towns and cities, which concentrated those who drank too much; and an increase in the practice of binge drinking caused alarm among native-born middle-class reformers, who considered themselves responsible for promoting both public morality and personal responsibility. They charged that the consumption of alcohol by men not only victimized women and children but also threatened to undermine the stability of society and the integrity of the home and family.[8]

Jane's support of the temperance movement focused on the impact of drunkenness on women and the fact that their disenfranchisement gave them no way to protect themselves from the consequences of alcohol abuse. She held tavern keepers responsible for the social consequences of alcoholism. In an 1849 editorial, she suggested that a good way to end drunkenness was to burn down taverns. "This will be called incendiary doctrine," she admitted, "but desperate diseases want desperate remedies."[9] When her friend Robert M. Riddle reminded her in the columns of his *Pittsburgh Daily Commercial Journal* that there were laws against the destruction of other people's property, she replied that the laws protecting taverns were not really laws and had no weight or authority because they lacked moral force: "The grog shop is a direct attack upon woman's right to life, liberty and the pursuit of happiness. She has no means of reaching the evil but open rebellion." Denied their rights as citizens to influence city ordinances regulating the sale of liquor, women, like Boston's Sons of Liberty, had no choice but to resort to vigilantism, she wrote. "We believe firmly that women have as good a right to knock in the heads of whiskey barrels, break bottles, and rid out dram-shops, as the Boston boys had to break up tea chests. The laws forbidding it are no more binding on them than were the Tea and Stamp acts on the old colonists. They were not represented in making them!"[10]

She eventually admitted that her suggestion that "dram-shops" be burned was imprudent and misguided, but she stood by her position that half of society did not have the right to pass laws for the other half without their consent and continued to argue that it was the duty of any "woman who sees a rumseller, for his own gain converting her natural protector into an object of terror and loathing . . . to remonstrate with said rumseller, and to restrain him peaceably if possible, forcibly if need be. It is her duty to protect her home from his rapacity, by such means as nature has provided, since the state has robbed her of such weapons as would be efficient in a legal conflict. A worm, an insect, a bird has the natural right and instinct to protect her home, and has a woman less?" she asked.[11]

Jane's commitment to abolition also tended to focus on how women were affected by slavery. By the time she was born, the Pennsylvania legislature had abolished slavery in the state, and her church had taken a strong position against the peculiar institution, forbidding its members to own slaves or to worship in fellowship with those who did.[12] The Covenanters were not the only religious group to oppose human bondage. The Quakers had been among the first groups to denounce slavery as a sin. Early antislavery advocates tended to support a gradual approach to emancipation, but by the 1830s many abolitionists were advocating a more radical approach, the immediate end to slavery. Convinced that slavery was an abomination, Jane supported the efforts of the so-called "immediatists." Although she never joined an antislavery organization, she was a passionate advocate of the cause and was willing to dedicate her life as a journalist to promoting abolition.[13]

Jane was ideologically committed to abolition but personally removed from slavery until 1838, when she and James moved to Louisville, Kentucky. There she was forced to confront the reality of human bondage. What seems to have bothered her the most about what she saw was the degree to which the existence of slavery demeaned and degraded both black and white women. In her memoir, she summarized her view of slavery by presenting a litany of horror stories to illustrate the unimaginable physical brutality and the debasement of the human spirit she observed during her short stay in Louisville. In her opinion, slavery made a travesty of regard for female virtue and motherhood. Across the street from the boardinghouse where she and James rented rooms, she met a northerner who owned a female slave by whom he had fathered five children. "The older two he had sold, one at a time, as they became saleable or got in his way," she reported. "On the sale of the first, the mother 'took on so that he was obliged to flog her almost to death before she gave up.' But he had made her understand that their children were to be sold, at his convenience, and that he 'would not have more than three little niggers about the house at one time.' "[14] Then there was the story of Liza, "a tall, handsome quadroon," who rejected her master's advances because of her love for another slave, Jo. "To punish both," Jane wrote, "the young master had Jo tied up and lashed until he fainted, while Liza was held so that she must witness the torture, until insensibility came to her relief. This was done three times," Jane continued. Jo was eventually sold "and Liza herself bound to the whipping-post, and lashed until she yielded and became the mother of . . . two beautiful boys."[15]

While in Louisville, Jane claimed to have seen female slaves beaten and tortured, their labor exploited, and their souls neglected by men and women who called themselves Christians. "An old rheumatic cook, Martha," was sent to the workhouse to be whipped because she could not see to do her work, and a white woman disciplined her cook by nailing the woman's ear to a fence with a ten-penny nail.[16]

Living in Louisville also taught Jane that slavery had a negative influence on white women. She was convinced that slavery made sexual predators out of white men, who considered any woman fair game if she was not under the immediate protection of another white man. Women who ventured out alone were likely to be subjected to advances "so lascivious as could not be imagined on American free soil," she reported.[17] Furthermore, she believed that women who found it necessary to support themselves were by virtue of that fact assumed to be sexually available. When her husband's business began to fail, Jane said that she sought employment with a Louisville dressmaker who explained that Jane would be "insulted at every step" if she worked for a living. But Jane had no choice. After setting herself up as a corset maker and seamstress, she claims to have been propositioned as she strolled on the sidewalk outside her boardinghouse and to have been insulted by inappropriate remarks from the husband of one of her customers.[18]

Because of the time she had spent in Kentucky, Jane spoke with some authority on the subject of slavery after returning to Pittsburgh and beginning to edit the *Saturday Visiter* in late 1847. Her primary goal in starting the paper was to promote the cause of abolition. In it, she argued that the U.S. Constitution sought to guarantee the blessings of liberty to the people, that slaves were people, and that the Constitution could not "establish both liberty and slavery to the same people at the same time." To the degree that the Constitution "fixes the curse of slavery upon one human being . . . it is not worth straw enough to burn it," she wrote.[19]

On those grounds, like many other northerners, she opposed the Fugitive Slave Act, passed as part of the Compromise of 1850, which made it easier for southern slave owners to regain custody of their runaway slaves. The only editor in Pittsburgh to express her contempt for the law's provisions and to argue that Americans should openly resist its enforcement, she carried on a heated debate on the subject in her paper with her friend and colleague, Riddle.[20] He believed that honoring the provisions of the Fugitive Slave Law was the price that Americans had to pay to preserve the Union. Assuring his readers that he deplored the existence of slavery and had great sympathy for the plight of those in bondage, he nevertheless maintained that those responsible for enforcing the law had an obligation to pursue, arrest, and return fugitive slaves to their owners and that citizens who opposed the law had no right to interfere with such actions.[21] While Jane was willing to acknowledge that Riddle was a man of "generous impulses and great goodness of heart" who would do anything in his power to help a slave, she was appalled by his position and argued that his willingness to see the provisions of the law carried out made him complicit in efforts to perpetuate slavery.[22]

Whenever she could, Jane attacked slavery in the *Visiter*.[23] The demise of her paper did not diminish her dedication to the cause. After she moved to St. Cloud in 1857, she again had access to public opinion through the columns of a newspaper and lost no time rooting out and exposing sources of proslavery sentiment.

Among the first to be subjected to her scrutiny was St. Cloud's slave-owning Presbyterian minister, the Reverend Thomas Calhoun. Calhoun had emigrated from Tennessee with at least one female slave and had married the sister of St. Cloud's foremost citizen and Jane's political rival, Sylvanus Lowry. In a September 1858 letter intended to embarrass and humiliate the Presbyterian cleric, she wrote in the *St. Cloud Democrat*, "Previous to your organizing a Presbyterian Church in this place, I had some conversation with you about uniting with that society. I stated to you that I could not conscientiously unite in church-fellowship with a voluntary slave holder. You professed a strong disapproval of the whole system of slavery; and detailed your plans for emancipating your slaves." A good deal of time had passed since their conversation, she noted, and he had done nothing but return a slave woman and her young son to

Tennessee. What had happened to them? she asked him in the most public forum she could find.[24]

Calhoun had no wish to engage in a public debate with Jane in a matter he considered his private business. But, as might have been expected, she was not willing to drop the matter. In a second published letter to Calhoun written about six weeks later, she accused him of hypocrisy and defended her right—indeed, her obligation as a Christian—to hold him to account. He should, she wrote, "appreciate any earnest call to rid yourself of the odious suspicion of traficing 'in slaves and souls of men.'"[25]

Calhoun died as a result of an accident in February 1859. God may have been willing to forgive his sins, but Jane was not. Unwilling to let him rest in peace and convinced that "the people of Minnesota" had "a right to know whether" their state was being used as "slave breeding soil; and whether men may here raise babies for the Southern market," she continued her efforts to discredit him by providing her readers with a detailed description of his slaveholding activities. He claimed, she wrote, that he opposed slavery and that when he decided to move to Minnesota he had considered freeing his slaves. His excuse for not doing so was that Tennessee law forbade emancipation. He claimed that he offered his slaves the opportunity to emigrate with him to Minnesota but that only one was willing to accompany him. So he brought her with him, intending to emancipate her. Instead of doing so, however, Jane suggested that he took advantage of the ambiguous status of slaves in the territories and kept the woman as his slave. Eventually, Jane alleged, he took the bondswoman back to Tennessee, where he sold her along with one of her children and used the money to buy "a handsome barouche, horse and harness."[26]

Jane's commitment to abolitionism went beyond the desire to see all slaves freed. She was also determined to do what she could to insure that whites and blacks shared all the opportunities, privileges, and responsibilities that U.S. citizenship was supposed to guarantee. Before the Civil War, she conducted a campaign to integrate Pittsburgh's public schools, writing on one occasion in the *Saturday Visiter* that "the idea of the two races not being educated together on account of the different color of the skin is quite as ridiculous to us as to partition them off according to the color of the hair. . . . White people and black ones go to the same communion table, and most likely they will go to the same heaven or hell and a common school will be a good place to take lessons for the common occupation of a common heaven."[27]

Time did not diminish her determination that whites and blacks should live, work, and play together. While living in Washington, D.C., in 1865, she wrote a letter, published by the *Boston Commonwealth*, complaining that white ladies were discriminating against black ladies of her acquaintance by refusing to admit them to a sewing circle. Signing herself, "Jane G. Swisshelm, General Disturber of the Peace," she eventually reported the matter resolved. With tongue in check, she wrote, "We colored folks—I was always reckoned to have a 'good deal of color'—can meet and sew with colorless folks without either party acknowledging the equality of the other. Our society is entirely democratic. Women with red hair and thin lips are not to be excluded on that account, and the only trouble, in future, is likely to be objections to the shape of my nose."[28]

On these two issues Jane was an integrationist. In her journalism, she tried to convince her readers that skin color was an insufficient reason to deny people the right to be judged on their merits. Jane did not believe that all people were "equal," but she did believe that all people, no matter their color or the shape of their noses, should have equal opportunities to prove themselves worthy of respect and to take advantage of the social, economic, educational, and political opportunities that citizenship was supposed to provide.

In the same spirit, Jane supported the woman's rights movement. Her attitudes toward gender relations seem to have been complicated by her socially conservative religious background and her domestic problems. She worried, for example, about the movement's potential impact on the balance of independence and dependence that characterized gender relationships and on the way masculinity and femininity were conventionally defined. She wrote that while she believed that "the creator gave but one sphere" for the occupancy of men and women and "gave them mutual interest in guiding each other," she was convinced that men and women were innately different.[29] She believed that women had a right to male deference and that men had a duty to take care of women.[30] When in 1851 Riddle accused women who wore bloomer dresses in public of being immodest notoriety seekers and thereby abdicating their claim to respectability and womanliness, Jane responded that he had abdicated his manly obligation to defend women from public ridicule. Reminding her readers that she too opposed wearing the new costume, she nevertheless considered his comment ungentlemanly and his criticism unwarranted. "We have a pretty intimate acquaintance with the private character of quite a number of the ladies who are leaders in this new fashion," she wrote, "and know that their reputation for modesty and moral worth is above rational impeachment. . . . We hate the dress most thoroughly, but respect the women who introduced it and are laboring for its adoption. . . . The fact that they are mistaken in their calculations is no reason why their reputations should be assailed."[31]

Despite her troubled domestic situation, she did not object in theory to the idea that women should depend on men for support and protection. She found it "pleasant to feel under obligations to people we love," she wrote in an August 1849 essay.[32] Later the same year, she wrote, "We claim all the reasonable care, attention and deference from our male friends, that gentlemen are accustomed to accord to ladies."[33] She rejected out of hand Elizabeth Cady Stanton's suggestion that in the pursuit of equality women should declare their independence from men. "We want no such bill of rights as E.C.S. appears to assert proclaimed in our own house," she wrote in 1851. "There is a little army of big men there, and we are rather a small woman, and if they get it into their heads that we ought to take care of ourself, harness horses, cut firewood, cradle grain, make hay, drive the team, and tend the sawmill we should have a sad time of it."[34] She found it hard to believe that "there are sensible women who seriously wish to disclaim all dependence on man—who would claim equal physical strength for the sexes. . . . We never saw any woman's rights woman who did not *practically* claim all the protection, and attention, and deference, on account of her sex, that we claim."[35]

However much Jane wanted to preserve what she considered to be the privileges and immunities that derived from being female, she was sympathetic to the goals that the leaders of the woman's rights movement laid out at their first convention, held in Seneca Falls, New York, in the late summer of 1848. She agreed with the organizers of that meeting that women should not be relegated to second-class citizenship, should have access to a wider variety of educational and vocational opportunities, and should have the right to control both their property and their wages and that the only way that women could protect their legal and political interests was to have the right to vote.

In her mind, preserving one's femininity and demanding access to the privileges and responsibilities of citizenship were not mutually exclusive, and the pursuit of that particular goal would do nothing to undermine the differences between men and women. "Perfect freedom for women— political and social equality of the sexes—would tend to strengthen, not weaken their distinguishing traits," she argued in 1851. And she was convinced that in the end, more rights for women "would make man more manly and woman more womanly."[36] "Let the men keep their big bones, and tough muscles, and rough skins, and athletic employments, and peculiar dress and all that belongs to them," she wrote, "Woman has her own peculiar gifts that are quite as good as his, and quite different from them."[37]

Jane's primary contribution to the woman's rights movement was to use her skills as a journalist to promote the cause and monitor the activities of its advocates. In the beginning, Jane supported the idea of holding conventions to discuss the plight of women and to devise strategies for improving their condition. She published a short article on the Seneca Falls convention.[38] Two years later, both she and James placed their names on a call welcoming those interested in the issue of woman's rights to attend a convention in Worcester, Massachusetts.[39] Neither she nor her husband attended the meeting, but she reprinted detailed reports of the convention proceedings taken from the *New York Tribune*.[40] In May 1851 she traveled to Akron, Ohio, to attend the woman's rights convention held in that city.[41] And later that year she published extensive reports about the second Worcester Convention.[42] Along with her brother-in-law, William, she signed the call for the Syracuse Convention held September 8–10, 1852. And she published extensive descriptions of its proceedings.[43]

But as time progressed, she became disillusioned with the leaders of the woman's rights movement. Among other things, she objected to the propensity of woman's rights advocates, many of whom were involved in other reform activities, to use woman's rights conventions to discuss issues that she considered to be unrelated to women. The problem arose when the issue of slavery was introduced into the discussion of woman's rights at the 1850 Worcester Convention. "The convention was not called to discuss the rights of color; and we think it was altogether irrelevant and unwise to introduce the question," she wrote in the *Visiter*. It was important to pursue one reform at a time, she argued, and she warned that associating woman's rights with antislavery risked alienating the support of those who supported woman's rights but had no interest in abolition. She maintained that woman's rights reformers should stick to their own agenda. "The question of the rights of colored men is already before the people," she reminded her readers. "Let it work out its own salvation in its own strength."[44]

Parker Pillsbury, a supporter of both abolition and woman's rights, immediately responded. He was particularly troubled by her position because she was one of the few editors on whom abolitionists could count for sympathy. He pointed out that race was an integral part of the woman's rights question because black as well as white women were being deprived of their rights.[45]

Jane quickly defended her position. She was not insensitive to the fact that black women needed more rights, she wrote, but "the women of this glorious Republic are sufficiently oppressed without linking their cause to that of the slave. . . . There is no kind of reason why the American prejudice against color should be invoked to sink woman into a lower degradation than that she already *enjoys*—no kind of reason why the car of emancipation, for the slave, should have been clogged by tying to its wheels the most unpopular reform that ever was broached, by having all the women in the world fastened to its axle as a drag." Neither the cause of women nor the cause of slaves had much popular support, she reminded Pillsbury and her readers. "The question of woman's right to equal privileges with the other sex, is like a little boat launched upon a tempestuous river. It may carry woman into a safe harbor, but it is not strong enough to bear the additional weight of all the colored men in creation. True, they may get on board, if they covet the honor of the company already there; but the chance is the whole concern sinks." She remained a committed abolitionist, she assured her audience. "As an individual we have done all we felt able to aid the colored man. We would still lend him an oar or show him how to make one," she wrote. But she did not want him in woman's boat. When the convention shifted its focus away from woman's rights, she felt as if her trust had been betrayed. "The call to the Convention was explicit. It was to discuss the rights of *Sex*. We signed that call . . . and had no thought it was to be converted into an abolition meeting. . . . We feel as if our name had been used for a purpose for which we did not give it." And she pledged to remember this "breach of trust" the next time anyone asked her to sign another call.[46]

There was more to Jane's disillusionment with woman's rights conventions than her objection to the leaders' tendency to lose their focus. Her personal experience as a delegate to the Akron Convention in May 1851 was not entirely satisfying. Organizers seem to have welcomed her with open arms, placing her on the business committee and allowing her to make speeches from the podium.[47] She subsequently wrote that she had been impressed by the delegates, describing them as "the finest collection of the sex we have ever seen." But they refused to support her contention that distinct differences existed between the sexes and that those distinctions should be honored.[48] Moreover, Jane left the convention feeling that its presiding officer, Frances Gage, had not competently handled her duties as president. True to form, Jane criticized Gage in the *Visiter*: "She is a most dignified and elegant woman . . . but she is not acquainted with parliamentary rules, and when women undertake to do business after that fashion they ought to do it well."[49] Gage, who wrote under the name Aunt Fanny and regularly published columns in the *Visiter*, did not appreciate Jane's criticism. Nor did others who had attended the convention and wrote to Jane in support of Gage.[50] Having expressed her opinion, however, Jane refused to back down, observing that because of their propensity to be "led by their feelings and affections [rather] than their judgments," women tended to give "any honor at their disposal to the one they like best." She acknowledged that Gage had considerable literary ability and a "fine personal appearance," but neither of those assets was, in Jane's opinion, a quality necessary in "a good presiding officer."[51]

Concerned more with action than with what seemed to her to be endless discussion, Jane began to question the usefulness of conventions as instruments of reform. "The great fault we find with these Conventions is, they say too much about 'equality,' and do not explain what is meant by equality! They deal in generalisms, and too many of them. . . . If the women who hold Conventions would pick out some one particular thing they want to do, and stick to that like shoemaker's wax to a blanket, they would get that done, but so long as they keep on spreading out resolutions which, like sunset clouds, spread from pole to pole, they will never do much but make folks stare," she wrote in January 1851.[52] Later that year she wrote, "Holding conventions as a means of promoting any object has always appeared to us like working an engine on a boat while the wheels are unshipped! It is a good way to let off steam, but before it can propel the boat the crank must be attached to the wheels. . . . Conventions appear to us rather more apt to create contentions amongst the friends of a measure, than any unanimity of action. . . . Nothing in the history of these conventions proves to us that they are the best means, or in fact any means at all, of reaching the end desired. . . . *No State, so far as we are informed, has made any legislative advance on this question since these conventions began.*"[53] Conventions, she concluded, had no practical effect on the status of women in the United States.[54] But being unenthusiastic about conventions, however, did not diminish her commitment to the cause of woman's rights, and she continued to cover the issue in her newspapers, both in Pittsburgh and St. Cloud.

Despite her propensity to criticize the leaders of the woman's rights movement and to find fault with their strategies and activities, Jane continued to support most of their goals. The issue about which she felt most strongly was married women's property rights, but she also supported the idea that women should have access to higher education and vocational training as well as opportunities for honorable employment.[55]

OHIO WOMEN'S RIGHTS CONVENTION,
HELD AT AKRON, MAY 28TH AND 29TH, 1851.

Caricature of the delegates to the 1851 Akron Woman's Rights Convention, *New York Pictorial Picayune*, January 1, 1852. (Courtesy of the Library of Congress, Washington, D.C.)

She hired women to work in her newspaper offices and encouraged other editors to do the same.[56] And she campaigned for equal pay for equal work.[57] She was convinced that circumstance rather than ability prevented women from excelling in art, science, and literature,[58] and she enthusiastically supported the idea that women should vote and hold office, writing, "We believe it is women's right and duty to exercise the political franchise—to sit in legislative halls, not merely as ornaments, like a painting or piece of statuary, but as lawmakers."[59] In 1850, she published a letter in Amelia Bloomer's *The Lily* in which she argued that although women with small children should remain at home, older matrons would make good legislators.[60] Five months later, she published another letter arguing that women should have the right to vote because they had "natural individual rights which require the protection and guarantee of society. In every relation [women have] separate and individual interests that need to be represented." Women, she argued, should help write the laws that they were expected to obey. This responsibility, she continued, could not be assumed by others.[61]

Jane campaigned for the immediate abolition of slavery. But she was a gradualist when it came to promoting woman's rights. Women, she believed, should attempt to advance their cause as opportunities presented themselves. "An ounce of experience is worth a ton of speculative opinion. Let us be content to get along step by step, and see how we like the ground and prospect before us at each succeeding one," she wrote in the *Pittsburgh Saturday Visiter* in 1851.[62] She never wavered from that general position. In 1880 she wrote that women's legal disabilities should be reduced "little by little, as experience should show was wise" and that women weakened their cause by making "impracticable demands." The strategy she recommended was to "make no claim which could not be won in a reasonable time. Take one step at a time, get a foothold in it and advance carefully." She believed that women should first be granted suffrage on the municipal level. "Suffrage in municipal elections for property holders who could read, and have never been connected with crime, was the place to strike for the ballot," she wrote. And she admonished the suffragists to "say nothing about suffrage elsewhere until it prove successful here."[63]

By the time she moved to St. Cloud in 1857, Jane had mapped out her position on the issue of woman's rights. In the process, she had set herself apart from such leaders of the movement as Elizabeth Cady Stanton, Parker Pillsbury, Frances Gage, and Lucy Stone by arguing with them over ideology and strategy or insulting their leadership skills. Nevertheless, after settling in Minnesota, she continued to support the movement both by publishing news of its activities and by lecturing on the subject of woman's rights.[64]

The leaders of the woman's rights movement respected Jane's writing ability and her power to promote their cause. Some of them found her witty and "sparkling" and enjoyed it when she "seized" with her "metaphysical tweezers" those who opposed woman's rights. Bloomer admired

Jane's "dare-devil independence" and fearlessness, and Stanton characterized Jane as a "genius." But Bloomer, Stanton, and others were put off by
Jane's lack of collegiality and her unwillingness to work with them; furthermore, they wished that she would show more appreciation for their
work and for their unwavering commitment to the cause. Consequently,
they tended to hold her at arm's length. Stanton put it mildly when she
wrote, "We like [Jane], although she is forever saying something we wish
unsaid." Matilda Joslyn Gage was less willing to mince words. Responding to Jane's public criticism of Stanton, Victoria Woodhull, and other
woman's rights advocates, Gage characterized Jane as a "Judas." From the
columns of the *Chicago Tribune*, Gage proclaimed Jane a "traitor" who was
willing to resort to slander to promote her interests.[65]

In the absence of pre–Civil War woman's rights organizations, the
movement was held together by the leaders' mutual esteem, affection,
and trust, cemented during periodic visits and through frequent correspondence. Jane spent little time with other activists, and they did not
find her contentiousness endearing. Although Stanton and the other
movement leaders did not always agree with each other and were willing
to debate issues relating to ideology or strategy, they believed that to
appeal to as many people as possible, disagreements had to be held to a
minimum. Jane, conversely, thrived on controversy.

Jane appears to have had little influence on the activities and strategies
of the early woman's rights movement, but after the Civil War, woman's
rights advocates began to develop the kind of narrowly focused, step-by-
step, practical approach that she had originally advocated. Upset that the
Fourteenth and Fifteenth Amendments to the Constitution guaranteed
freedmen the right to vote but did not expand suffrage to women, members of the Anthony-Stanton faction of the woman's rights movement,
many of whom had been abolitionists, began to lose interest in former
slaves and to concentrate exclusively on advancing the cause of women.
And while woman's rights supporters continued to hold conventions,
they increasingly devoted their time to the practical matter of petitioning
and lobbying for woman's suffrage on the municipal and state as well as
national levels. The Victoria Woodhull affair, which tainted the woman's
rights movement by associating it with the practice of free love, provided
even more incentive for woman's rights advocates to modify their demands and narrow their focus beginning in the 1870s. By the early twentieth century, suffragists finally adopted a strategy that Jane would have
supported when they began to emphasize the idea that women differed

fundamentally from men and had specific gendered interests that only the vote would protect.[66]

Jane spent her career as a journalist championing the interests of those she believed to be in need of her help. In the process, however, she exposed the kinds of tensions and contradictions that characterized a reformer's life. Misdirected efforts that distorted the philanthropic spirit and competition for scarce resources as well as personal rivalries and the pursuit of self-interest all plagued the world of social reform.[67] Nothing better illustrates those tensions and contradictions than Jane's campaign to punish the Dakota Sioux Indians of Minnesota for their 1862 uprising and her attack on Horace Mann's niece, Maria, over the administration of an orphan home in Washington, D.C., in early 1865.

Jane arrived in Minnesota in 1857 with a highly romanticized image of the Indians, a benevolent attitude toward them, and boundless optimism about their ability to assimilate. Her ideas regarding them were similar to those of many other northeasterners. "Before going to Minnesota," she wrote in her memoir, "I had the common [James Fenimore] Cooper idea of the dignity and glory of the noble red man of the forest."[68] She saw Native Americans as both good and bad, noble yet uncivilized, virtuous and uncorrupted but heathen and savage.[69] She intended to adopt a benevolent attitude toward whatever natives she encountered and pledged that those "unsophisticated children of nature" would never "want for salt while there was a spoonful in my barrel." She hoped to befriend them "by caring for their sick children, and aiding their wives."[70]

Abolitionism reinforced her belief that the native inhabitants of Minnesota needed whatever help she could give. Like other antislavery advocates, including Lydia Maria Child, William Lloyd Garrison, and Lucretia Mott, Jane was predisposed to view the condition of Indians as analogous to that of slaves. She defined both as races apart and felt that both were victims of white exploitation and violence.[71] "Our government," she wrote, "is rolling up a fearful responsibility in permitting them to be robbed and demoralized by the brutal whites who seek their ruin."[72]

Although abolitionists were interested in and sympathetic toward the Indians, only a few reformers had any personal contact with Native Americans. Moreover, any concerns about them were often tangential to the more immediate goal of freeing the slaves. As a result, slavery opponents tended to reduce the struggle between white settlers and Native Americans to a clash between the weak and the strong and to assume that civilization would eventually prevail over savagery. Thus, despite harboring concerns about the fate of the Indians, abolitionists failed to develop any coherent, practical program for dealing with Native Americans before the Civil War.[73]

Jane was among the few well-known antislavery advocates to settle on the frontier; consequently, concern about the Indians and their relationship with whites had more immediacy for her than for those she had left behind. So while her abolitionist background fostered her interest in Indians and prompted her benevolent feelings toward them, it provided little in the way of help in devising practical strategies for living among them.

Busy establishing herself as a force to be reckoned with in Stearns County's business and political life, Jane paid little attention to the native inhabitants of Minnesota following her arrival in St. Cloud and devoted little space in her newspaper to discussion of their affairs. She eventually came to distinguish among the Dakota (whom she called the Sioux), the Ojibwa (whom she called the Chippewa), and the Winnebagos. But despite her original plans to help the natives, she made little effort to acquaint herself with the members of any of these groups.[74] The town of St. Cloud served as a physical and cultural buffer between her and the indigenous population. For her, most Indians were merely a part of the frontier landscape, shadowy figures who occasionally materialized on the streets of St. Cloud or lurked on its outskirts.

When confrontations between the Dakotas and the settlers came to her attention during her early years in St. Cloud, her reports were ethnocentric but otherwise generally evenhanded. She was critical when Indians appropriated the property of settlers, and she tended to view the natives as "lazy." But she counseled tolerance and patience, noting that it was "wiser and better to suffer loss, than to have any serious personal difficulty with the Red man." Critical of the way whites treated Native Americans, she wrote, "It may be that the Indians and whites have different understandings of the treaty by which they sold their lands; and it may be that consideration has not been fully paid to them." And acknowledging that "whites are the stronger and wiser party," she called for forbearance as well as justice and fair treatment for the Dakotas.[75]

Before the rebellion, Jane tended to view Minnesota's natives as exotic curiosities and irritating nuisances, more of a danger to each other than to whites. Any "refined and intelligent" housewife could get rid of them with little more than a broom or pitchfork, she claimed.[76] She, like most of the settlers in frontier Minnesota, was thus completely unprepared for the violence that began on August 17, 1862. On that day, four hungry

Dakotas, after arguing about whether to steal some eggs, attacked a farm-house near the town of Acton, Minnesota, and killed five settlers.[77]

Within days after the initial incident, the Dakotas attacked settlements and forts all along the Minnesota River in southern Minnesota, killing settlers, stealing their property, and burning their homes. Whites fled the area, carrying with them stories of horror and atrocity and swelling the populations of towns and cities to the north and east, including St. Cloud.[78]

The Dakota Uprising was unexpected, but, in retrospect, it should not have been. The Dakotas were hungry. Forced to give up their land eleven years earlier, some had begun to farm. But nature was not kind to them, and their crops failed in 1862. Other natives continued to hunt but encountered hostility from whites who resented and feared the presence of Indians off the reservation. The Treaty of 1851 had guaranteed the Dakotas compensation for land ceded to the federal government: these annuities were scheduled to be paid in June 1862. By August, however, there was still no sign of the money or the services that federal officials had promised. The land hunger of white settlers and real estate speculators continued as troops from Minnesota headed for the battlefields of the Civil War, leaving the state's white citizens unprotected and vulnerable.[79]

Situated above St. Paul and the falls at St. Anthony on the Mississippi River, St. Cloud lay more than one hundred miles from Fort Ridgely, the center of the uprising.[80] Still, Stearns County was not well protected. So, despite her immediate sense of security, Jane warned the citizens of St. Cloud to take precautions in case the Dakotas moved north or the Winnebagos and Ojibwa, who lived nearby, decided to join the conflict.

Throughout the Dakota War, which lasted for only a few months, she continued to publish her weekly paper. In the beginning, her response to the affair was relatively calm. While she clearly wanted to provide her readers with the latest news, she tried to avoid spreading rumors and relied on as much firsthand information as she could get.[81] But as time passed, it became increasingly difficult to obtain accurate and up-to-date information, and she began to anticipate what she considered to be an inevitable Indian attack on St. Cloud. "We may reasonably expect an attack here at any time of the day or night," she wrote, and "it is little short of insanity to expect any assistance from State or national sources." So she called on the town's residents to prepare to defend themselves and outlined plans to fortify the Baptist Church, offering to pay part of the cost of doing so.[82]

Like most civilians unaccustomed to the kind of inhumanity sanctioned by war, Jane was appalled by the acts of brutality described by the survivors of Indian attacks. The Green Lake postmaster told her that the Dakotas had "cut the heads off" of two members of his party, "set them up in the road and placed their hats on. They took the skin off entire from the face and front part of Mr. Larenson's head with both the ears. They cut off Mr. Buckland's right hand, set his snuff box by his face, placed the finger and thumb in the box with a pinch of snuff between them and propped the hand so as to keep it in that position, and so left them."[83]

Her increasingly inflammatory rhetoric was intended to galvanize public opinion against the Indians, prevent complacency on the part of St. Cloud's citizens, mobilize them to take increasingly elaborate steps to protect themselves, and assert herself as a community organizer. She had always tended to champion the cause of anyone she considered to be a victim. Believing that Minnesota's farming families were in no position to defend themselves, she used her position as a newspaper editor to voice their concerns and demand retribution for their suffering. And she did so with a ferocity that was excessive, even for her.

By the time the conflict had ended, she viewed the Dakotas as little better than beasts of prey and attempted to convince her readers, Minnesota politicians, and federal authorities that something drastic needed to be done to preserve the white settlers' safety. Describing the marauding Indians as "crocodiles" and "red jawed tigers whose fangs are dripping with the blood of innocents," she advocated removal of the Dakota from the land that had been guaranteed them by the Treaty of 1851. And the woman who had once called for an end to capital punishment in Pennsylvania demanded that those who refused to move be exterminated.[84] "It is folly to fight Indians as we would European soldiers," she wrote. "Let our present Legislature offer a bounty of $10 for every Sioux scalp, outlaw the tribe and so let the matter rest. It will cost five times that much to exterminate them by the regular modes of warfare and they should be got rid of in the cheapest and quickest manner."[85] Because of their acts of "butchery," the rebellious Dakotas had become merely "organized bands of murderers and as such, have by all laws human and divine forfeited their right to life."[86] "A Sioux has just as much right to life as a hyena, and he who would spare them is an enemy to his race," she concluded.[87]

The U.S.-Dakota Conflict ended in December. Federal authorities hanged thirty-eight Dakotas who had been convicted of participating in the rebellion.[88] Many more natives, including women and children, were imprisoned or forced to move further west. But Indians remained in Minnesota, so the question of frontier security continued to rage among the white citizens of the state. Determined that Minnesota settlers would never again have to worry about protecting themselves from the Indians, Jane decided to put her nephew, William B. Mitchell, in charge of running the *Democrat* and travel to Washington to convince Lincoln to take a stronger stand against Minnesota's native inhabitants.[89] There she delivered a series of public lectures on the problem. If more Dakotas were not brought to justice, she warned from the podium, "our people will hunt them, shoot them, set traps for them, put out poisoned bait for them— kill them by every means we would use to exterminate panthers. We cannot breathe the same air with those demon violators of women, crucifiers of infants. Every Minnesota man, who has a soul and can get a rifle, will go to shooting Indians; and he who hesitates will be black-balled by every Minnesota woman and posted as a coward in every Minnesota home."[90] Despite her provocative and inflammatory rhetoric, she found that her audiences were more curious than concerned about either the Dakotas or their victims. Distracted by the Civil War, they did not seem interested in the West and appeared to be bored by the subject of Native American depredations.[91]

Unable to make any headway in Washington, Jane used the columns of the *St. Cloud Democrat* to suggest that the citizens of Minnesota should resort to vigilante justice. The people should see to it, she wrote, "that for every white person killed three red skins shall die, and then organize hunting parties of from two to ten, kill the number and send Little Crow [the leader of the Dakotas] the scalps in evidence that the threat has been executed."[92] A few months later, in May 1863, she assured her readers that settlers who felt threatened by the Dakotas had "a right to choose the means by which they will secure themselves in their right to life and liberty, to pursue their lawful avocations."[93]

Between her arrival in Minnesota in 1857 and her departure in 1863, Jane's ethnocentric but high-minded and benevolent reform mentality collided with the reality of frontier life. And that collision transformed her into an anti–Native American vigilante. Along with her baggage and her daughter, she brought to Minnesota the belief that the Indians were powerless victims of historical circumstance whose culture was condemned to extinction and who needed whatever material assistance and legal safeguards benevolent whites could provide for them. The U.S.-Dakota conflict provided the lens through which she came to appreciate the power of the Indians to resist the civilizing process and the limits they imposed on white ability to control them. By rebelling in the late summer of 1862, the Dakotas reversed the power structure that had been so carefully crafted by federal government agents, Minnesota state officials, and ordinary white settlers. The natives challenged white authority by contesting the settlers' claims to the land, threatening their safety, and rejecting their law. Jane was willing to champion the interests of those she believed to be powerless, but the violence of Dakota attacks on Minnesota farm families suggested to her that those who needed her advocacy were not the Indians, whom she had once considered to be innocent victims of white greed and mistreatment and the deserving focus of compassion or charity, but the white settlers. Faced with Dakota resistance to what she considered to be the inevitable advance of civilization, she called on white men to take the law into their own hands.

Jane's comments about the Indians were characterized by a peculiar kind of racism. It is true that as long as she believed that the Indians posed an immediate threat to white setters, she wanted to see them exterminated. But she seems to have been more concerned about specific aspects of their behavior, situation, and culture than about their race. She believed that their attacks on Minnesota farmers were unjustified, and she was critical of the reservation system, which gave Native Americans claim to land that she did not believe they needed or used and to annuities that allowed them to live without "working." She placed great value on labor and was wont to quote the biblical injunction, "By the sweat of thy brow thou shalt eat bread." Therefore, she found objectionable what she considered to be their unprovoked aggressiveness, their undeserved privilege, and their ability to live without engaging in the kind of activity that in her mind qualified as work. As a result, she was prone to equate Indians with southern slave owners: "The Indian and the Slaveholder have been the aristocrats of American society. They have been fostered and fed and kept in idleness like a den of rattlesnakes and cage of pet panthers until grown strong and insolent they have simultaneously broken loose to sting and tear those who have fed and fondled them. *Both races must be exterminated* or learn the art of working for a living, and find some other occupation for their activity, than in plotting and executing treason and murder."[94] Like her contemporaries, Jane thought in racial categories, but she did not always privilege the white race over others. When it came to black-white relations, she was an integrationist. And she believed that white slave-owning southerners who supported the treason of secession and waged war against the Union were just as objectionable as Indians who killed settlers.

Jane's distorted sense of justice and the moral outrageousness of her demands had little appeal in St. Paul. Political and military authorities, many of them her personal friends, were not willing to implement the kind of draconian policies she advocated. So she decided to remain in Washington and to continue her career as a journalist by sending regular dispatches back to the *Democrat* so that her readers could have up-to-date information on the conduct of the Civil War.

Posting letters back to St. Cloud combined with her official duties in the quartermaster general's office and her volunteer nursing activities left her little free time. But sometime after her arrival, she became interested in helping to ameliorate the condition of contraband and freed slaves. The plight of former slaves in Washington was particularly desperate. The capital city was not a pleasant place to live during the war. Noisy and bustling, it was populated by transient and often rowdy soldiers, refugees, government contractors, lobbyists, clerks, legislators, and job seekers. In a letter to her readers, Jane described Washington as over-crowded, smelly, and dirty: "The streets and open spaces in Washington are plentifully besprinkled with dead horses, dead dogs, cats, rats, rub-bish and refuse of all kinds. . . . The street in front of the President's house and War Department has a gutter heaped up full of black, rotten mud, a foot deep and worth fifty cents a cart load for manure. It appears to be a matter of national pride that the President is to have more mud, and blacker mud, and filthier mud in front of his door than any other man can afford. Five Points [one of New York City's worst neighborhoods], when I saw it, was clean compared to Pennsylvania Avenue in front of the Executive mansion."[95]

Without the means to support themselves, runaway or abandoned slaves roamed the teeming streets of Washington, sleeping in doorways or alleys and scavenging food wherever they could find it. In response to the situation, the federal government began building temporary refugee camps to provide the former slaves with somewhere to live. But in trans-ferring contraband families in and out of various camps, orphaned chil-dren or those separated from their parents were often left behind to fend for themselves. Aware of their distressed circumstances, a small group of Washingtonians in 1863 formed the National Association for the Relief of Destitute Colored Women and Children.[96] Jane joined the organization and became one of its officers.[97] To assist the group, Secretary of War Edwin M. Stanton authorized the confiscation of an eighty-acre estate owned by Richard S. Cox on Georgetown Heights and ordered that it be given to the society.[98]

In possession of a large furnished house and with support from the federal government, funds obtained from philanthropists in the North, and money derived from leasing the land the group now held, the society modified the house and built temporary outbuildings to house, feed, and educate about eighty occupants. While the trustees of the organization were willing to raise money to support the home, they did not intend to spend much time on the premises, so they hired a matron to manage the asylum and then began to look for a teacher.[99]

The woman chosen to supervise the orphans' educational activities was Maria Mann, niece of noted Massachusetts educator Horace Mann. After accepting the teaching position at the orphan home, the quiet and reserved Maria turned to her family to help her raise funds for the orphan school. With the support of Horace's wife, Mary Peabody Mann, and her sister, Elizabeth Palmer Peabody, a Transcendentalist educator and founder of the kindergarten movement, Maria raised money to buy school supplies and secondhand desks.[100]

By the time Maria arrived in Georgetown to begin teaching in September 1863, the orphan home had admitted sixty-two children, many of them infants. Living in crowded and unsanitary conditions, most of the children were already infested with parasites and were in generally poor health, suffering from consumption, scurvy, and other forms of malnutrition as well as chronic diarrhea, smallpox, measles, and camp fever.[101] Mann first taught her pupils in the parlor, but by January 1864 a barracks serving as a dining room, laundry, schoolroom, and dormitory was completed.[102] The constant influx of children, however, meant that remodeling and renovation had to continue.

About a year after Mann's arrival, the officers of the orphan asylum hired Lucy N. Colman as matron. A widow from New York, she was an abolitionist and woman's rights advocate who had worked as a teacher and had both helped to integrate the public schools of Rochester, New York, and campaigned against corporal punishment of students.[103] Strong willed and accustomed to wielding authority, Colman dedicated herself to assuring that the orphan children for whom she was responsible got the best of care.

When Colman arrived in Georgetown in the late summer of 1864, the orphan home was in a state of chaos. The barracks that had served as a dormitory had been taken down to make room for new construction. The beds for all the boys had been moved into the house, and all of the children then living at the home slept together in two or three rooms, including the parlor. Only one stove remained for cooking and boiling water. The grounds had been dug up, and when the children returned from playing outside, they brought dirt and mud with them. Bad weather forced the staff to keep the children indoors, crowded into the dining room, kitchen, and cellar. And because Maria Mann had been out of town for part of the summer, the orphans had been left to entertain themselves.[104] Under the circumstances it is not surprising that Colman found the children largely out of control.

Colman faced the herculean task of putting the affairs of the orphan asylum in order. Her first step was to assert her authority over the other members of the staff. She told Mann that she was to have no authority outside the classroom. Colman held the staff responsible for the lice and other unidentifiable creatures that infested the children's bodies and called in an army surgeon to provide advice on the best way to rid the orphans of the parasites.

The relationship between Colman and Mann deteriorated rapidly. Mann refused to share a room with Colman and, in a fit of pique, verbally abused her, calling her "a spiritualist, a woman's rights woman, and a free lover."[105] Colman responded by locking Mann out of the house.[106]

After only three weeks at the orphan home, Colman sent a letter to the administrative committee of the National Association for the Relief of Destitute Colored Women and Children, charging Mann with insubordination and with cruelly treating the children in her care.[107] Colman alleged that Mann forced the orphans to work on Sunday, denied them food when they were disobedient, and cut off their water supply because they wet their beds. Mann also reportedly forbade the children from using the front parlors and prohibited them from eating fruit from the orchard. Colman also charged that Mann had physically abused a sick child by turning him out into a storm because he could not control his bowels and that he had died as a result.

The administrative committee responded to the charges against Mann by appointing three male trustees to investigate conditions at the home. After their inquiry, two of the three agreed that Mann had been unduly severe with the children and disrespectful to her superior, Colman. They advised the board to ask for Mann's resignation. The third member, George E. Baker, recommended that both Colman and Mann be fired.

Colman resigned within the month and almost immediately found a position as superintendent of eleven freedman's schools in the Washington area.[108] But, committed to the well-being of her former charges, she paid her dues to the orphan association to maintain her membership and provide as much support for the children as possible. Instead of following Colman's example, Mann remained at her post. Outraged by the charges against her and horrified at being the subject of public discussion, she called on the members of her family to marshal their considerable resources and come to her defense to help her keep her job.

The Manns and the Peabodys were friends with some of the most powerful and influential people in the Northeast. To protect Maria's reputation, Elizabeth Peabody wrote to William Cullen Bryant, the editor of the *New York Evening Post*, explaining the situation and asking him not to mention the affair in his paper.[109] The family also appealed to Massachusetts Governor John A. Andrew, who sent his private secretary, Albert G. Browne, to Washington to look into the matter.[110] With the support of such a notable group of people, the family felt sure that Maria's reputation as well as her position would be secure.

All was quiet for the next few weeks. But Peabody and the Reverend William Henry Channing, nephew of William Ellery Channing and Washington's Unitarian minister, arrived at the association's annual meeting on January 10, 1865, prepared for trouble.[111] And trouble is what they got. Jane also attended the meeting, and after the annual report had been read, she interrupted the proceedings to repeat Colman's charges against Mann and to denounce the executive committee for ignoring the recommendation that she be asked to resign. For Jane, the conflict between Colman and Mann was more than just a personnel matter. It confirmed her belief, derived from her work in Union field hospitals, that internal politics, professional rivalry, and the pursuit of self-interest could seriously undermine efforts to help those in need. The dispute also reinforced her inclination to be suspicious of the powerful and well connected. And, finally, the incident served as just another example of the kind of "robbery and cruelty" that she believed characterized public and private philanthropy in wartime Washington.[112]

At Channing's suggestion, the board appointed a new committee to review the situation, but Jane was not satisfied. She dispatched a letter to the *Washington Evening Star* that accused Mann of committing "atrocious abuses" and Channing of prejudging the case without hearing all the evidence.[113] Thoroughly humiliated and embarrassed by the charges against her, Mann resigned the day after the meeting. Convinced that she could still be of service to Washington's freed population, she took the money she had raised and the supplies she had collected and leased land near the corner of Seventeenth and M Streets, where she set up a school devoted to education of young people of color.[114]

Predictably, Jane was unwilling to let the matter rest. Believing that

Mann had not been sufficiently held to account for her misdeeds, Jane wrote "Margaret Merlyn," a fictionalized account of the affair that appeared in the *St. Cloud Democrat*. "Margaret Merlyn" tells the story of the orphan home; its inattentive board of managers; and its cruel teacher, Miss Augusta Ironton, whose smug self-assurance derives from her powerful friends and her access to money. Margaret Merlyn is the virtuous heroine, devoting her life to prosecuting a "war against those systems of crime and robbery and wrong which make the great old earth a prison house of sighs to so many thousands of her children."[115]

Jane's attack on the Dakota Sioux in Minnesota illustrates the tensions inherent in the pursuit of social reform. She believed that her role as a reformer required her to champion the cause of the powerless. In this case, however, she believed that the white settlers rather than the Dakota needed a champion. However misdirected her campaign to remove Minnesota's Dakota Indians if possible and exterminate them if necessary to assure the safety and well-being of Minnesota's farmers, her actions were consistent with her Calvinist obsession with sin, guilt, and punishment. Her attack on Maria Mann also exposed the fault lines that separated reformers from one another and the tensions that constituted an integral part of the world of reform and philanthropy. Jane was a lightning rod for controversy. She had a knack for prompting debates that often deteriorated into personal quarrels. And to the chagrin of other reformers, she did not hesitate to expose the internal struggles that sometimes plagued reform organizations and drove wedges between those who might otherwise have worked together to bring about social change. She claimed membership in a community filled with sometimes competitive, single-minded reformers who were often as determined to promote themselves and their particular approaches to curing society's ills as to serve the interests of those in need. Jane did not hesitate to criticize other reformers when she thought doing so was necessary. She was just as incapable of ignoring what she considered to be an injustice as she was of restraining her rhetoric. She was unwilling to be taken for granted. And she loved a good fight. Her strongly expressed opinions and her propensity for engaging in controversy served the cause of reform by identifying and prompting public discussion of the social problems of her day. In the process, however, she offended and alienated many people who were willing to spend their time and money trying to make the world a better place. Consequently, her contributions to reform were not always positive.

CHAPTER SEVEN

RESPECTABLE

BUT NOT

GENTEEL

*It is a wintery Sabbath morning in the late 1870s;
the Reverend Joseph Hunter, holding forth from his
Covenanter pulpit to an intent, albeit half-frozen
congregation.*

*Suddenly, a small, grey wisp of a woman shiveringly
arises from her pew, well up front, marches determinedly
down the aisle and out of the church, hurries across the
snowy road to a nearby house and soon returns with a
rag rug over her arm.*

*Regaining her seat, she wraps the carpet about her feet
and resumes her devotions, oblivious to the fact that she
has created a disturbance and done something "queer."*

*All her life she has been creating disturbances and doing
"queer" things. Wilkinsburg is both ashamed and proud of
her, whose life for all her drab little figure, runs like a thread
of gold through the prosaic history of the village.*

*This frail human being with the straightly parted hair,
severe and querulous face, penetrating grey-blue eyes and
disdain of "form" is Mrs. Jane Grey Swisshelm.*

*By far the most interesting figure in Wilkinsburg, she
came and went, threading paths of ephemeral fame, "dining
with those in high places." Yet ever was she drawn back to
the village, mingling with the townsfolk. A unique being
and lonely by reason of it.*

*Elizabeth Davidson and Ellen McKee, "Jane Grey
Swisshelm: The Queer Woman Crusader of
Wilkinsburg,"* Annals of Old Wilkinsburg, *1940*[1]

That was the problem, of course. When it suited her, she viewed social form with disdain, saying what she thought and doing what she pleased without concern for convention. Her behavior made her interesting but also could be a source of embarrassment for her friends and family. She insisted on defining herself on her own terms, and such nonconformity resulted in a distinctiveness that gave her an ambiguous position in polite society.

One of the characteristics of life in the nineteenth century was the ease with which people with the necessary resources could improve their social position. The shift from an economy based primarily on agriculture to one based increasingly on industry and commerce brought with it the rise of a culturally powerful middle class, which by the 1850s was large enough to the set ideal standards for public and private behavior.[2] Those who conformed to those standards could lay claim to what was commonly known as middle-class respectability.

Life in America's growing cities heightened sensitivity to class issues. In small towns and farming communities, where everyone knew everyone else, it was relatively easy to determine where a person belonged in the social structure. But urban life was characterized by a certain degree of anonymity, which made placing someone else and establishing a place for oneself more difficult. That did not mean, of course, that those who lived in the country were immune from concerns about who was respectable and who was not. But the rural or small-town definition of "respectability" was usually broad enough to include prosperous farmers and artisans who, despite performing manual labor and by necessity associating with less prosperous neighbors, met the other requirements for claiming middle-class status.

In both the city and the country, concerns about acquiring the trappings of gentility pervaded the lives of members of the middle class who had social aspirations. Gentility implied means and accomplishment, along with a refinement that superseded that of people who were merely respectable. Building on reputations for integrity, industry, and affluence, members of the middle class who wished to be considered genteel had to work quite self-consciously to acquire elegance and grace as well as the outward and material symbols of whatever was considered good taste at the time. Such a person might be expected to exhibit, at the very least, outward evidence of advanced education, a refined aesthetic sense, a knowledge of the intricacies of an increasingly complicated social etiquette, and an interest in fashion. While claims to respectability were based on reputation, claims to gentility were based on leaving an impression. The genteel were, in that sense, always on display. Despite its superficiality, gentility bestowed social power on those credited with possessing it. And a great many people, both male and female, considered gentility an important resource in making their way in the world.[3]

As a young woman, Jane's claim to middle-class respectability stood on relatively firm ground. Her grandfather and father were educated small businessmen and skilled artisans, and her husband was heir to a large farm. They were propertied church members who were well regarded in the Pittsburgh area. Therefore, her claim to respectability derived from their reputations as men of substance and integrity. Furthermore, her work as a reformer and newspaperwoman regularly put her in the position of associating with some of the most prominent men and women of her day. By the 1860s, she was on a first-name basis with Indiana Congressman George Julian and his wife and knew both U.S. Senator Charles Sumner and Secretary of War Edwin Stanton. She had met President Abraham Lincoln and his wife, was a good friend of prominent author E. D. E. N. Southworth, and had working relationships with a great many social reformers. She entertained prominent Minnesota politicians in her St. Cloud home and was entertained by them in St. Paul.[4]

Jane possessed many of the qualities necessary to justify a claim to gentility. She had an education and was well-read. She was an accomplished artist and had a "classic" sense of fashion in clothing based on an appreciation of clean lines, a good fit, and high-quality fabric.[5] She could be gracious when she felt like it. And she possessed—but did not always exhibit—a knowledge of the rules of social etiquette and the kind of good manners that were required of anyone who hoped to be welcomed into genteel society.

But Jane was not socially ambitious. Throughout most of her life, she expressed contempt for superficiality and the social conventions that limited women's opportunities to express themselves, support themselves, and represent their own interests. And her behavior and self-presentation were governed by that contempt. She was outspoken and publicly contentious. She had an interest in politics and economics in an age that defined those two areas of public life as off-limits to anyone who considered herself to be a "true woman." She was more prone to lecture than to engage in casual conversation. She demanded access to public space at a time when the ideal woman was supposed to center her life on her home and her church. Jane was divorced rather than married. She provoked discord rather than harmony. And while it is clear that she had a refined aesthetic sense, her appearance did not betray that fact. She dressed like a Quaker, wore her hair severely pulled back from her face, and did nothing to visually enhance her claim to womanliness. Consequently, the social space she occupied lay somewhere between respectability and gentility.

Jane seems to have been somewhat ambivalent about the importance of the material trappings of gentility. It was not that she failed to appreciate the aesthetic, social, and physical comfort they offered. Although she did not dress fashionably, she appreciated the beauty and durability of fine silk.[6] And after she left James, she was willing to go to court to retrieve her piano from his house.[7] But she appears to have been as comfortable living in her old log home at Swissvale as in visiting the White House, and she was more interested in what people thought about important issues and on which side of the moral divide her friends and acquaintances could be found than in whether they knew which fork to use at the dinner table.

Nowhere was her ambivalence expressed more openly than in what she called "Letters to Country Girls," an advice column published in the *Pittsburgh Saturday Visiter* in the late 1840s and early 1850s and intended for farmers' daughters.[8] Several of her letters expressed disdain for what was considered genteel, describing dissipated urban girls as "loung[ing] around reading novels, lisping about the fashions and gentility, thumping some poor hired piano until it groans again, and putting on airs to catch husbands." By the hundreds, she reported, these girls "parade the streets in feathers, flowers, silks, and laces." Their hands, she charged, were as "soft and white as uselessness can make them." While their mothers did the housework, they lay in bed, read silly books, took music and French lessons, spent their fathers' money, and abused their fathers' credit on extravagances of every kind. Urban girls spent their evenings trying to entrap "witless" young men into marriage. The purpose in life of such girls, she claimed, was to "lay their empty heads on somebody's pillow, and commence their empty life with no other prospect than living at somebody's expense—with no higher purpose than living genteely, and spiting the neighbors."[9]

In writing her advice column, Jane joined a host of other female social critics who were determined to set ideal standards of behavior for young women. The most notable of these domestic advisers included Catharine Beecher, the author of *A Treatise on Domestic Economy, for the Use of Young Ladies at Home, at School,* and Lydia Maria Child, who wrote *The American Frugal Housewife, Dedicated to Those Who Are Not Ashamed of Economy.* Both Beecher and Child offered young women living in towns and cities advice ranging from the management of their health and the care of brass kettles to the best way to endure poverty. These authors agreed, as Child put it, that gentility and "attention to the graces of life" were desirable but that acquiring them should not interfere with a young lady's practical domestic education.[10]

When Jane began her "Letters to Country Girls" in the *Visiter*, she acknowledged that "there has been a great deal of paper spoiled in writing lectures about women's duties, and there is no end to the directions to young ladies to teach them how to behave." But, she reminded her readers, most of the advice that women such as Beecher and Child offered was directed toward the urban middle class. "Few people write much to you country girls, who make butter and milk cows," she observed.[11] Jane was more interested in influencing women who on occasion might have to exchange their rolling pins for pitchforks than in affecting women who spent the morning supervising domestic servants and the afternoon shopping and paying social calls. Country women had a double burden, she argued. Like urban, middle-class women, they were responsible for taking care of their husbands and children, but their families' physical and financial well-being almost always depended on these girls' willingness occasionally to work as farm laborers. Doing so helped to define what it meant to grow up as a respectable and responsible "country girl." Any woman "who would loll about idly, or trifle away her time while her father or brother was oppressed and hurried with his harvesting, corn planting, hoeing, or hay making," she charged, was "mean, selfish, and lazy" and abdicated her claim to being the country version of the true woman.[12] Jane acknowledged that while country women needed to know how to keep fleas out of carpets and save time churning butter, they also needed to know something about what was generally considered to be "men's business." "Many a family has been brought to bankruptcy," she warned, "because the women of it were quite too feminine to know whether they were living upon their own or their creditors' means."[13]

At the same time, however, Jane insisted that farm women needed to conform to some of the prevailing ideas about what constituted femininity, particularly in the area of personal hygiene. "You girls do not wash yourselves more than once a month, and some of you not that often!" she complained. The result, she said, was that their skin was "clogged with impure, foul matter." No "matter how much floor-scrubbing or tin-scouring" they did or "how many clean clothes" they put on, women who didn't bathe daily were simply "dirty."[14] And being dirty was unacceptable.

Jane also faulted country women for tending to discount the importance of their appearances. Because they failed to wear bonnets to protect themselves from the sun and made no effort to protect themselves from the baking influence of wood fires, "the faces of some women," she observed, "look like a rennet-bag that had hung six weeks in the chimney corner." The problem was, she observed, that when women who wanted to protect their skin tried to take care of their hands or wore a sunbonnet, they faced accusations of being "proud and stuck up." She felt that such criticism reflected a kind of reverse snobbery and argued that a woman's hands needed to be soft and pliable to be useful. "Hands hardened by cold weather or desensitized by constant immersion in scalding hot water are not fit for sewing or writing or holding a baby or dressing a wound," she argued.[15]

In her "Letters," Jane offered women who lived and worked in the country advice and information that she believed would improve the quality of their lives. But in so doing, she did not see herself as encouraging them to be something they were not. Her definition of what it meant to be a country woman had no room for the pretense and display that accompanied the quest for gentility. She knew that that no matter how much land these country women's families owned, no matter how much money they had in the local bank, no matter how elaborate their Sunday dresses and bonnets, no matter how expensive the rugs or ornamental the needlework in the parlors of their farmhouses, most respectable country girls were likely to become nothing more—and nothing less—than respectable country women. Country life was not conducive to the pursuit of gentility if only because there were little leisure time, few forms of public entertainment, and a dearth of truly cultivated people with whom to associate. That being the case, Jane's advice was intended to encourage her middle-class rural female readers to construct their gendered identities within a social context that called for respectability but discouraged the pursuit of gentility. The key to a productive and happy life, she suggested, was to balance self-improvement with the duty to work hard and serve others.

Jane's advice reflected her circumstances as she understood them. Her personal covenant with God made concern about worldly position and the regard of others irrelevant to the conduct of her life and the construction of her female identity. A high regard for respectability and disdain for the pursuit of gentility freed Jane to pursue newspaper work and social reform. And as she did so, she took no one else, including her daughter, into account. She made sure that Zo received a good education as she was growing up. But it was not until Jane ended her career as a newspaper editor and returned to Pittsburgh that she began to think seriously about what the future might hold for Zo, who was rapidly approaching adulthood.

Zo's childhood could not have been easy. During her first five years, she lived in a household characterized by hostility, psychological warfare, and constant turmoil. After Jane took her daughter to Minnesota, Zo was surrounded by an adoring aunt, loving cousins, and two uncles who were men of substance. Nevertheless, it would have been impossible for her to have escaped the pain and embarrassment associated with being the object of local gossip. She was, after all, the daughter of a woman who deserted her husband, moved to St. Cloud and almost immediately became involved in a quite public and violent controversy with the one of the city's most highly regarded citizens, and constantly provoked social and political controversy through her paper. Furthermore, Zo's parents' divorce was of such public interest that the editor of the *New York Tribune* took pains to carry an announcement of the matter.

It is not terribly surprising, then, that Nettie turned out to be a sensitive little girl, prone to feelings of insecurity and plagued by a sense of personal vulnerability. Even Jane recognized this in her daughter. In a letter to her sister, Elizabeth Mitchell, Jane wrote that Zo was "easily wounded, & the wounds hard to heal." Jane acknowledged that Zo had developed ways of dealing with snubs and whispers and did her best to try to hide her feelings but predicted, "Life will be a hard passage to her."[16] Because Jane was unwilling to make major changes in her life, she could do little to protect Zo from feeling victimized by local gossips.

When Jane returned to the Pittsburgh area from Washington, D.C., in 1866, she rented a small cottage with two rooms and a good well in Wilkinsburg, between the Covenanter church and the railroad station. Nettie enrolled in a school in Pittsburgh, while Jane waited for the settlement of her suit against James Swisshelm regarding her claim to part of Swissvale. She had very little money at the time, but that did not stop her from thinking about how she might further her daughter's prospects. "If either my book or suit succeed," she wrote to her sister, Elizabeth, in St. Cloud, "I think I will take Nettie to Paris to go to school one year. . . . I should rent a room or two furnished & board ourselves. Tuition is less there than here & living no higher." Getting Nettie away from Wilkinsburg was becoming important to her because her daughter's position in country society was being threatened by James's attentions to his housekeeper. James's disapproving mother had thrown the woman out of the house, but Jane reported that "he has got that Hannah & her mother in one of the Mill houses & has made a public scandal running after her."

Returning to the Swissvale area had subjected Nettie to further personal embarrassment and scandal. To spare her daughter any more public humiliation, Jane was determined to "take her out of this" when the lawsuit was settled.[17]

Jane won her suit in 1868, gave up her rented house in Wilkinsburg, and moved into the Swisshelm homestead. There she did what she could to make a home that her daughter would find both comfortable and congenial.[18]

But life with Nettie was not be to confined to residence in the country. Unable to give up her public activities, Jane returned to Minnesota. By January 1869 Nettie was ensconced in the Mitchell household and attending school with her cousins in St. Cloud while Jane traveled to St. Paul to lecture on woman's rights, to visit Governor Alexander Ramsey and his wife, and to propose that the state legislature pass a measure providing married women with both the right to sign contracts and the right to custody of their children.

During this visit, Jane's inattention to matters of personal finance became yet another source of embarrassment for Zo, who was forced to write to her mother to inquire about whether her tuition had been paid. The principal of Zo's school had announced her name as one of eight students whose parents had not paid the necessary fees. Jane immediately wrote to St. Cloud, asking that her nephew, William Mitchell, investigate the matter. She clearly could not remember whether she had paid Zo's tuition and consequently asked Mitchell either to pay the bill or to demand an apology if the bill had already been paid: Nettie "must not be insulted before her schoolmates by a fellow like" the principal, Jane wrote. If the bill had been paid and the principal refused to admit his mistake, she ordered Will to take Nettie out of the school and arrange to provide her with lessons at home.[19] But the damage had already been done, and Zo had once again suffered embarrassment, this time because of her mother's inattention to the details of her care.

Part of the problem seems to have been the lack of a clear understanding concerning who bore financial responsibility for that care. In 1872, for example, Jane asked her brother-in-law, Henry Z. Mitchell, "Will you please enquire if Mr. Swisshelm has paid Dr. Webber's bill for attendance on Nettie & if he has not will you collect the interest due on Kennedy's notes & hand the money to the Doctor?" The bill apparently had originally been sent to Jane, but she was out of town when it arrived, so Nettie "referred the matter to her father & said nothing" about it to her mother.

James thought the charges were too high and either refused or neglected to pay the bill.[20]

Jane was sensitive about the issue of female dependence. She felt strongly that women should be prepared to support themselves, and she was determined to prepare Zo to do so. "Through many difficulties I have kept on educating my own child that she may earn her living, & render the world *quid pro quo* for the bread she eats, & if I had millions would never try to help anyone to live without work," she wrote.[21] Despite her good intentions, however, it is not clear what she thought she was preparing Zo to do. Rather than teaching Zo a practical trade such as printing, Jane merely continued to send her daughter to school and to encourage her interest in music.

During the early 1870s, Jane and Zo spent their time in various places— living in their Swissvale home and their cottage called Zozonia in Indiana County, Pennsylvania; visiting the Mitchells in St. Cloud; and living in Chicago. Zo, described as "very sweet and a gentle" young woman "with dove eyes and languid manners," apparently liked spending time with the Mitchells and thoroughly enjoyed the cultural life of Pittsburgh and Chicago.[22] But she seems to have been less satisfied with country life. Listening to the wind blow through the willow trees at Swissvale or living in relative isolation at Zozonia simply did not compare to attending a concert or the theater, and she was bored. She wrote to a friend that she was literally "buried" in the country. The fact that there was nothing to do and no one with whom she wanted to socialize tried her patience and taxed her social skills. She complained that the people she saw on a daily basis "don't know anything except raising pigs and then eating them. . . . I think sometimes when one of these big boobies come[s] stalking in, that I could receive President Grant with more grace. The most of them are so desperately ignorant that any one is exceedingly well educated if they can do a hard example in arithmetic. . . . Their education is so one sided. They have no general information at all." She also found them devoid of religious sensibility and lacking in anything resembling serious religious training.[23]

Whether or not Jane intended it, Zo was slowly developing the sensibilities of a genteel young lady, self-conscious about her feelings of superiority toward what she considered to be the country bumpkins with whom she was forced to associate at Swissvale. A serious young women with few distractions and uninterested in what she considered to be frivolous pleasures, "where the object is mere amusement," she spent a great deal of time practicing her piano and waiting to attend classical music concerts in Pittsburgh, her preferred form of entertainment. Nettie admitted that she liked minstrel shows and giggled over the "silly songs" she heard there. But she dismissed actors and their craft as "ephemeral." Her approach to classical music and the musicians who performed it was romantic in the extreme: "I like to go to hear some genius, who has struggled through years of labor and patient endurance, to attain some one thing."[24]

Having grown beyond the rural culture that prevailed at Swissvale, Zo was restless but does not appear to have considered striking out on her own. For the moment, she was destined to stay with her mother. The two women could not have been more different, and living together may have been something of a strain. Whereas Jane was assertive, Zo was retiring. Whereas Jane enjoyed being the center of attention, Zo tried to avoid it. Jane made things happen; Zo was a fatalist and simply let things happen. She once wrote philosophically, "I used to be so troubled because things did not turn out as I thought they should, but I have got to feel now that 'what is, is right' and then in the end I sometimes find, though I don't have everything, I have some things which I did not expect."[25]

Zo must have been relieved when she and her mother moved to Chicago in early 1876. Having leased out her house and land in Pennsylvania to raise some cash, Jane rented rooms in the Windy City and began work on her autobiography while Zo boarded with the family of Dr. W. H. Thomas, a Presbyterian minister.[26]

Jane apparently had never given up the idea that Zo would benefit from spending time in Europe. So on April 1, 1876, she, Zo, and Elizabeth's daughter, Jean Mitchell, boarded a steamship in New York. They sailed to London and then traveled to Leipzig, in Saxony, where Zo planned to spend two years studying piano. When the trio arrived on April 27, they rented a furnished apartment from two mantua makers in a handsome new building at 22 Gustav-Adolph Strasse on the outskirts of the city. Jane and the girls were very pleased with their lodgings. Their two rooms were filled with comfortable furniture. When the sun shone, the light filtered through the lace curtains at the windows and formed shadowy designs on the highly waxed floors. The white woodwork surrounding the doors and windows glistened, and the walls and ceilings were covered with frescoes.[27]

The decision to study in Leipzig was not made casually. The city was an important center for music education during the 1870s, with a renowned music conservatory, founded by Felix Mendelssohn in the 1840s, that attracted talented students from all over Europe and the United States.[28]

When a grand piano had been rented and delivered to Zo, she began taking hourlong music lessons from a local instructor who held her to high standards of performance, complimenting her on her "grosz talent" but criticizing her for having "nein tecnique."[29]

Nettie typically spent most of the day practicing while Jane wrote travel letters for the *Chicago Tribune* and Jean kept them company.[30] When they were free, the three women attended classical music concerts as well as the opera and spent hours wandering through the city's art galleries. When they went to the circus, both girls fell madly in love with the owner's son, who, according to Jean, performed in a pair of tights. Jane laughed at them for raving over the shape of his legs. When Zo took an interest in drawing, Jane hired a drawing master to instruct her. Jane, Zo, and Jean took German lessons, but none of them appear to have been particularly good language students. So on Sundays, they typically attended a chapel where English was spoken.[31]

As their stay lengthened from weeks to months, Jane and the girls began to associate with the members of the American expatriate community in Leipzig, which included William Sloane, a young Covenanter from Pittsburgh. Though reared with all of the seriousness with which Covenanter parents reared their children, he was something of a "man about town," charming and handsome. "He is just splendid," Jean wrote to her sister, "Knows everything and a little more—yet is not priggish. We are all dead struck after him. Aunty worst of the lot—and Nettie and I giggle privately to ourselves at the way she monopolizes him."

Jane had apparently decided that the young man would make an ideal husband for her daughter. But although he was attentive, the relationship did not flourish, in part because Jane was so determined to impress him. As a result, no one else had much of a chance to engage him in conversation when he called. "I thought after he'd been told the war and hospital stories—all the woman's rights views—the history of the St. Cloud Democrat—Visiter—the first public appearance—the explanation of the lawsuit and . . . a few scattering personal experiences there would be a little rest—but such is not to be, there's always something to dilate upon," Jean complained. In the process of talking to him, however, Jane found that he had what she considered to be unenlightened attitudes toward women and their need for more rights. Disenchanted, she decided that he simply would not do as a prospective son-in-law. So, according to Jean, the "matrimonial enterprise" simply "flickered" out.[32] Sloane left Leipzig in August, traveling to London and Paris and then home to Pittsburgh. Jean did not particularly miss him, but Zo had apparently been smitten. According to her cousin, she talked about him incessantly and vowed "eternal allegiance" to him.[33]

Ultimately, it turned out that losing Sloane was no loss at all. Indeed, according to Jean, he was "a first class fraud," a parasite who lived off his ability to charm. "He was the most plausible, deceptive creature," she wrote, "forever prating about his conscientious scruples and his principles and he wasn't in the least troubled with either. We have found since [his departure] that he has borrowed money of everybody that would lend it; he went off in debt to everybody that would trust him both here and in Berlin." Because he was charming, attentive, and a product of a good Covenanter home, Jane had placed great trust in him. She loaned him money and even asked him to serve as her banker while in Leipzig. He not only failed to repay his loans but also helped himself to a great deal of the money that she had left in his hands. It was no wonder, Jean wrote, that the three women seemed to spend so much money during the time they associated with him.[34]

Jane's naïveté regarding Sloane is in some ways surprising. She was quite aware that the world was full of scoundrels who in one way or another were likely to misrepresent themselves and that unattached women constituted the primary prey of such men.[35] She had been the victim of her husband and mother-in-law's attempt to defraud her of her claim to Swissvale and had written about the consequences of placing confidence in the untrustworthy. Nevertheless, when it came to establishing relationships with others, she tended to be open and confiding. Part of her forthrightness resulted from the fact that she was quite egocentric and typically spent more time talking about herself, her accomplishments, and her adventures than in assessing the sincerity of new acquaintances. And her lack of personal concern about the superficialities that often accompanied life among urban sophisticates made her oblivious to the possibility that she could be unduly influenced by a person's style and manner.

Her personal sincerity made her vulnerable in a place such as Leipzig. When she arrived, she must have felt very much out of her element. She had never been out the United States, spoke no German, had no friends, and had limited personal resources. Sloane, a Covenanter from Pittsburgh who spoke German and knew the city and its people, befriended them, arranged for their housing, and helped them to negotiate daily life. His much appreciated attentiveness apparently made it difficult for Jane to distinguish between appearance and reality, and she was taken in.

After Sloane's departure, the three women settled into what seemed to be an endless routine of attending concerts and art exhibitions. The girls made friends easily and seem to have enjoyed themselves. Jane, however, became increasingly restless. There was little for her to do each day, and she had few good things to say about either Germany or its people. "We do not like the folks or the fashions very well and will be glad to go home when the time comes," she wrote to her lawyer shortly after arriving.[36] She also hated the "wretched" weather, describing it to her sister as "soggy and shivery and blistery and raw and damp and generally detestable."[37] Even her new gray flannel wrapper with its red lining did not seem to keep her warm enough.[38] Because she did not understand the language, she was irritated by what she described as the "everlasting incomprehensible gabble" that she heard from morning until night. And she detested German food, which gave her indigestion. So as she escorted the girls from place to place and watched her money supply dwindle, she began to make plans to return to Pittsburgh for a few months.[39]

Before leaving, Jane found her daughter and niece a new set of rooms, run by a respectable widow and conveniently located closer to the center of town near the opera house, the concert hall, shopping, an ice cream parlor, and Zo's music teacher.[40] Leaving them with enough money to cover their expenses, she traveled via Cologne to Liverpool, boarded the steamship *Italy*, and on October 4 sailed for New York. Jean and Zo celebrated Jane's departure with ice cream and chocolate cakes. Jean wrote to her sister, "Between you and me and another hay stack, I was not inconsolable at the Aged's departure." Because Jane had been unwilling to really immerse herself in German culture or, as Jean put it, to "get among the Dutch and be of them," it had not been possible for the girls to feel like they were really in a foreign country. According to Jean, "It was simply no living in Europe at all, and only a bad imitation of America the way we had to do when she was with us. She couldn't live among the Germans and we could learn nothing and have no real good of our stay here unless we did mingle with the people and be of them."[41] With Jane gone, Jean and Zo intended to make the best of the opportunity that living among the "Dutch" could offer.

Now on their own, the girls went shopping and continued to immerse themselves in the city's cultural life.[42] They bought long, three-buttoned kid gloves to wear out in the evening, and Zo purchased a full-length sealskin coat. They socialized with musicians and listened to them perform. But when it came to learning to appreciate fine art, they were left to their own devices. In November 1876, as they stood gazing at a large, dark painting hanging on a gallery wall, Zo remarked scornfully, "I wouldn't give five cents for a cart load of that sort!" Jean, who agreed that the work was not the least impressive, took a closer look. Turning to her cousin, she reported with considerable chagrin that it was signed by Van Dyck. "We are not educated up yet to the old picture point," Jean told her sister. "Now we did giggle over this startling display of ignorance."[43]

Both of the girls enjoyed being in Europe, but Zo was beginning to get homesick. So when spring arrived, they decided not to wait for Jane to return and booked passage for the United States.[44] Although she was anxious to go home, Zo dreaded the thought of having to live at Swissvale, instead preferring to go to St. Cloud. But Jane was at Swissvale, so Zo had no choice in the matter. Her cousin felt sorry for her. "Poor girl," Jean wrote, "she hasn't much to make life happy and bright."[45]

Given her apparent unwillingness to strike out on her own, Zo had to trade the excitement of living in a major center of European culture for the quiet solitude of life in the country. Because of her musical training, she was occasionally invited to give concerts in Pittsburgh. And when she did so, she received good reviews in the *Pittsburgh Commercial*. Her audiences found her charming and were so enthusiastic about her performances that they demanded encore after encore. One reviewer was particularly impressed "by her exceedingly fine execution. Sitting near her, as we did," he said, "it seemed as though she had about two dozen fingers on each hand, and every one going at double quick."[46] But the excitement of performing did not make up for the tedium of everyday life on the farm.

In July 1878, Jane leased her Swissvale property so that she and Nettie could move to Princeton, New Jersey, where they rented a small house. Zo taught piano, and she and her mother enjoyed picnics, afternoon teas, and excursions with friends. It became increasingly clear, however, that Chicago was the place where money was to be made, so Jane and Zo moved to Illinois.[47] There Jane and her daughter again lived separately, Zo boarding with the Thomases and Jane renting rooms elsewhere.[48]

At about this time, Zo apparently renewed her acquaintance with Ernest L. Allen, who had grown up with her in St. Cloud. Trained as a lawyer, he lived in Chicago and was the successful northwestern division manager of the Royal Insurance Company of Liverpool.[49] Ernest's parents were from Pittsburgh and had been among the earliest subscribers to the *Pittsburgh Saturday Visiter*. His father had died when he was six, and his mother, Nancy, moved with her two sons to St. Cloud to be near friends and relatives from Pittsburgh who had emigrated to Minnesota.

When Nancy Allen arrived in St. Cloud, Jane met her old friend at the wharf and provided Nancy and her children with room and board until they were settled. Nancy eventually moved in next door and supported her family by teaching, running a boardinghouse, and opening an ambrotype gallery.[50] Ernest and Zo attended school together. Jane remembered that when he was about eight, he would bring Zo home from school on his sled and was so possessive that on one occasion he "flog[ged] another little fellow for daring to escort her."[51]

There is no record of how Jane felt when Zo announced her plans to marry Ernest. Given the fact the Zo had made no real effort to support herself, Jane no doubt had to accept the possibility that marriage was Zo's best prospect for economic and social security. So when Ernest and Zo set the date for their wedding, Jane returned to Swissvale and set about creating an elaborate dress for her daughter to wear. Spreading out the yards of creamy white silk that would eventually be gathered into a skirt, she started to embroider. For part of the pattern, she used a wall hanging and botanical prints and photographs from *Harper's Monthly* magazine. For the rest, she copied flowers plucked from her garden. Around the bottom of what was to be the skirt, she embroidered five large water lilies on their pads. Different stitches representing plant stalks ran all the way up the skirt to the waist. The front of the dress featured a row of graduated tiger lilies as well as tent-lily leaves, grasses, oak leaves, acorns, roses, asters, tulips, and morning glories. When all of the intricate embroidery was completed to her satisfaction, Jane backed the silk with Lawndale muslin, placed wool wadding between the two fabrics, and waited for her neighbor, Daniel Double, to bring the quilting frame he was constructing so she could finish the dress.[52]

Patience was not one of Jane's virtues. As the days passed and Double did not appear, she grew weary of waiting and sent him a poem:

Oh Daniel Double! Daniel Double
You surely will get into trouble
Be blown up busted like a bubble
Be beaten into smallest rubble
Then bound like dry and worthless stubble
And get, beside a horrid name
If you do'nt bring my quilting frame

You said "first rainy day I'll make it
And to your house will straightway take it."
This bargain fair—why did you break it?
The road was plain, then, why forsake it?
The weather, sure, is not to blame

> One day it rained and next day the same
> A third day ditto—so for shame!
> Just come along and file your claim
> For bringing home that quilting frame.

She then waited for his response. "He brought the frame," she wrote, "and looked very gruff. I praised it and said 'did you get a letter about it?' 'Yes,' he replied slowly 'I got a letter!' 'Well! I hope it did not make you angry!' 'No' he said slowly and glancing, with sharp inquiry, into my face, 'It did'nt m-a-k-e m-e a-n-g-r-y; for ye see, I thought ye was in fun.' 'Oh yes of course I was in fun' and the little joke, being explained he grew quite cheerful and left in good humor." With a typical lack of humility, she added, "I was always very successful as a humorist."[53]

Jane finished the dress, adding a lacy, high-necked bodice; big, puffy sleeves; and a train. The result was stunningly beautiful. When her affairs were in order and the dress packed, Jane returned to Chicago. The wedding took place on December 19, 1881, at 7:30 in the evening in one of the parlors of the fashionable Palmer House Hotel. A group of fifty guests looked on as Zo and Ernest said their vows. One hundred more people attended the reception. When the festivities had ended, the bride and groom left on a wedding trip to Washington and New York and then returned to Chicago to live.[54] Jane stayed in Chicago to await their return and to help her daughter settle into her new role as the wife of an insurance executive and young Chicago matron.

The new bride was determined to become a part of genteel Chicago. By the 1880s, the city had more than recovered from the devastating 1871 fire. Its population of more than five hundred thousand continued to grow as thousands of immigrants flocked to the city, where jobs on the railroads, in the meatpacking plants, and in the grain and lumber industries were available. Service industries abounded. Insurance companies bankrupted by the fire were replaced by others, including the Royal Insurance Company of Liverpool, which Ernest represented. Housing ranged from the great mansions of Cyrus McCormick, Marshall Field, George Pullman, Philip Armour, and Potter Palmer to workers' cottages and tenements inhabited by the very poor. Young, socially ambitious, middle-class couples who wanted to live in the city could rent suites of rooms in one of Chicago's hundreds of respectable boardinghouses so that they could keep up appearances without immediately investing their resources in real estate.

By the time Zo married, Chicago was truly metropolitan. Its middle

Jane Grey Swisshelm as an older woman, ca. 1870. (Photo by Whitney's Gallery, courtesy of the Minnesota Historical Society, St. Paul)

Jane Grey Swisshelm's daughter, Zo, in her wedding dress, 1881. (Photo by Max Platz, courtesy of the Minnesota Historical Society, St. Paul)

Ernest Allen, the husband of Zo Swisshelm, ca. 1880. (Photo by Steffens, courtesy of the Minnesota Historical Society, St. Paul)

Jane and Elizabeth Allen, Jane Grey Swisshelm's granddaughters, ca. 1900.
(Photo by Langhorne, courtesy of the Minnesota Historical Society, St. Paul)

class, like men and women all over the country, joined groups whose purposes ranged from self-improvement to benevolence. There was an Amateur Musical Club for Zo and an Illinois Women's Press Association for Jane. And those with social aspirations could take lessons in music, dancing, and elocution.

The social elite supported the Young Women's Christian Association and Woman's Christian Temperance Union and sponsored such cultural organizations as the symphony, the art museum, and the theater. During the winter, marriageable daughters were presented to society at elaborate debutante balls, with proceeds going to favored charities. For those social events too large for the mansions that dotted the landscape, the Fremont House and the Palmer House, where Zo and Ernest were married, provided the required space and elegance.[55]

Although Jane had never been personally concerned with associating with the "right people," she recognized the importance to Ernest's business of cultivating the friendship of the socially prominent. Along those lines, Jane believed that as Ernest's wife, Zo had a responsibility to minister "to his importance in the world."[56] But while Jane understood all of this in principle, she found herself increasingly uncomfortable with the prospect that if she remained in Chicago, she too might be expected to minister to his interests.

Her problems began even before Ernest and Zo returned from their wedding trip. While they were gone, she wrote to the *Chicago Tribune*, describing Zo's wedding dress and commenting on her relationship with her new son-in-law. A friend of the young couple sent them a clipping of the published letter while they traveled and expressed surprise that Zo's mother "could have been guilty of so gross a violation of the rules of good taste as to write it." Zo and Ernest were mortified. Jane wrote of her faux pas to her sister and reported that only necessity had enabled her son-in-law "to return to Chicago and face the ignominy." Both he and Zo were literally sick with "neuralgia of the stomach" over the incident, Jane added.[57]

Jane's life with Zo and Ernest became increasingly difficult. Zo did not approve of the way Jane managed servants and did not believe that she knew how to behave in polite company.[58] Jane had always been opinionated and outspoken and had never been particularly discreet when it came to engaging in ordinary conversation. She found particularly disconcerting the matter of paying formal social calls, one of the rituals that characterized urban life. Calling was intended to regularize personal relationships and assure ease of social intercourse among the genteel. The ceremony of presenting one's calling card, having it accepted, and then being welcomed into the parlor of an established member of society was a way of measuring a person's social acceptability.[59] Primarily a female activity, calling kept "society" running smoothly, but it also provided women with contacts and information that their male relatives might find useful in pursuing their economic or political interests. In other words, calling was serious business and, in the words of historian Catherine Allgor, "was about keeping and augmenting power" on any number of levels.[60]

As in other U.S. cities, calling was an integral part of upper-middle-class Chicago social life. Jane had no objection to paying calls, but she was not used to sharing center stage with her daughter. "It was funny to go calling and announced as Mrs. Allen and another lady by the servant who took the names upstairs," Jane wrote to her sister.[61] The former editor enjoyed having her name cause a stir when it was announced, but Zo's new friends and acquaintances, primarily concerned with the here and now, did not seem aware of or much interested in Jane's history and importance as a journalist and reformer. And Zo insisted that Jane not bore listeners to tears by telling them all about herself. To add insult to injury, according to Jane, Zo also forbade all discussion of family matters because she feared that her mother would "tell some family secret." The trouble was, Jane told her sister, that given Zo's standards, everything about the Swisshelm family was a secret.[62]

From Jane's point of view, parlor talk in Chicago must have been excruciatingly tiresome and boring. To avoid embarrassing her daughter, she had to listen attentively as the ladies with whom she was forced to associate discussed clothes, shopping, children, parties, and their husbands' careers. She was not likely to have heard a word about such topics as political corruption and the design of city sewers.

Sensing that she needed to be more of a social asset to her daughter and son-in-law, Jane willingly submitted to etiquette lessons from Zo and tried to behave in polite company. But after months of trying to conform to Zo's expectations, Jane decided to return to Pennsylvania. She did not object to Zo's demands: "The daughters must educate the mothers up to new standards, and it is so sweet to feel their dear hands that we are quite willing to be beaten into shape like a pillow or kneaded and rolled and cut out like a batch of cookies. If it were my business in life to be nice I'd enjoy my education," she said. She understood that when she lived with Zo and Ernest, she could not behave any way she wished. "While there was but us two, it was not so much a matter that I failed to get my lessons and I did not strain my attention on them." But as the mother of Mrs. Ernest Allen, Jane wrote of feeling like "a bull in a china shop," fearful of moving around freely or of forgetting where she was and what she could or could not say.[63] The strain was simply too much. Living in Chicago made Jane feel as if she were being held hostage to "Zo's tastes."[64] Jane knew that Ernest was just as sensitive to her lapses in polite discourse and behavior, and she regretted those lapses because her daughter and son-in-law found them so embarrassing. She became desperate to get away from the "many proprieties and respectabilities" that formed an integral part of the life that Zo and Ernest had chosen.[65]

In the end, Jane decided that Zo and Ernest would be better off without her: "They two should be one," she wrote. "The union will be much more perfect without any attempt to make it three ply." She considered Ernest to be "just and generous" and believed that he would take care of Zo. "I am only to[o] happy that she has such a protector," Jane wrote, for without one, she felt that Zo was "about as defenseless as an oyster without a shell."[66]

Jane had submitted to Zo's attempts to teach her mother to be a proper lady, but the lessons had been for naught. Jane had humiliated herself, her daughter, and her son-in-law in a failed attempt to claim a place among Chicago's socially ambitious, and she chose to give up trying to recast herself as a gentlewoman and to live life on her own terms.

Fed up with spending her time in what she called "the etiquette infant class," Jane returned to Pittsburgh to resume what she considered to be her work. She wrote to her sister, Elizabeth, from Swissvale that "those who fear my voice can keep out of reach; & those who want to use it can at $50 an hour." She lectured at the Pittsburgh Opera House on the labor question and wrote a series of letters to the *Pittsburgh Dispatch* on municipal corruption.

Suspecting that her sister was lonely, Elizabeth asked Jane to come to Minnesota, but Jane declined. Fearing that her time was running out, she wrote, "I must be about my Father's business. If I staid with you I should simply listen to your talk or talk to you & this would not pay in its effect upon the long ages which are crowding up in the march of time & on which I must make my impress or go to the Last Judgment with my talent in a napkin."[67] She had not yet fulfilled all of her obligations to God and needed to spend what time she had left completing her work.

Zo desperately missed her mother. When she wrote of her feelings, it broke Jane's heart. "If by staying with you I could prevent your being lonesome I would, probably, have undone every duty that I might save you from this nightmare, but a bitter experience has taught me that you cannot possibly be more lonesome than with me, & that you cannot, well, have companionship likely to cause you more annoyance. We see & estimate things so differently that it is quite out of the question for me to avoid being a source of apprehension to you all the time we are together. You never know when I am going to hurt someone's feelings or do something to make myself ridiculous. If I should give my whole attention to avoid such results they would be no less likely to occur. I am not fit for society, & no one knows this better than I. I have no desire to occupy a place for which I know myself to be unfit. My work in the world lies in another field, & I cannot & will not neglect it in a vain effort to be someone else than myself." She had public work to do, she reminded Zo— fraud to expose and public services to organize in Pittsburgh. Jane wrote to her daughter that she hoped to teach "people how to live" by lecturing in the Opera House or Library Hall on Sunday afternoons. She was confident in her ability to make a real difference in the world, and she was determined to carry on.[68]

So Jane remained at Swissvale. There she lived with the Summs, who rented most of her house and ran the farm. While her work took her to Pittsburgh, she took great pleasure in her life in the country and in the log house that she had first inhabited as a young wife. From her kitchen door, she could see a grand panorama of rich, velvety green fields with hills and mountains looming in the background. Inside, she could walk from one light-filled room to another.[69]

The Swissvale homestead had once sat in its valley in serene isolation. It was isolated no more. Shortly after the Civil War, the Dickson-Steward Coal Company opened a mine on land purchased from Jane's neighbors, John McKelvey and John Hann. Company managers hired between fifty and sixty men and boys to work in the mines and built housing and stables nearby. In the early 1870s, the Allegheny Car and Transportation Company began to manufacture railroad freight cars at a factory built in the Swissvale area. Nearby stood the Edgar Thompson Steel Works. And in 1880, the Homestead Steel Company began operation.[70] The world was closing in on her. Jane reported to her sister, "I take my medicine at night by the light of the Westinghouse Gas Well. You can see the great sheaf of flame from the hill top as you go to the station & hear the roar, here, & a mile further off."[71]

As Pittsburgh businessmen began to move to the city's suburbs, they headed toward Swissvale. James Swisshelm sold about fifteen acres to Sol

Schoyer Jr., a Pittsburgh attorney, and another twenty-five acres close to the Pennsylvania Railroad right-of-way to R. H. Palmer, a merchant in the city. Jane's neighbors eventually included John Dickson, one of the owners of the Dickson-Steward Coal Company; a contractor; a Pittsburgh wholesale grocer; an insurance executive; a doctor; a Presbyterian minister; a judge; and the owner of a feed store.[72]

With the exception of the Dicksons, Jane had little or nothing in common with many of her new neighbors. Instead of associating with them, she sought the company of old friends who were as interested in social reform as she was.[73] She enjoyed being with people who knew her and were willing to put up with her idiosyncrasies, her impatience, and her sometimes acerbic wit. When she was not trying to change the world and teach people how to live, she spent her time painting and writing. She regularly attended church, entering her pew and gently nodding to those around her. She would typically remove her bonnet and place it on the floor of the aisle while she waited for the service to begin. Her exceedingly plain church dress caused one of her follow congregants to observe that "her whole appearance was that of one to whom fashion or the desire of personal adornment had no appeal." Despite her gray hair and wrinkled skin, she carried herself with dignity and a quiet air of self-satisfaction. Her figure remained thin, and she reminded those who knew her "of a bird by her alert and changeful movements."[74]

She enjoyed entertaining visitors, who found her hospitable and unpretentious. She was never ruffled when someone called out of the blue. One day when she received unexpected visitors, she simply rose "without apology or embarrassment, with a kind of stateliness, not assumed," wrote one of them. "She asked her callers to find chairs, while from a tumbler she removed her teeth to her mouth" and then chatted pleasantly while she showed the visitors a painting she had just finished that was resting against the fireplace.[75]

Jane was happy living at Swissvale surrounded by old friends and neighbors, but she missed her daughter. In February 1883 she traveled back to Chicago. Shortly after her arrival, Ernest left on a business trip. Zo, who was either pregnant or had just given birth to her first child, mostly stayed home with her mother, although she spent some evenings playing piano in what Jane characterized as "stylish clubs." Jane came down with a terrible cold during her stay, but her physical discomfort did nothing to restrain her sense of the ridiculous. The doctor, she reported to her sister, had prescribed brandy and quinine. So it was on his orders, she explained, that she intended to remain perpetually drunk until she was cured: "My only danger lies in the possibility of getting sober between drams."[76]

Jane remained in Chicago until May and then returned to Swissvale to fix up the house and prepare for a short visit from Zo and her daughter.[77] By July both Jane and Zo were back in Chicago. Zo had not particularly enjoyed her visit to Pennsylvania. She had been sick for part of the time and found living in her mother's home something of a trial. She wrote to Elizabeth Mitchell that the tenants had let the property deteriorate and that the house was in such bad shape that burning it down was the best course of action. But, Zo confessed, it had some economic value. "Mother will keep control of it herself after this & rent half the house, & try & get enough out of it pay the taxes, & there seems to be no trouble to get tenants."[78]

With her health slowly failing, Jane spent the winter in Chicago with Zo, Ernest, and the baby. In April 1884, Jane wrote to her sister that Zo was planning to spend the summer at Swissvale and that Ernest was arranging to close the Chicago house and store most of their furniture. While his wife and daughter were away, he planned to stay in Chicago and move into a boardinghouse.[79]

Jane returned to Swissvale, never again to see Chicago. In early July, she wrote "The Bloody Shirt" and sent the article to the *Pittsburgh Gazette* for publication. But all of the old fire and energy were gone. When she became ill on July 12, she called for her doctors, John and Robert McClelland. Despite their ministrations, however, she fell into a coma. Elizabeth Mitchell rushed from St. Cloud to be at her sister's bedside, where she found Ernest, Zo, their daughter, a nurse, a hired girl, and two neighbors running the household.[80]

On July 21, Jane died of "ulceration of the bowels." She was sixty-eight. As she had instructed, her body was wrapped in an old-fashioned winding-sheet and laid out in her writing alcove at Swissvale. Riding in carriages and buggies or walking on foot, her friends and neighbors as well as Pittsburgh's literati streamed down the winding, sumac-bordered lane to her crumbling log house to pay their last respects. In subdued whispers they gathered around her silver-trimmed walnut coffin festooned not with flowers but with artistically arranged twigs and branches. There Jane lay, all in white, her long gray hair draped around her shoulders.[81]

On the morning of July 24, Jane's old friend, the Reverend Thomas, arrived on a train from Chicago to conduct her funeral service. That afternoon, he delivered her eulogy. Her body was interred in Allegheny Cemetery.[82] Death did not diminish her attachment to her slowly deteriorating home. An image of the house was carved into the back of her tombstone, a permanent reminder of her love for the property.

Jane was as comfortable living in a primitive, rough-hewn log house in the country as in a tastefully decorated set of rooms in Leipzig, Saxony. And while she did not begrudge her daughter a superior social position, she had no desire to do what was necessary to accompany Zo on what Jane knew could be a long and tortuous road to acceptance among Chicago's social elite. Jane had associated with people whose claims to gentility were unimpeachable, not because she had social aspirations but because associating with such men and women was essential to carrying out what she perceived to be her mission in life. She had been accepted by them not because she had the resources and pedigree of a gentlewoman but because she was a lively and interesting social activist who had public influence as a newspaper editor.

While others with more ambitious social aspirations might have found frustrating her somewhat ambiguous position in society, it suited her well. She had early on dedicated herself to a life of usefulness in the pursuit of what she believed to be God's business. No matter how she behaved in any particular circumstance, Jane Grey Swisshelm maintained a reputation for being unself-consciously honest and hardworking. And she sacrificed her personal resources in terms of both energy and money to carry out God's will as she understood it. Her enemies may have on occasion questioned her judgment and considered her to be seriously misguided, but they never undermined her claim to respectability. So although she often transgressed middle-class gender conventions by engaging in "unfeminine" and "ungenteel" behavior, her failure to conform does not appear to have significantly affected the regard in which others held her. As she grew older, her associates may have considered her somewhat eccentric, but there is no evidence to suggest that they viewed her peculiarities as grounds for avoiding her.

That did not mean, however, that she remained unaffected by the anxieties concerning class and social status that plagued many of her contemporaries. While her daughter was growing up, Jane ignored some of the social conventions that served as the basis for defining what it meant to be a woman among the respectable and genteel. But when Zo reached adulthood and sought marriage, Jane was forced to seriously consider her behavior's impact on those around her. Motherhood complicated her class sensibilities. In the end, her insistence that she not be held to conventional standards of feminine behavior became a wedge that came between her and the person she most loved.

When she made her adolescent promise to spend the rest of her life as God's "thistle-digger in the vineyard," she expected her way to be strewn with difficulties. As an adult, she was willing to give up physical comfort and economic security and to expend a considerable amount of emotional and intellectual energy to fulfill her covenant with God in pursuit of eternal salvation. She knew that she would have to make sacrifices along the way but could never have anticipated that she would be asked to forfeit the company of her only child to preserve her personal integrity and that of her life's work.

She should not have been surprised that she was asked to make such a painful and distressing sacrifice. She wrote in her autobiography, published only four years before she died, that the God she served was jealous and unwilling to share her love with anyone.[83] Her love for Zo was great, and there is no way to measure the degree to which acknowledging that love caused Jane moments of extreme anxiety. Her response to that anxiety seems to have been that while she was determined to secure Zo's future, Jane was equally determined to remain focused on the importance of her work. Once Zo was happily married and economically secure, Jane turned away from Chicago society to focus once more on the more mundane world of ordinary people and the need to fulfill her personal covenant with God in the time allotted to her.

Jane once commented that she had never known members of any religious group who were as "humble" and "self-distrustful" as Pittsburgh's Covenanter Presbyterians. She was brought up, she said, to think that "such a worm of the dust as I, could be aught to the Creator but a subject of punishment."[84] Jane spent her adult life sealed in a covenant relationship with God, hoping that she had been elected to go to heaven but convinced that, in the end, no amount of effort on her part could assure her salvation. Like her Calvinist forebears, she lived with the excruciating pain of self-doubt and the sense that there would never be enough time to do what God expected of her, all the while believing that what she did would make no difference to him at all. She could, however, take comfort in the thought that she had made a difference in the lives of those less fortunate than herself and that she had championed causes that she considered both worthy and just.

If that was her goal, she would have been gratified by an incident that occurred only a few days after her death. A member of Pittsburgh's Post

128 of the Grand Army of the Republic approached Nelson P. Reed, the editor of the *Pittsburgh Commercial Gazette*, holding the May 25, 1863, issue of the *Gazette*. "This paper has an article about Lady Jane," the man said, "that the boys would like to see republished." The article was one that Jane had written from Campbell Hospital in Washington, begging northern civilians to send supplies to the soldiers under her care. The Civil War veteran and his friends had been in the hospital, remembered what she had done for them, and wanted to do something to honor her. Reed granted their request. On July 25, 1884, he republished the article under the title "Lady Jane."[85]

AFTERWORD

Jane Grey Swisshelm was one the most widely read and versatile female journalists in mid–nineteenth century America. She was a provocateur, a propagandist, and a polemicist. Her style was distinctive enough to cause comment. One editor described it as "poetical, piquant, and pithy." Another noted the "boldness" of her "unsparing hand."[1] She was not the only woman at the time to make a place for herself in the world of commercial journalism, but few of her contemporaries had careers as long as hers, and most could not claim the kind of diverse readership that she commanded.[2] Not only did she publish and edit four newspapers between 1847 and 1866, but her news stories, prose, editorials, social and political commentary, and letters to the editor appeared in such high-circulation dailies as the *New York Tribune*, the *New York Times*, and the *Chicago Tribune* as well as the *Atlanta Constitution*, the *Washington Evening Star*, and the *Boston Commonwealth*; reform periodicals such as *The Lily* and *The Liberator*; and special-interest newspapers such as the *Kaleidoscope*, the *Ohio Cultivator*, and the *New England Farmer*. Her critiques of society, her unrestrained rhetoric, and her ability to stir up controversy attracted readers, which in turn increased circulation and maximized profits. Consequently, other editors published what she wrote, sometimes adding their own editorial comments.

As a journalist, Jane was in a position to publicize the goals of social reformers and to promote their activities. During her first few years as a newspaper editor, she provided a medium through which people living in western Pennsylvania could debate the issue of capital punishment. Her pre–Civil War campaign against drinking combined with the efforts of other temperance advocates helped to lay the groundwork for the formation of the Woman's Christian Temperance Union and the eventual passage of the Eighteenth Amendment to the U.S. Constitution. Along with editors and agitators such as William Lloyd Garrison and Frederick Douglass, she promoted the antislavery cause in the press. Immediately following the Civil War, she did what she could to promote the interests of the freed slaves in the pages of *The Reconstructionist*. Jane was thoroughly committed to the cause of woman's rights. She was not a systematic or original thinker and found it impossible to work closely with other woman's rights advocates. But she spent a great deal of time and energy trying to promote various aspects of the woman's rights agenda. She argued in her editorials that women should have the right to control their property, to the custody of their children, and to vote and run for office. She supported the ideas that women should have access to education and vocational training, that opportunities for employment for women should be expanded, and that women should receive equal pay for equal work. On a practical level, she helped to integrate the male-dominated printing trade by hiring female printers and did what she could to help to create an environment in government offices and military hospitals that would accommodate the presence of women.

Jane also tried to expand what it meant to be both respectable and feminine. Her success in challenging gender prescriptions and transgressing gender boundaries depended on both personal agency and circumstance. Jane's background as a Covenanter Presbyterian and her personal covenant with God helped to insulate her from the consequences of her failure to observe middle-class gender conventions. The fact that she believed that she was doing God's work immunized her to some degree from the pain and humiliation that accompanied contemporary criticism of her. She understood the gender implications of her actions but tended to discount them as factors that might have inhibited her behavior. Indeed, she sometimes seemed to revel in the abuse she received for her gender transgressions. In a sense, she used the anxiety that she elicited and the criticism that she received as a way of measuring her success in doing what she thought God wanted her to do. She took a certain degree of pride in her ability to withstand the pain of martyrdom. Like anyone else, Jane wanted to be liked and needed to be loved, but when push came to shove, she was willing to forgo the companionship of her daughter to fulfill her covenant obligations.

At no prior time in U.S. history had discussions about women's nature and status been as public or as comprehensive as in the 1840s and the years that followed. Jane and others like her benefited from those discussions. When Lucretia Mott, Martha Coffin Wright, Elizabeth Cady Stanton, Jane Hunt, and Mary Ann McClintock sat in McClintock's parlor in Waterloo, New York, on July 16, 1848, and decided to call a woman's rights convention in nearby Seneca Falls, they set in motion a reconsideration of women's role in American society that was unprecedented in its scope and duration. The resolutions passed at that convention exposed the sources of gender inequality and called for dramatic and fundamental changes in women's legal, social, political, and economic status. The convention delegates both literally and rhetorically challenged social conventions that applied to women and in so doing opened the door for those women who wanted or needed to explore new ways of expressing their femininity. In the process, these pioneers prompted a public and often acrimonious debate about how to define masculinity and femininity. This cultural environment provided women such as Jane with unprecedented opportunities to expand the boundaries of how womanhood and manhood were expressed and how men and women related to each other.

Opportunity combined with expedience to provide a context that allowed Jane to subvert gender conventions without sacrificing her claim to femininity. Her first transgression occurred when she decided to challenge her husband's authority by refusing to convert to Methodism. Had James been in a position to force her to do so, he no doubt would have. But his position as a man was limited both by her conviction that he had no control over her in matters of conscience and by his economic circumstances as a dependent. His mother was the head of his household. Jane's entry into the male world of journalism was expedited by the fact that the bankruptcy of the *Albatross* left Pittsburgh's abolitionists with no newspaper. They had no alternative to supporting her desire to edit a political paper, even though in so doing they were quite consciously endorsing a transgression of gender boundaries. Robert M. Riddle clearly understood the gender implications of what he was doing when he agreed that Jane could use his office and his presses to publish the *Pittsburgh Saturday Visiter*. The same can be said of the men and women who supported her editorship of the *St. Cloud Visiter/Democrat*, her participation in partisan politics, and her work as both a clerk and a volunteer nurse.

Most middle- and upper-class Americans considered gender conventions that restricted women's activities to be relatively rigid. But these conventions were rigid only where there was no need for women to step outside the bounds of domesticity. In reform movements and such places as frontier Minnesota and wartime Washington, the need for competently rendered female services trumped gender proscriptions and established an environment in which the definitions of masculinity and femininity could be renegotiated.

Finally, the ambiguity of Jane's social class designation helped to reduce the tension that typically accompanied the transgression of gender boundaries. Throughout her adult life, she straddled the relatively blurry line between the middle class and the respectable working class. She sometimes worked for profit and sometimes worked for wages, and she was as comfortable associating with the social elite as with the printers she employed. In the process of critiquing society, she often stepped outside the bounds that defined what it meant to be a lady, and her enemies responded to her behavior by denying that she had any claim to middle-class respectability. But with her typical self-assurance, she simply refused to accept their assessment as valid. When her daughter finally married, Jane could no longer ignore the class implications of her actions but ultimately rejected the demands placed on her by Zo's social ambition. Throughout Jane's life, she always thought of herself as a lady, never gave up the claim that she was in every way worthy of the high regard of rich and poor alike, and formulated strategies designed to insure that she received the respect she thought she deserved.

Jane's life dramatizes the pressure points in gender relations that existed in the nineteenth century, helping those of us in the twenty-first century to understand more clearly what possibilities for self-making and self-expression existed for women in her day, how women took advantage of those possibilities, and what the consequences were. By divorcing her husband, living as an unmarried woman responsible for supporting herself and her child, and suing him for fraud, Jane claimed the right to the same sort of social and economic independence that gave men a privileged position in U.S. society. In her work as a journalist, printer, government clerk, and nurse, she helped to make a wide variety of jobs acceptable for women who needed to support themselves and their families without giving up their claim to "true womanhood" as defined by the middle class. By demanding a place for herself in the male world of partisan politics, she at the very least forced men to consider what benefits might be derived from giving women a larger role in political life. In both her journalism and her fiction, she exposed private struggles to public view and discussed power relations among women and between men and women. She appropriated a vigorous writing style and expanded the rhetorical choices available to women in their efforts to critique society, expose hypocrisy, justify women's participation in politics, and promote social reform.

Jane was not without her warts. She was most assuredly a bundle of contradictions. On one hand, she worked hard to free the slaves in the South and, when they were freed, was determined to see that their civil rights were protected. On the other hand, she led a campaign to displace and if necessary exterminate the Dakota in Minnesota. She could be charming and witty one moment and cruelly sarcastic the next. She was well-meaning and honest, but she was also rigid, opinionated, and pig-headed. She was a bigot when it came to Pittsburgh's Catholics. At the same time, however, she was an early supporter of integrated education. She, like most people, was in some ways deeply flawed, but she differed from many people in that she was quite willing to acknowledge that fact. Her Calvinist religion held that to be flawed was to be human and offered no hope for her salvation except through God's grace. Although she believed that there was little or nothing she could do to earn a place in heaven, she was determined to fulfill the terms of the covenant she was convinced she had made with the Lord at the time of her adolescent conversion experience.

Jane was proud of who she was and of what she tried to accomplish. To leave a permanent record of her activities and preserve a place for herself in the collective memory that comprises U.S. history, she published a memoir shortly before she died. It received considerable attention and acclaim at the time, but within a few years of her death, her name was no longer a household word, and by the early twentieth century few people remembered her.[3] Consequently, although she is not completely absent from the grand narrative of U.S. history, she has had no prominent place in it.

Women's historians have done little to improve Jane's historical profile. Since the 1970s, feminist historians have rescued from obscurity women who dedicated their lives to reform. But Jane is not among them. Part of the problem is that she burned her personal papers. Her sister and some of her friends saved a few of her letters, but they are scattered all over the country, making research on her life tedious, time-consuming, and expensive. Unlike other early woman's rights advocates such as Lucy Stone, Susan B. Anthony, Elizabeth Cady Stanton, Lucretia Mott, and Julia Ward Howe, Jane had no friend or relative willing to devote the time and energy necessary to preserve her memory.[4] The person most likely to have done so was the shy and retiring Zo, but she was embarrassed by her mother's activities and took no pleasure in the fact that Jane was a noted and controversial public figure. When Zo married Ernest Allen, she retired into domesticity, and after the birth of two daughters, she died.

Other factors have also contributed to Jane's relative obscurity. She is not entirely appealing to write about. Moreover, the approach that women's historians have taken to studying the long campaign to guarantee more rights for women has tended to be organizationally based and concerned primarily with identifying woman's rights advocates and examining how they worked together in groups as well as with discussing their collective philosophy; exploring how they organized to gain political, economic, and legal rights; analyzing the advocates' strategies; and assessing their collective accomplishments.[5]

Jane was as dedicated as anyone to the cause of woman's rights. But while she occasionally attended woman's rights conventions, she did not join woman's rights organizations. So she never really became a member of the network of activists that has attracted so much scholarly attention. Incapable of compromise, she was an infuriatingly self-righteous, opinionated, and harshly judgmental renegade. Uncooperative, uncollaborative, and often unsisterly, she was fiercely independent and consistently lay bare the divisions, multiple voices, and conflicting perspectives that characterized nineteenth-century reform movements. Thus, despite her ability to identify and articulate feminist issues, despite her willingness to sacrifice herself and her resources for the cause of woman's rights, despite the fact that she promoted the cause of women through journalism, and despite her personal efforts to expand educational, vocational, and political opportunities for women, she remained on the margins, aloof from the sense of sisterhood that bound woman's rights advocates together both before and after the Civil War.

Social change typically comes slowly and in increments. It occurs when there is an aggregate change in individuals' attitudes and behavior patterns. One of the things that makes Jane's life so compelling and significant is that she was willing to break down barriers that prevented nineteenth-century women from realizing their potential. Sometimes intentionally, sometimes unintentionally, she exposed the tensions that ideas about gender brought to social, economic, and political life. She was part of an aggregate of women who renegotiated the terms of their marriages; asserted their right to control their property; forced educators, employers, and public officials to provide women with a wider variety of vocational opportunities and access to a larger role in public life; and obliged people to reconsider their attitudes toward race, class, and gender relations. Caroline Maria Nichols Churchill, an early resident of St. Cloud who subsequently moved further west, acknowledged Jane's contribution to those efforts by writing in the *Denver Queen Bee*, "Our first ideas of the wrongs which women suffer from the absolute power of a ruling class were put in shape by reading the *St. Cloud Democrat*, edited by Mrs. Swisshelm."[6]

By the time Jane died in 1884, the line between a woman's private life and her public one was becoming increasingly blurred. As new opportunities for advanced education, economic independence, personal autonomy, self-gratification, and public service opened for women, a new set of gender conventions gradually fell into place. Predictably, a great many people opposed those changes. The degree of disorientation and anxiety that shifting ideas about gender brought with them could be measured by the amount of discussion such changes elicited.[7]

One of Jane's acquaintances said that she "blazed the trees through the forest as guides for others."[8] In so doing, she was a pioneer of sorts. In her adult life she helped to lay the groundwork for what by the turn of the century would become known as the "New Woman"—a woman who was educated, economically self-sufficient, often unmarried, and determined to make her mark on the world.[9] In that sense, Jane Grey Swisshelm stands as a symbolic transitional figure, a bridge between the gender conventions of the mid–nineteenth century and those that emerged in the twentieth.

NOTE ON PRIMARY SOURCES

For a historian, the early stages of research are a particularly exciting time, filled with a frenetic kind of activity—reading what has already been written on your topic, visiting archives, and writing letters of inquiry to anyone who might be able to help you locate the sources you need. It is also a period filled with a heightened sense of anticipation and with the feeling that there are no limits to what you can find out about your subject. Each small discovery—sometimes only a scrap of paper or an indirect reference—can lead to a much bigger one. And each new discovery provokes more questions than it answers. Under such circumstances, a comment like the one that follows can bring the period of excitement that sometimes spills over into euphoria to a screeching halt: "I . . . burned the private journal kept in girlhood, and the letters received from my brother, mother, sister and other friends. . . . At the office I had received, read and burned, without answer, letters from some of the most prominent men and women of the era; letters which would be valuable history to-day [and] therefore [have] no private papers."

Jane Grey Swisshelm wrote those words on page 164 of the memoir she published in 1880, shortly before her death. She claims to have destroyed her diary and family letters to preserve her privacy from the prying eyes of the "female help" and "farm laborers" with whom she lived. She does not explain why she destroyed her professional papers and correspondence.

The destruction of such documents does not make a researcher's life easy. It requires the casting of an extremely wide net in order to compensate. For me, the working assumption was that if "some of the most prominent men and women of the era" wrote to her, she must have written to some of them. And if they were prominent enough, they probably kept those letters, and someone else probably preserved them by depositing them in an archive or library.

This proved to be the case. Over a period of about eight years, I found references to and/or letters from Jane in the Horace Greeley Papers (New York Public Library), the Pickard-Whittier Papers (Houghton Library, Harvard University), the Joshua Giddings and George Julian Papers (Library of Congress), the Mann Family Papers (Antioch College Library), the Zabina Eastman Papers (Chicago Historical Society), and the Holt-Messer Papers and the Jane G. Swisshelm Papers (Schlesinger Library, Radcliffe Institute for Advanced Study). Other references and letters appear in the microfilm collections of the Stanton-Anthony Papers (ed. Patricia G. Holland and Ann D. Gordon, Wilmington, Del.: Scholarly Resources, 1991) and the Charles Sumner Papers (ed. Beverly W. Palmer, Alexandria, Va.: Chadwyck-Healey, 1988).

The largest number of primary materials relating to Jane is to be found at the Minnesota Historical Society. The William B. Mitchell Papers include a few letters to and from Jane, her sister, and her other relatives as well as a variety of family legal documents and a number of short original manuscripts. Miscellaneous references to Jane and her activities are contained in the Ignatius Donnelly Family Papers, the John Gillan Riheldaffer Papers, the Sylvanus Lowry Family Papers, the Mortimer Robinson Family Papers, the Alexander Ramsey Family Papers, and the Minnesota Republican Party Papers. The Minnesota Historical Society also has census data, a collection of newspapers, and a collection of photographs of Jane and members of her family as well as typescripts of articles written by Jane and published in the *Woman's Journal*, the *Boston Daily Journal*, the *Massachusetts Ploughman*, the *Boston Evening Traveller*, the *New York Daily Tribune*, and the *Chicago Tribune*.

The Stearns County Historical Society in St. Cloud, Minnesota, has a collection of newspaper clippings relating to the Mitchell family. And the Consolidated Correspondence of the Quartermaster General in the National Archives and Records Administration in Washington, D.C., has a small file relating to her appointment as a clerk during the Civil War.

Although the Carnegie Library in Pittsburgh has no original papers relating to Jane, references to her can be found in the Pennsylvania Room. The most useful was a folder of clippings consisting primarily of George T. Fleming's twenty-article series on Jane as a Pittsburgh author that appeared in 1919 in the *Pittsburgh Gazette-Times*. Much of the material in the articles was taken from Jane's autobiography, but Fleming does include some information from William B. Mitchell and others. The microfilm room at the Carnegie Library has the Pittsburgh census and early Pittsburgh city directories as well as various Pittsburgh newspapers.

The Library and Archives Division of the Historical Society of Western Pennsylvania in Pittsburgh has original copies of the *Pittsburgh Saturday Visiter* as well as the *Family Journal and Saturday Visiter*; a folder of photographs relating to Jane; a folder of her papers; two folders relating to Jane in the William Black McClelland Papers, including papers referring to her 1876 patent application for a heating apparatus; the papers of the Women's Club of Pittsburgh; and her self-portrait.

Papers relating to the various lawsuits in which she or members of her family were involved, tax records, wills, marriage records, and death records are available at the Pittsburgh City-County Building.

Copies of the *Pittsburgh Saturday Visiter*, the *St. Cloud Visiter*, and the *St. Cloud Democrat* are available on microfilm. Only five copies of *The Reconstructionist* are extant. Individual copies are available at the American Antiquarian Society in Worcester, Massachusetts; the Western Reserve Historical Society in Cleveland; the National Archives in Washington, D.C.; Houghton Library, Harvard University, Cambridge, Massachusetts; and the Wisconsin Historical Society in Madison.

Jane's newspapers are a particularly rich source of information. Journalism was much more personal in the nineteenth century than it is today. Jane wrote most of the original copy that appeared in her papers, and her style was at once conversational and pedantic. By reading her letters, editorial columns, and "Explanatories," it is possible to find out what she thought about the social, economic, and political issues of the day as well as when she was sick, when she was out of town, when she was in financial straits, and when the ordinary events of daily life interfered with her editorial duties.

Jane also published poems; short stories; serialized novels; *Letters to Country Girls*, a collection of essays taken from her *Pittsburgh Saturday Visiter*; and a memoir, *Half a Century*. Her autobiography is immensely valuable. It must, however, be used with care. Jane said in the preface that she intended to provide her readers with a "history" of slavery and abolition, of the federal government's indifference regarding the care of Union soldiers, and of the early woman's rights movement. Her final purpose, she said, was "to illustrate the force of education and the mutability of human character, by a personal narrative of one who, in 1836, would have broken an engagement rather than permit her name to appear in print . . . and who, in 1850, had as much newspaper notoriety as any man of the time." The tale that Jane told in her memoir was the story of her quest for a public life. In the first few chapters, she described her childhood, acknowledged the degree to which her Covenanter background influenced both her private and public actions, and explored the sources of tension in her marriage. But most of the book was devoted to her public activities as a newspaper editor, reformer, and nurse. When she discussed her role in public life, she allowed discussion of her private affairs to intrude only when it clarified or justified her desire to step outside the bounds of what was considered to be woman's sphere.

Jane's version of her life story can be read on more than one level. Written from memory, it sometimes obscures as much as it reveals. Jane's memory, like that of most autobiographers, was both unreliable and selective. She embellished some of her life experiences and ignored others. And what she chose to ignore is as revealing as what she chose to emphasize. For example, she never mentioned becoming a mother. Motherhood was glorified in the nineteenth century, and bearing a child was the ultimate confirmation of a woman's femininity, so this omission is striking. Yet Jane rarely referred to her daughter in her memoir and never called her by name.

Jane made her first reference to Zo when describing the controversy she had provoked between herself and the Catholic hierarchy of Pittsburgh in 1855 (155). Subsequent references were just as offhand: Jane referred to taking "baby" to see Charles Sumner (158) and to her daughter as being "much-coveted" and her birth as "long-delayed" (165). She described taking her "baby" (who was by then about five) with her when she deserted her husband (167). She wrote that in late 1862 she decided to leave Minnesota and return to the East to live, "that our daughter, then old enough to live without me, might spend a portion of her time with her father" (234). And finally, Jane wrote that during her sojourn in Washington, she became seriously ill but that the receipt of a letter from her "daughter" and the thought of leaving "my child an orphan" brought forth such a "gathering of scattered life-force" that she recovered (355–56).

What are we to make of these brief references? What do they say about how Jane constructed both her self-image and her public persona? One conclusion is that Jane was extremely ambivalent about being a mother. That this should have been so is not terribly surprising. While Zo may have been "much-coveted," it is not at all clear that Jane derived significant personal pleasure from her role as a mother. Zo's birth meant that Jane had fulfilled her biological destiny as a woman. But fulfilling the obligations of motherhood seemed to pose some problems for her. It was not that she was unaware of her responsibilities; indeed, after Zo was born, Jane turned over the editorial responsibilities for the *Visiter* to Robert M. Riddle. But within a few months she was back at the helm. There is no way of knowing for certain why she decided to resume her duties as editor so soon after the birth of her child, but in so doing, she abdicated her child care responsibilities to others without acknowledgment or apology.

Zo's presence not only interfered with Jane's work (or what she preferred to think of as God's work) but also complicated her life in other
ways. Jane was clearly willing to sacrifice herself and her reputation to
pursue her reform goals, and there is no evidence to suggest that she was
terribly concerned about the possible repercussions of her words and
actions on the adult members of her family. But their impact on Zo was
another matter. The memoir's first allusion to Zo occurs when Jane's attack on Pittsburgh's Catholics prompts concern for her daughter's safety.
As Jane put it, "the discussion [of Catholic ritual] marked me as the
subject of a hatred I had not deemed possible. . . . So bitter was the feeling,
that when my only baby came great fears were felt lest she should be
abducted" (155). This melodramatic comment indicates an awareness that
she could not afford to be cavalier about the safety and sensibilities of her
daughter. But although she expressed motherly concern for her child's
well-being, she did so in a way that was both inaccurate and self-serving.
In her description of the situation, she misstated the chronology: Zo was
born in 1852, not in 1855. During the conflict between Jane and Pittsburgh's Catholics, Zo was not an infant whose ill-timed birth inadvertently placed her in the wrong place at the wrong time. She was a toddler
who was allegedly at risk because her mother could not or would not back
away from a fight. However willing Jane may have been to acknowledge
this to herself, she was not willing to do so in public. Instead, she blamed
destiny, thus diverting attention away from her responsibility for Zo's
well-being.

Jane may also have found her love for her daughter a source of considerable anxiety. She believed that God had taken her brother and father
from her as a result of her love for them (35), and she traced the cause for
the discord in her marriage back to the same source: "I knew 'that jealous
God,' who claimed the supreme love of his creatures, was scourging me
for making an idol and bowing down before it—for loving my husband"
(45). How dangerous, then, was loving her daughter? How could she
monitor that love to protect Zo from God's wrath and herself from the
grief that the loss of her daughter might entail? Is it any wonder that her
autobiography does not dwell on her daughter's role in her life? Keeping
Zo in the background, there but rarely acknowledged, may have been a
way of protecting both herself and her child from potential suffering.

Given the trajectory of her life and the way she chose to report it, it was
not in Jane's interest to remind her readers that she had a child. For any
number of reasons, it would have been easy for them to have concluded,
had they been so inclined, that she was, if not a "bad" mother, at least an

inadequate or inattentive one. Nothing in her autobiography romanticizes the sacredness of the relationship between mother and child. Despite the fact that she married a man whose family could have supported her, she refused to give up her career in journalism, stay home, and take care of her baby. And when Zo was about five, Jane moved with her daughter to St. Cloud, thus depriving her child of the company of her father, because Jane could no longer bear to be James Swisshelm's wife. Thus, she may have dwelt so little on this particular aspect of her life as a way of preserving her self-image as a "good" mother. She may have believed that the less said, the better.

She apparently felt the same way about discussing the years between 1866 and the publication of her memoir in 1880. If she intended what she wrote to stand as testimony to what she thought was important, her life ended when she left Washington and returned to Pittsburgh to sue James for her portion of Swissvale. After having devoted more than a hundred pages to a detailed description of her activities as a nurse, she abruptly ended her life story by noting that in the summer of 1866 she became concerned about the fact that James and his mother were selling off parts of their farm, to which she had legal claim. She said that she had made no provisions for retirement, had "made up my mind to poverty," and, having been fired from her position in the quartermaster general's office, "was without visible means of support" (362). So she sought the advice of her friend, Edwin Stanton, who told her she was being foolish and should do something to protect her interests. Following his advice, she sued her former husband. "The decree of the court was in my favor," she wrote in the last sentence of her book, "and through it I have been able to rescue the old log block-house from the tooth of decay, and to sit in it and recall those passages of life with which it is so intimately connected" (363).

Her abrupt conclusion is puzzling for a number of reasons. First, she did not, as she implied, spend the 1870s and 1880s living in quiet retirement at Swissvale, dwelling on memories of the past. She remained interested in social reform, continued to write and publish, lived for a time in both New Jersey and Chicago, traveled to Europe, and periodically visited her sister.

It is impossible to determine with any certainty why she failed to discuss these years. One possibility is that she simply felt she had accomplished what she wanted to accomplish as an author. She had provided her readers with a "history" of slavery, abolition, bureaucratic indifference, and the woman's rights movement, and she had shown how she changed from a woman hesitant to seek public attention to one who reveled in "notoriety." Given her goals, she may have felt that it would serve no purpose, literary or otherwise, to outline the activities that she pursued after her Pennsylvania Supreme Court victory. Her memoir was about her public life, and when she gave up her editorship of *The Reconstructionist*, her career as a newspaper editor had ended.

There may have been a less straightforward reason for her to have implied that her legal triumph over James was important only because it gave her the opportunity to preserve an old house and live there in relative solitude. It was out of character for Jane not to celebrate a victory. Take, for example, her argument with her mother-in-law over the willow tree that grew at Swissvale. Mary Elizabeth ordered the willow dug up and transplanted in a nearby swamp because she said she was afraid its roots would get into the millrace. Jane loved the tree and was determined to preserve it. So the next morning, she took a willow cutting and planted it where the original tree had been. Two days later, her mother-in-law had it removed. Not one to give up easily, Jane planted more cuttings. In the end, some of her cuttings "were permitted to remain," and, as she proudly put it, "Swissvale is now noted for its magnificent willows" (79). She also reveled in her victory over Sylvanus Lowry, James Shepley, and their cronies in St. Cloud. After settling the Shepleys' lawsuit against her by signing a document agreeing not to publish articles or editorials relating to the destruction of her press in the *St. Cloud Visiter*, she closed down the paper, opened a new newspaper called the *St. Cloud Democrat*, and "into the first editorial column copied verbatim, with a prominent heading, the article from the *Visiter* on which the libel suit was founded." "It seems strange that those lawyers should have been so stupid. . . . No famous victory was ever before turned into a more total rout by a more simple ambush, and by it I won the clear field necessary to the continuance of my work," she wrote (195).

Simply put, Jane was a gloater. Yet when she defeated her husband in the highest court in the state of Pennsylvania, she had little to say about it. She did not even use her victory as one last piece of evidence to demonstrate that while their property might be protected under law, women needed to maintain vigilance in pursuit of their economic self-interests.

In this case, internal conflict over her complicated relationship with her ex-husband may help to explain why she had so little to say about the outcome of the lawsuit. She exposed her ambivalence about James when, on one hand, she romanticized their courtship and called him her "black knight" (40) yet on the other said that he made her so unhappy that she had to desert him or "die" (168). She accused him of insensitivity and

disloyalty, but although she went to great lengths to document his failings as a husband, she felt compelled to assure her readers that "there
never was a time when my husband's strong right arm would not be
tempered to infantile gentleness to tend me in illness, or when he hesitated to throw himself between me and danger" (46). And it appears to
have been important for her to believe that, despite their estrangement,
he continued to think of her with affection if not love. She wrote, "Years
after I left him, he said to our neighbor, Miss Hawkins, when speaking of
me: 'I believe she is the best woman God ever made'" (168). It seems never
to have occurred to her that he might have resented her for having caused
so much turmoil in his life. If Jane found it difficult to think that her ex-
husband might harbor ill feelings toward her, what, then, was she supposed to make of the painful fact that he had attempted to defraud her?

The lawsuit had both public and private implications for her. It stood
as public testimony to the success of her long campaign to guarantee
married women's property rights. And by giving her clear title to property
at Swissvale, the court secured her financial future. In that sense, it was
fitting that the lawsuit was one of the last things she mentioned in her
memoir. But her legal victory also stood as a reminder of her failure to
nurture James's willingness to love her and to protect her interests in an
age when doing so was considered to be one of women's primary responsibilities. The implications of her desertion and divorce may have been
easy to discount when she lived in Minnesota and Washington. But the
area around Swissvale was full of people who knew the intimate details of
her personal life and where the consequences of her personal failure and
James's betrayal of her interests were most obvious. When she moved
into the old homestead, Jane was living with her daughter in close prox-
imity to both her ex-husband and his mother. At that point, Jane may
have felt there was nothing to be gained by gloating over James's public
humiliation at the hands of the Pennsylvania Supreme Court. Her victory
was a matter of public record. She had what she wanted—clear title to her
land. She could go about her business knowing that she had the means to
support herself should the profits from her writing prove inadequate.
And she had guaranteed Zo the opportunity to seek the company of her
father and grandmother whenever she wanted. If that was the case, dwelling on the victory in the memoir could serve no useful purpose. Jane had
won the lawsuit and could afford to be magnanimous. The public image
that she was quite self-consciously constructing could only benefit from
such high-mindedness.

Jane's autobiographical self-portrait reveals a woman with a compulsive need for public affirmation. Generally speaking, she tended to justify her personal attributes and actions, particularly those that others were likely to find most objectionable, on the grounds that she was an instrument of God rather than an independent agent. Jane's memory may sometimes have been untrustworthy. And her literary style was often melodramatic. While her memoir might not be a "true" story from a historian's point of view, it may have been as "true" a story as Jane could tell. In that sense, it is not strictly a story of her life but a literary construction of the meaning she gave her life. Parts of her story are verifiable. When that is the case, she appears to have done what she said she did. It is when she attempted to deal with motivations, both her own and that of others, that her reliability is most open to question. But because her memoir reveals what she thought about herself, her background, her activities, her accomplishments, and her mistakes, it provides information available from no other source.

NOTES

Abbreviations

ECM	Elizabeth Cannon Mitchell
FJSV	*Family Journal and Saturday Visiter*
HAC	Jane Grey Swisshelm, *Half a Century* (Chicago: Jansen, McClurg, 1880)
JGS	Jane Grey Swisshelm
JM	Jean Mitchell
McFP	McClelland Family Papers, Historical Society of Western Pennsylvania, Pittsburgh
MFP	William B. Mitchell Family Papers, Minnesota Historical Society, St. Paul
MHS	Minnesota Historical Society, St. Paul
PDCJ	*Pittsburgh Daily Commercial Journal*
PSV	*Pittsburgh Saturday Visiter*
SCD	*St. Cloud Democrat*
SCV	*St. Cloud Visiter*

Prologue

1. I will allude to the way that Jane both consciously and unconsciously defined for herself what it meant to be a woman in a society that clearly differentiated between what was masculine and what was feminine. I use the term "gender" to refer to the way ideas about sexual differences are and have been used to organize society and structure the relationships between men and women. My approach is based on the assumptions that ideas about gender (what it means to be feminine or masculine), while based on biological characteristics, are largely social constructions that are learned; that gender in American society is and has been a binary and hierarchical construct; that individual gender identities shift over time as people adapt the ideas about gender that they have been taught to their own needs; that at any one period of time there is more than one prevailing gender ideal; and that constructing a gender identity is an ongoing, lifelong process. Useful discussions of these ideas appear in Judith Lorber, "'Night to His Day': The Social Construction of Gender," in *Paradoxes of Gender* (New Haven: Yale University Press, 1994), 13–36; Judith Butler, *Gender Trouble: Feminism and the Sub-*

version of Identity (New York: Routledge, 1990), 163–80. For discussions of the relationship between the construction of gender and history, see Joan W. Scott, "Gender: A Useful Category of Historical Analysis," *American Historical Review* 91 (December 1986): 1053–75; Kathleen M. Brown, "Brave New Worlds: Women's and Gender History," *William and Mary Quarterly*, 3d ser., 50 (April 1993): 311–28.

Chapter 1

1. Swisshelm's autobiography, *Half a Century*, which covers the first fifty years of her life, was written in the late 1870s and was published in Chicago by Jansen, McClurg in 1880. It is a critical but not ideal source. I have tried whenever possible to verify what she wrote in her memoir by using other sources. In those cases where there were no other records available, I have had to depend on her unsubstantiated testimony. This is particularly true of my discussion of her early life and her work as a volunteer nurse during the Civil War. In such cases, I remind my readers that I am dependent upon her autobiography by prefacing what I have to say with such phrases as "according to Jane" or "in her memoir." For a more complete critique of *Half a Century*, see the Note on Primary Sources.

2. The literature on the Second Great Awakening is voluminous. For a good introduction, see Nathan O. Hatch, *The Democratization of American Christianity* (New Haven: Yale University Press, 1989); Robert H. Abzug, *Cosmos Crumbling: American Reform and the Religious Imagination* (New York: Oxford University Press, 1994).

3. Ian B. Cowan, *The Scottish Covenanters, 1660–1688* (London: Victor Gollancz, 1976); T. C. Smout, *A History of the Scottish People, 1560–1830* (New York: Scribner's, 1969), 62–71; James Kerr, *The Covenants and the Covenanters: Covenants, Sermons, and Documents of the Covenanter Reformation* (Edinburgh: R. W. Hunter, [1895]), 11–36; Abbott Emerson Smith, *Colonists in Bondage: White Servitude and Convict Labor in America, 1607–1776* (Gloucester, Mass.: Peter Smith, 1965), 180–87.

4. Thomas Macaulay, *The History of England from the Accession of James the Second*, 5 vols. (London: Longman, Green, Longman, Roberts, and Green, 1863), 3:142–43.

5. Ibid., 188–89, 191, 197–201, 228–37; R. F. Foster, *Modern Ireland, 1600–1972* (London: Allen Lane, 1988), 601–2.

6. *HAC*, 11.

7. R. J. Dickson, *Ulster Emigration to Colonial America, 1718–1775* (London: Routledge and Kegan Paul, 1966), 5.

8. Ibid., 1–18, 62, 77, 78; Foster, *Modern Ireland*, 212–16.

9. Dickson, *Ulster Emigration*, 223, 224; Henry Jones Ford, *The Scotch-Irish in America* (Hamden, Conn.: Archon, 1966), 269.

10. *City Directory of Pittsburgh* ([Pittsburgh]: n.p., 1815), 74; George T. Fleming, "Bits of Biography—Jane Grey Swisshelm," *Pittsburgh Gazette Times*, March 30,

1919, clipping in Jane Swisshelm File, Pittsburgh Authors, Pennsylvania Room, Carnegie Library, Pittsburgh.

11. W. Melancthon Glasgow, *History of the Reformed Presbyterian Church in America* (Baltimore: Hill and Harvey, 1888), 78–79; Andrew E. Murray, *Presbyterians and the Negro: A History* (Philadelphia: Presbyterian Historical Society, 1966), 129.

12. John Walker Dismore, *The Scotch-Irish in America: Their History, Traits, Institutions, and Influences; Especially as Illustrated in the Early Settlers of Western Pennsylvania and Their Descendants* (Chicago: Winona, 1906), 129–42, 181–82; Ford, *Scotch-Irish in America*, 288; R. F. G. Holmes, *Our Irish Presbyterian Heritage* (n.p.: W. G. Baird, 1985), 73; Elizabeth Davison and Ellen McKee, eds., *Annals of Old Wilkinsburg and Vicinity: The Village, 1788–1888* (Wilkinsburg, Pa.: Group for Historical Research, 1940), 214–16.

13. Mark H. Welchley, ed., *Pittsburgh, Pa., Gazette: Genealogical Gleanings, 1786–1820*, vol. 1 (n.p.: n.p. 1983), item 884. On July 17, 1801, George Cochran, a master chair maker in Pittsburgh, placed an ad in the *Pittsburgh Gazette* announcing that his apprentice, Thomas Cannon, age eighteen, had run away.

14. Welchley, *Pittsburgh*, items 1496, 229.

15. Clara E. Duer, ed. and comp., *The People and Times of Western Pennsylvania: Pittsburgh Gazette Abstracts*, 3 vols. (Pittsburgh: Western Pennsylvania Genealogical Society, 1988), 3:310.

16. Lease between Samuel Ewalt and Thomas Cannon, Pittsburgh, March 29, 1806, Box 3, MFP; *City Directory of Pittsburgh*, 16.

17. "Mrs. Swisshelm," *Chicago Tribune*, December 24, 1881, p. 11.

18. *HAC*, 30. Jane was born in 1815 (*HAC*, 10). William was three years older than Jane (*HAC*, 14). Swisshelm discusses Elizabeth's birth in *HAC*, p. 15. The only other sibling that she names is her sister, Mary (*HAC*, 19).

19. Ibid., 8–9.

20. Lease between Thomas Cannon and Benjamin Bloomfield, May 1, 1816, Box 3, MFP. Jane dates their move to Wilkinsburg as April 1816 (*HAC*, 11).

21. *HAC*, 11, 12; Davison and McKee, *Annals*, 391, 195–96.

22. James Horner, "Reminiscences of Early Wilkinsburg," *Western Pennsylvania Historical Magazine* 10 (July 1927): 182–83; Davison and McKee, *Annals*, 36, 48; Leland Dewitt Baldwin, *Pittsburgh: The Story of a City* (Pittsburgh: University of Pittsburgh Press, 1937), 235.

23. *HAC*, 7.

24. Glasgow, *History*, 304. The Covenanters did not build a church in Wilkinsburg until 1845 (Davison and McKee, *Annals*, 211).

25. *HAC*, 12.

26. Fleming, "Bits of Biography," *Pittsburgh Gazette-Times*, March 16, 1919, clipping in Jane Swisshelm File.

27. *HAC*, 13–15, quotation on 14.

28. Ibid., 11–12, 15, 19. For a discussion of how the depression affected Pitts-

burgh, see Richard C. Wade, *The Urban Frontier: Pioneer Life in Early Pittsburgh, Cincinnati, Lexington, Louisville, and St. Louis* (Chicago: University of Chicago Press, 1964), 163–68.

29. "Dr. Black's Funeral," *PSV*, November 3, 1849, p. 166; "The Memory of Dr. Black," *PSV*, November 3, 1849, p. 167.

30. Glasgow, *History*, 299, 300, 440–42.

31. *HAC*, 18–19.

32. "Rev. Dr. Black," *PSV*, October 27, 1849, p. 162; *HAC*, 19.

33. *HAC*, 12.

34. Ibid., 19–20. In her memoir, Jane incorrectly gave the date of her father's death as March 23, 1823. The 1826 City Directory lists Thomas Cannon as a chair maker whose shop was located at Wood and Smithfield (S[amuel] Jones, comp., *Pittsburgh City Directory for 1826* [Pittsburgh: Johnston and Stockton, 1826], 112). Some documents in the MFP indicate that on March 10, 1827, the executors of Hance Scott's estate appointed Thomas Cannon to rent out the house the Scotts had owned on Sixth Street. On May 22 of the same year, Thomas transferred his power of attorney in this matter to his wife, Mary. His hand was clearly shaking when he wrote out this transfer, no doubt as a result of his illness, and he probably died shortly after that date; see appointment document and power of attorney document in Box 3, MFP.

35. *HAC*, 20, 30–32, quotation on 32.

36. Ibid., 21–29; Virginia K. Bartlett, *Keeping House: Women's Lives in Western Pennsylvania, 1790–1850* (Pittsburgh: University of Pittsburgh Press, 1994), 125; Thomas Cushing, *History of Allegheny County*, 2 vols. (Chicago: Warner, 1889), 2:125; Baldwin, *Pittsburgh*, 214–15; Isaac Harris, *Harris' Business Pittsburgh Directory for the Year 1839* (Pittsburgh: A. A. Anderson, 1839), advertisement. Jane described the school in an 1848 story she published under a pseudonym; see Jennie Deans [JGS], "The Haunted Church," *PDCJ*, January 27, 1848, p. 1.

37. *HAC*, 26–27.

38. Ibid., 29–30.

39. Ibid., 35–38.

40. Ibid., 40–45, quotation on 43–44.

41. Ibid., 80–82. For a description of the meetinghouse, see Davison and McKee, *Annals*, 196–97.

42. *HAC*, 85–86.

43. Ibid., 35.

44. Ibid., 45.

45. Ibid., 80–86.

46. Ibid., 67.

47. "The Syracuse Convention," *PSV*, September 25, 1852, p. 142; "Communication," *PSV*, August 12, 1848, p. 1; "Women in Male Attire," *PSV*, June 15, 1850, p. 86.

48. "Woman's Legal Disabilities," *PSV*, October 25, 1851, p. 158.

49. *HAC*, 4.

50. "Aunt Fanny, Bloomer Dresses, and Woman's Rights," *PSV*, August 23, 1851, p. 118.

51. Ray Allen Billington, *The Protestant Crusade, 1800–1860: A Study of the Origins of American Nativism* (Chicago: Quadrangle, 1964); Jenny Franchot, *Roads to Rome: The Antebellum Protestant Encounter with Catholicism* (Berkeley: University of California Press, 1994).

52. "The Pittsburgh Catholic" and "Bishop O'Conner's Lecture," *PSV*, January 27, 1849, p. 6.

53. *HAC*, 151–53; for examples of this debate, see "Bishop O'Conner and the Public Schools," *PSV*, February 5, 1853, p. 10; "Bishop O'Conner and the Public Schools," *PSV*, March 5, 1853, p. 26; "The School Question and Sectarian Press," *PSV*, April 9, 1853, p. 46; "The Pittsburgh Catholic and Public Schools," *PSV*, April 30, 1853, p. 58; "The Catholic and Common Schools," *PSV*, May 21, 1853, p. 70.

54. "The Allocution of the Pope," *PSV*, April 2, 1853, 42.

55. "Cathedral Ceremonies," *FJSV*, June 30, 1855, p. 5; *HAC*, 153–55.

56. "Cathedral Dedication," *FJSV*, July 14, 1855, p. 5. For another critical response, see "What Is to Be Thought of Mrs. Swisshelm," *FJSV*, August 11, 1855, p. 5.

57. "Catholic Ceremonies and 'The Catholic,'" *FJSV*, August 11, 1855, p. 5.

58. The outfit consisted of trousers with legs gathered around the ankles and a loose-fitting tunic. For a discussion of the bloomer costume and responses to it, see Gayle V. Fischer, *Pantaloons and Power: Nineteenth-Century Dress Reform in the United States* (Kent, Ohio: Kent University Press, 2001).

59. "The Bloomer Costume," *PSV*, August 2, 1851, p. 106.

60. "The Bloomer Dress," *PSV*, September 27, 1851, p. 138.

61. "Women in Male Attire," *PSV*, June 15, 1850, p. 86.

62. "The Sex of Dress," *FJSV*, February 9, 1856, p. 5.

63. "Mrs. Swisshelm on Copes," *FJSV*, September 29, 1855, p. 5. Swisshelm discusses her relationship with Pittsburgh's Catholics in *HAC*, 150–55.

64. Rebecca Broadnax Hicks, "Mrs. Jane Swisshelm," *Petersburg (Virginia) Kaleidoscope*, August 22, 1855, p. 255. My thanks to Cheryl Junk for sharing this source with me.

Chapter 2

1. Ernest S. Craighead, "The Swisshelm Home in Edgewood" (speech delivered on December 9, 1948, at the annual meeting of the Edgewood Historical Society), pp. 1–2, 16, Historical Society of Western Pennsylvania, Pittsburgh; *HAC*, 29–30; *Golden Progress: History and Official Program of the Fiftieth Anniversary Celebration of Swissvale, Pennsylvania, 1898–1948* (n.p.: Executive Committee for the Fiftieth Anniversary Celebration, 1948), 4, 27; "The Old Homestead," *St. Cloud Journal Press*, July 31, 1884, p. 2. James remarried in September 1869 at the age of fifty-eight to a woman thirty-seven years his junior, with whom he had a son, James. James Sr. inherited the farm in 1875, when his mother died (U.S. Manuscript Census for

1870 for Wilkins Township, Allegheny County, Pennsylvania, roll 1299, p. 633; Craighead, "Swisshelm Home," 6; Helen Beal Woodward, *The Bold Women* [New York: Farrar, Straus, and Young, 1953], 86; "Mrs. Mary E. Swisshelm," *Pittsburgh Commercial Journal* deaths index, Carnegie Library, Pittsburgh).

2. *HAC*, 23, 39-40; William B. Mitchell to J. L. Washburn, March 4, 1915, quoted in Abigail McCarthy, "Jane Grey Swisshelm: Marriage and Slavery," in *Women in Minnesota: Selected Biographical Essays*, ed. Barbara Stuhler and Gretchen Kreuter (St. Paul: Minnesota Historical Society Press, 1977), 348n.

3. Willoughby Babcock, "Gateway to the Northwest: St. Paul and the Nobles Expedition of 1859," *Minnesota History* 35 (June 1957): 255; "A Pen Picture," *St. Cloud Journal Press*, November 26, 1874, p. 3; Madelon Golden Schilpp and Sharon M. Murphy, *Great Women of the Press* (Carbondale: Southern Illinois University Press, 1983), 83; William B. Mitchell, *History of Stearns County*, 2 vols. (Chicago: H. C. Cooper Jr., 1915), 1:65.

4. Craighead, "Swisshelm Home," 1-2; *HAC*, 50.

5. A. Gregory Schneider, *The Way of the Cross Leads Home: The Domestication of American Methodism* (Bloomington: Indiana University Press, 1993), 199.

6. Riley Moffat, *Population History of the Eastern U.S. Cities and Towns, 1790–1870* (Metuchen, N.J.: Scarecrow, 1992), 192.

7. Richard C. Wade, *The Urban Frontier: Pioneer Life in Early Pittsburgh, Cincinnati, Lexington, Louisville, and St. Louis* (Chicago: University of Chicago Press, 1967), 11-12, 46-47; John Ingham, "Steel City Aristocrats," in *City at the Point: Essays on the Social History of Pittsburgh*, ed. Samuel P. Hays (Pittsburgh: University of Pittsburgh Press, 1989), 268; *Pittsburgh in 1816* (Pittsburgh: Carnegie Library, 1916), 22-24.

8. S[amuel] Jones, comp., *Pittsburgh City Directory for 1826* (Pittsburgh: Johnston and Stockton, 1826), 12, 39. The state legislature did not authorize the establishment of public schools until 1834. See Thomas Cushing, *History of Allegheny County*, 2 vols. (Chicago: Warner, 1889), 1:669-70; Leland Dewitt Baldwin, *Pittsburgh: The Story of a City* (Pittsburgh: University of Pittsburgh Press, 1937), 214; Robert I. Vexler, *Pittsburgh: A Chronicle and Documentary History, 1682–1976* (Dobbs Ferry, N.Y.: Oceana, 1977), 93.

9. Jones, *Pittsburgh City Directory for 1826*, 11, quotation on 41; *Pittsburgh in 1816*, 17.

10. *Pittsburgh in 1816*, 20; Ann[e] Royal[l] in Vexler, *Pittsburgh*, 104.

11. *HAC*, 21-25, quotation on 23.

12. Ibid., 38-41, quotations on 40.

13. Ellen K. Rothman, *Hands and Hearts: A History of Courtship in America* (New York: Basic, 1984), 31-35.

14. *HAC*, 41.

15. Henry Jones Ford, *The Scotch-Irish in America* (Hamden, Conn.: Archon Books, 1966), 286-88.

16. Schneider, *Way of the Cross*, 174.

17. See Howard P. Chudacoff, *The Age of the Bachelor: Creating an American Subculture* (Princeton: Princeton University Press, 1999); Lee Virginia Chambers-Schiller, *Liberty, a Better Husband: Single Women in America: The Generations of 1780–1840* (New Haven: Yale University Press, 1984).

18. The technical term for a married woman's legal status under common law was "femme covert." Although under common law married women had no independent legal identity, they preserved some of their legal rights under the law of equity. For further discussion of this matter, see Hendrik Hartog, *Man and Wife in America: A History* (Cambridge: Harvard University Press, 2000), 119, 125.

19. Sylvia D. Hoffert, *When Hens Crow: The Woman's Rights Movement in Antebellum America* (Bloomington: Indiana University Press, 1995), 55–56.

20. "Women of Genius," *PSV*, November 24, 1849, p. 178.

21. *HAC*, 41.

22. Norma Basch, *Framing American Divorce: From the Revolutionary Generation to the Victorians* (Berkeley: University of California Press, 1999), 177.

23. Rothman, *Hands and Hearts*, 17–84; Karen Lystra, *Searching the Heart: Women, Men, and Romantic Love in Nineteenth-Century America* (New York: Oxford University Press, 1989), 157–91; E. Anthony Rotundo, *American Manhood: Transformations in Masculinity from the Revolution to the Modern Era* (New York: Basic, 1993), 109–28.

24. Rothman, *Hands and Hearts*, 64–71.

25. Rotundo, *American Manhood*, 92, 145–46, 166, 178; Rothman, *Hands and Hearts*, 59–60; Lystra, *Searching the Heart*, 136.

26. *HAC*, 41–42.

27. Ibid., 42–43, 45, quotation on 42.

28. Ibid., 45–50, quotations on 48, 49. Jane's self-portrait is archived in the Historical Society of Western Pennsylvania in Pittsburgh. A series of floral panels that she painted decorate an armoire owned by one of the members of her family.

29. Ibid., 50–51, 52, 60, 64.

30. Toby L. Ditz, "Shipwrecked or Masculinity Imperiled: Mercantile Representations of Failure and the Gendered Self in Eighteenth-Century Philadelphia," *Journal of American History* 81 (June 1994): 51–80.

31. *HAC*, 63–64.

32. Mary Cannon and Elizabeth Cannon to JGS, August 1, 1839, Box 1, MFP; Ephesians 22; *HAC*, 65–68.

33. *HAC*, 71, 73.

34. Ibid., 74, 78, 83, 79.

35. Ibid., 83.

36. Ibid., 84–87.

37. "The Locust's Song," *PSV*, July 21, 28, August 4, 11, 18, 25, September 1, 8, 15, 22, 29, October 6, 13, 27, November 3, December 1, 8, 15, 22, 1849.

38. Only a year earlier, Elizabeth Cady Stanton and Lucretia Mott had orga-nized the first woman's rights convention held in the United States. From that convention came the Declaration of Sentiments, which demanded that women be granted, among other things, the right to equal educational and vocational op-portunities, the right to control their own property, and the opportunity to rep-resent themselves through the right to vote. Based on the principle that women had a right to pursue and protect their own self-interests, the demands of wom-an's rights advocates threatened the foundation of male-dominated social, eco-nomic, and political life. See Hoffert, *When Hens Crow*, 2–3, 34.

39. Basch, *Framing American Divorce*, 45, 177–82; Michael Grossberg, *Governing the Hearth: Law and the Family in Nineteenth-Century America* (Chapel Hill: Univer-sity of North Carolina Press, 1985), xi–xii, 6–9, 19.

40. "Matrimonial Difficulties," *PSV*, September 15, 1849, p. 140.

41. "The Locust's Song," *PSV*, October 6, 1849, p. 150.

42. "Marriage and Divorce," *PSV*, August 3, 1850, p. 114.

43. Basch, *Framing American Divorce*, 72–80.

44. "Notices of the Press," *PSV*, January 26, 1850, p. 6; W[illiam]. S[wisshelm]., "Initiatory," *PSV*, January 19, 1850, p. 2.

45. "A Change" and "Explanatory," *PSV*, May 15, 1852, p. 66.

46. Hartog, *Man and Wife*, 30, 38–39.

47. *HAC*, 164–65.

48. Hartog, *Man and Wife*, 36–38.

49. James Swisshelm Divorce Petition, Deposition of William Shields, Of-fice of the Prothonotary, City-County Building, Pittsburgh; *HAC*, 165–68; Merril Smith, *Breaking the Bonds: Marital Discord in Pennsylvania, 1730–1830* (New York: New York University Press, 1991), 14, 35.

50. James Swisshelm Divorce Petition.

51. References to Swisshelm's trip to Pittsburgh appear in the *SCD*, July 19, 1860, p. 2; August 9, 1860, p. 2; August 16, 1860, p. 2; August 23, 1860, p. 2. She was back in St. Cloud by the middle of September (see *SCD*, September 20, 1860, p. 2).

52. James Swisshelm Divorce Petition, Deposition of William Shields.

53. James Swisshelm Divorce Petition and accompanying depositions.

54. *HAC*, 216–17.

55. "Laws of Marriage," *SCD*, May 29, 1862, p. 2.

56. Hartog, *Man and Wife*, 212.

57. *HAC*, 168.

58. See Janet Farrell Brodie, *Contraception and Abortion in Nineteenth-Century America* (Ithaca: Cornell University Press, 1994).

59. *HAC*, 46.

60. Ibid., 168.

61. Ibid.

62. "Mrs. Swisshelm's Funeral," *Pittsburgh Commercial Gazette*, July 24, 1884, p. 2.

Chapter 3

1. According to depositions attached to James Swisshelm's divorce petition, Jane purchased the watch in 1857. See James Swisshelm Divorce Petition, Office of the Prothonotary, City-County Building, Pittsburgh.

2. *HAC*, 46.

3. *Swisshelm v. Swisshelm*, 56 Pa. 475 (1867), in P. Frazier Smith, *Pennsylvania State Reports* (Philadelphia: Kay, 1869), 56:475–88; *HAC*, 30; Ernest S. Craighead, "The Swisshelm Home in Edgewood" (speech delivered on December 9, 1948, at the annual meeting of the Edgewood Historical Society), pp. 1–2, Historical Society of Western Pennsylvania, Pittsburgh.

4. E. Anthony Rotundo, *American Manhood: Transformations in Masculinity from the Revolution to the Modern Era* (New York: Basic, 1993), 168–69; Karen Lystra, *Searching the Heart: Women, Men, and Romantic Love in Nineteenth-Century America* (New York: Oxford University Press, 1989), 133–35; Robert L. Griswold, *Fatherhood in America: A History* (New York: Basic, 1993), 147.

5. For mention of Samuel's death and William's assignment, see *Swisshelm v. Swisshelm*; Henry Swisshelm to friends, June 8, 1856, Box 1, MFP.

6. *Pittsburgh in 1816* (Pittsburgh: Carnegie Library, 1916), 18; Richard C. Wade, *The Urban Frontier: Pioneer Life in Early Pittsburgh, Cincinnati, Lexington, Louisville, and St. Louis*, 163.

7. See the two-year lease agreement between Thomas Cannon and Benjamin Bloomfield, May 1, 1816. When this lease ran out, Cannon leased the house to Gordon Gilmore and then John Gilmore. The latter paid an annual rent of $310 (Box 3, MFP).

8. *HAC*, 11–12.

9. Wade, *Urban Frontier*, 177–78.

10. *HAC*, 11–12, 15.

11. See accounts payable to Samuel Ewalt, October 1, 1820–October 1, 1831, Box 3, MFP; *HAC*, 19–20.

12. *HAC*, 20–21, 30–31. Although Jane says that her mother eventually regained title to her father's Wilkinsburg property, real estate documents in the MFP indicate that on April 25, 1834, Mary Cannon bought a lot in Wilkinsburg from James and Sarah Ann Kelly for one hundred dollars (Box 3, MFP).

13. See power of attorney documents dated May 22, 1827, and November 12, 1827, Box 3, MFP.

14. *HAC*, 32.

15. Ibid., 72.

16. The *Pittsburgh City Directory of 1839* lists Mary Cannon as a seamstress with

a shop located on Sixth Street (microfilm of the 1839 *Pittsburgh City Directory*, p. 30, Carnegie Library, Pittsburgh).

17. *HAC*, 71–72.

18. Hendrik Hartog, *Man and Wife in America: A History* (Cambridge: Harvard University Press, 2000), 115–16.

19. Marylynn Salmon, *Women and the Law of Property in Early America* (Chapel Hill: University of North Carolina Press, 1986), 24, 32–35, 36, 82, 91–93, 186. For an earlier discussion of changes in married women's property law, see Charles W. Dahlinger, "The Dawn of the Woman's Movement: An Account of the Origin and History of the Pennsylvania Married Woman's Property Law of 1848," *Western Pennsylvania Historical Magazine* 1 (April 1918): 68–84.

20. *HAC*, 72.

21. Ibid., 45, 50.

22. JGS, "A Husband's Liabilities for the Support of His Wife," *New York Daily Tribune*, May 4, 1860, p. 5; *HAC*, 84.

23. *HAC*, 101–2; Thomas Cushing, *History of Allegheny County*, 2 vols. (Chicago: Warner, 1889), 1:580–81; *History of Allegheny County, Pennsylvania, 1753–1876* (n.p.: L. H. Evarts, n.d.), 139–40, Pennsylvania Room, Carnegie Library, Pittsburgh.

24. *HAC*, 102; Hartog, *Man and Wife*, 144. It is not clear how this issue was resolved. According to a mortgage assignment dated September 1, 1851 (Box 3, MFP), Jane and Elizabeth's trustees sold the land on May 27, 1845, for twenty-five hundred dollars.

25. *HAC*, 166.

26. Ibid., 102.

27. "Mrs. Swisshelm's Letter," *PDCJ*, October 28, 1847, p. 2; "Mrs. Swisshelm's Letter," *PDCJ*, December 11, 1847, p. 2; "Mrs. Swisshelm's Letter," *PDCJ*, February 17, 1848, p. 2.

28. Dahlinger, "Dawn," 74–78; *HAC*, 103–4. For information on the New York law, which served as a model for married women's property legislation in other states, see Norma Basch, *In the Eyes of the Law: Women, Marriage, and Property in Nineteenth-Century New York* (Ithaca: Cornell University Press, 1982); Peggy A. Rabkin, *Fathers to Daughters: The Legal Foundations of Female Emancipation* (Westport, Conn.: Greenwood, 1980).

29. 1848 Pa. Laws 372.

30. Dahlinger, "Dawn," 78–84.

31. *HAC*, 106.

32. "Salutory," *PSV*, January 20, 1849, p. 2.

33. *HAC*, 162–63; "An Introduction" and "Initiatory," *PSV*, January 19, 1850, p. 2.

34. *HAC*, 163; *Swisshelm v. Swisshelm*.

35. *Swisshelm v. Swisshelm*.

36. JGS, "A Husband's Liabilities."

37. *HAC*, 165; JGS, "A Husband's Liabilities."

38. *HAC*, 166; "Mrs. Swisshelm's Watch," *Boston Daily Evening Traveller*, March 12, 1860, reprinted from the *Pittsburgh Post* (typescript in MHS); James Swisshelm Divorce Petition, Depositions of William Shields and James McKelvey.

39. JGS, "A Husband's Liabilities"; "Mrs. Swisshelm's Watch," *Boston Daily Evening Traveller*, March 12, 1860.

40. Hartog, *Man and Wife*, 147.

41. Michael Willrich, "Home Slackers: Men, the State, and Welfare in Modern America," *Journal of American History* 87 (September 2000): 466; Hartog, *Man and Wife*, 156–57.

42. *HAC*, 166.

43. The *Boston Daily Evening Traveller*, March 12, 1860, picked up the story from the *Pittsburgh Post*. Jane, then living in Minnesota, read a story about the lawsuit in the *New York Tribune*, March 5, 1860, p. 5; for reference to this story, see JGS, "A Husband's Liabilities."

44. JGS, "A Husband's Liabilities."

45. *HAC*, 167.

46. *Swisshelm v. Swisshelm*.

47. *HAC*, 168.

48. *Swisshelm v. Swisshelm*.

49. *HAC*, 362.

50. For reference to this land, see Clarence D. Stephenson, *Indiana County 175th Anniversary History*, 5 vols. (Indiana, Pa.: A. G. Halldin, 1983), 4:274, 275. Stephenson claims that the land was given to Zo to keep it out of James's hands. Since fathers were considered the natural guardians of their children and their children's property, however, putting it in Zo's name would not have prevented James from claiming it unless Mitchell made specific legal provisions to do so.

51. *Swisshelm v. Swisshelm*; for a reference to her determination to get control of her share of the land, see JGS to ECM, March 27, 1867, Box 1, MFP.

52. For reference to her life in Indiana County, see Stephenson, *Indiana County*, 4:274.

53. For discussions of the economic value of women's work on farms, see Joan M. Jensen, *Loosening the Bonds: Mid-Atlantic Farm Women, 1750–1850* (New Haven: Yale University Press, 1986); Nancy Grey Osterud, *Bonds of Community: The Lives of Farm Women in Nineteenth-Century New York* (Ithaca: Cornell University Press, 1991). For a discussion of the economic significance of housework in the nineteenth century, see Jeanne Boydston, *Home and Work: Housework, Wages, and the Ideology of Labor in the Early Republic* (New York: Oxford University Press, 1990).

54. See, for example, "Employment for Women," *PSV*, May 14, 1853, p. 66. Jane also employed female printers and compositors whenever she could and encouraged other editors to do the same; see "Women and Printers," *FJSV*, August 4, 1855, p. 5; "Wanted," *SCD*, January 12, 1860, p. 2.

Chapter 4

1. The first edition of her paper came out on December 20, 1847. In her memoir she mistakenly gave the date as January 20, 1848 (*HAC*, 109).

2. Jane noted in her memoir that at the time the only man and woman who worked together in an office in Pittsburgh were a lawyer and his daughter, who served as his clerk. The office was apparently in their home. Jane described the father-daughter arrangement as "remarkable and very painful" (*HAC*, 107).

3. Charles Sellers, *The Market Revolution: Jacksonian America, 1815–1846* (New York: Oxford University Press, 1991).

4. E. Anthony Rotundo, *American Manhood: Transformations in Masculinity from the Revolution to the Modern Era* (New York: Basic, 1993), 209; Michael Kimmel, *Manhood in America: A Cultural History* (New York: Free Press, 1996), 26.

5. Rotundo, *American Manhood*, 201; for male ambivalence toward women, see 104–8.

6. Ibid., 196–97.

7. Joan M. Jensen, *Loosening the Bonds: Mid-Atlantic Farm Women, 1750–1850* (New Haven: Yale University Press, 1986); Nancy Grey Osterud, *Bonds of Community: The Lives of Farm Women in Nineteenth-Century New York* (Ithaca: Cornell University Press, 1991).

8. Changes in women's work have been of great interest to labor historians, who have focused on such issues as the degree to which working for wages brought economic independence to women, the influence of women's work on family relationships, and the development of working-class subcultures. For discussions of these issues for the nineteenth century, see Thomas Dublin, *Women at Work: The Transformation of Work and Community in Lowell, Massachusetts, 1826–1860* (New York: Columbia University Press, 1979); Mary H. Blewett, *Men, Women, and Work: Class, Gender, and Protest in the New England Shoe Industry, 1780–1910* (Urbana: University of Illinois Press, 1988); Christine Stansell, *City of Women: Sex and Class in New York, 1789–1860* (New York: Knopf, 1986); Joanne J. Meyerowitz, *Women Adrift: Independent Wage Earners in Chicago, 1880–1930* (Chicago: University of Chicago Press, 1988).

9. In using the term "middle class," I am referring both to the economic position of people and to their attitudes about who they were. The middle class refers to those whose social and economic position lay somewhere between the laboring poor and the very rich. The people in this group shared similar attitudes, beliefs, and experiences in such areas as work, consumption, residential location, membership in formal and informal groups, and family organization and child-rearing strategies. See Peter Gay, *The Education of the Senses* (New York: Oxford University Press, 1984), 17–44; Stuart M. Blumin, "The Hypothesis of Middle-Class Formation in Nineteenth-Century America: A Critique and Some Proposals," *American Historical Review* 90 (April 1985): 299–338.

10. For a discussion of the domestic ideal, see Barbara Welter, "The Cult

of True Womanhood: 1820–1860," *American Quarterly* 18 (Summer 1966): 151–74; Mary P. Ryan, *Cradle of the Middle Class: The Family in Oneida County, New York, 1790–1865* (New York: Cambridge University Press, 1981); Nancy F. Cott, *The Bonds of Womanhood: "Woman's Sphere" in New England, 1780–1835* (New Haven: Yale University Press, 1977). For a discussion of housework, see Jeanne Boydston, *Home and Work: Housework, Wages, and the Ideology of Labor in the Early Republic* (New York: Oxford University Press, 1990).

11. John F. Kasson, *Rudeness and Civility: Manners in Nineteenth-Century Urban America* (New York: Hill and Wang, 1990), 121–32.

12. "Female Employments," *PSV*, March 22, 1851, p. 36.

13. *HAC*, 63–64.

14. For a notice of the content of his Saturday edition, see "Local Matters," *PDCJ*, January 29, 1848, p. 2.

15. See, for example, "Mrs. Swisshelm's Letter," *PDCJ*, February 17, 1848, p. 2; on the *Visiter*'s availability in the *Journal* office, see *PDCJ*, January 17, 1848, p. 2; April 29, 1848, p. 2. Both Swisshelm and Riddle are listed as editors on the masthead of each of the editions of the *Visiter* issued in volume 2 (January 20, 1849–January 12, 1850). "A Change" and "Explanatory," *PSV*, May 15, 1852, p. 66, explain his role as editor from May 22, 1852, to August 21, 1852.

16. *HAC*, 107–8.

17. "Obituary," *SCD*, January 6, 1859, p. 2.

18. *HAC*, 110.

19. "Hon. James Riddle," *FJSV*, May 31, 1855, p. 5.

20. "Queer," *PSV*, January 29, 1848, p. 2; "Robert M. Riddle," *PSV*, February 5, 1848, p. 2.

21. "Hon. James Riddle," *FJSV*, May 31, 1855, p. 5.

22. "Notice," *PSV*, January 22, 1848, p. 2.

23. *HAC*, 110–11.

24. For discussion of this issue, see Virginia G. Drachman, *Sisters in Law: Women Lawyers in Modern American History* (Cambridge: Harvard University Press, 1998), 94–97, 208–11; Regina Markell Morantz-Sanchez, *Sympathy and Science: Women Physicians in American Medicine* (New York: Oxford University Press, 1985), 120–21; Rosalind Rosenberg, *Beyond Separate Spheres: Intellectual Roots of Modern Feminism* (New Haven: Yale University Press, 1982), 189; Linda Gordon, *Heroes of Their Own Lives: The Politics and History of Family Violence, Boston, 1880–1960* (New York: Viking, 1988), 66–67; Angel Kwolek-Folland, *Engendering Business: Men and Women in the Corporate Office, 1870–1930* (Baltimore: Johns Hopkins University Press, 1994), 174–76.

25. *HAC*, 111.

26. For reference to Fleeson, see *HAC*, 109; "Obituary," *SCD*, January 6, 1859, p. 2.

27. *HAC*, 109–10.

28. "The Saturday Visiter," *PDCJ*, March 18, 1848, p. 2.

29. *HAC*, III.

30. Ava Baron, "Contested Terrain Revisited: Technology and Gender Definitions of Work in the Printing Industry," in *Women, Work, and Technology: Transformations*, ed. Barbara Drygulski Wright, Myra Marx Ferree, Gail O. Mellow, Linda H. Lewis, Marea-Luz Daza Samper, Robert Asher, and Kathleen Claspell (Ann Arbor: University of Michigan Press, 1987), 62–63; Ava Baron, "An Other Side of Gender Antagonism at Work: Men, Boys, and the Remasculinization of Printer's Work, 1830–1920," in *Work Engendered: Toward a New History of American Labor*, ed. Ava Baron (Ithaca: Cornell University Press, 1991), 48–50; Ava Baron, "Women and the Making of the American Working Class: A Study of the Proletarianization of Printers," *Review of Radical Political Economies* 14 (Fall 1982): 26–27, 29.

31. Riddle ran for mayor of Pittsburgh during the winter of 1852–53. His position on labor issues and unionization is unclear. As a businessman, he was undoubtedly concerned with profit. Conversely, he needed labor's votes. His inconsistency on this issue was revealed in a ditty used by his political opponents to try to discredit him (Leland Dewitt Baldwin, *Pittsburgh: The Story of a City* [Pittsburgh: University of Pittsburgh Press, 1937], 308–9).

> Sing hey diddle, diddle!
> Hurrah for Bob Riddle
> The man for the working men he!
> He smiles in their faces
> With all his best graces
> As friendly as friendly can be,
> But when fortunes frown
> And the *wages come down*
> And labor is trodden in dust,
> The proud "upper ten"
> Claim the Journal man then
> And ever he's true to the trust.

32. "Special Notice," *PSV*, December 31, 1853, p. 193.

33. *HAC*, 157.

34. Ibid., 156–57, quotation on 157.

35. Ibid., 157; "Printing," *SCD*, October 21, 1858, p. 1; "Obituary of Robert M. Riddle," *SCD*, January 20, 1859, p. 2.

36. "Female Compositors," *PSV*, September 24, 1853, p. 143.

37. "Female Type Setters," *PSV*, November 26, 1853, p. 173, reprinted from the *PDCJ*.

38. See Cyrus Aldrich, William Windom, and H. Wilson to Edwin M. Stanton, February 12, 1863, in Jane Grey Swisshelm File, RG 92, Consolidated Correspondence File, Box 1100, Quartermaster General Papers, National Archives and Records Administration, Washington, D.C. The other twelve signatures appear at the bottom of the letter.

39. For information on Stanton in Pittsburgh, see Benjamin Thomas and Harold M. Hyman, *Stanton: The Life and Times of Lincoln's Secretary of War* (New York: Knopf, 1962), 45–60.

40. *HAC*, 104–5; JGS to the *SCD*, February 14, 1863, in *Crusader and Feminist: Letters of Jane Grey Swisshelm*, ed. Arthur J. Larsen (St. Paul: Minnesota Historical Society, 1934), 175–76.

41. B. Thomas and Hyman, *Stanton*, 68–70, 137.

42. *HAC*, 235. Swisshelm claims that she got her job the day after she renewed her acquaintance with Stanton in Washington, D.C. The letter recommending her for the job, however, is dated February 12, 1863.

43. For a profile of the "gentlemen" who worked in government offices before the war, see Cindy Sondik Aron, *Ladies and Gentlemen of the Civil Service: Middle-Class Workers in Victorian America* (New York: Oxford University Press, 1987), 13–39.

44. Ibid., 42–55, 70–71.

45. JGS to the *SCD*, November 13, 1865, in *Crusader and Feminist*, 307–8.

46. "The Lady Clerks in the Departments," *New York Times*, November 10, 1865, p. 4. Jane may well have written this letter.

47. "Women in the Departments," *The Reconstructionist*, December 14, 1865, p. 2.

48. JGS to the *SCD*, November 13, 1865, in *Crusader and Feminist*, 308.

49. "Love of the Beautiful," *The Reconstructionist*, December 14, 1865, p. 2.

50. JGS to General Charles Thomas, February–March 2, 1865, Jane Grey Swisshelm File, RG 92, Consolidated Correspondence File, Box 1100, Quartermaster General Papers. There is no record of Thomas's response. In a personal letter, Jane described Perkins as "a musical composer, grand, gloomy & peculiar, tall, thin, consumptive, sad, petulant, & world weary" (JGS to Mary Mitchell, March 7, 1865, Box 1, MFP). He was one of the seven people who boarded with her.

51. JGS to the *SCD*, August 20, 1863, in *Crusader and Feminist*, 255.

52. Jane identifies Baxter in JGS to the *SCD*, May 23, 1863, in *Crusader and Feminist*, 232; she identifies Kelly in JGS to the *SCD*, December 20, 1864, in *Crusader and Feminist*, 283.

53. Jane devotes 120 of 363 pages to a discussion of nursing and conditions in field hospitals. In the preface to her memoir, she says that one of her objectives in publishing her autobiography was to "give an inside history of the hospitals during the war of the Rebellion, that the American people may not forget the cost of that Government so often imperiled through their indifference" (*HAC*, 3). Jane's claims about the extent and importance of her work are confirmed by Joseph B. Holt, a friend of Jane's from Minnesota who served as the superintendent of a contraband camp in the Washington area during this period (JGS to the *SCD*, August 2, 1863, in *Crusader and Feminist*, 251). Holt visited her at Campbell Hospital and in a letter to his wife noted that Jane "spends her time night and day attending to the sick and wounded not only in her own ward but all through the Hospital. The Steward told me that he carried her to another Hospital the other

day where she found a poor fellow suffering from [a] wound in the brest. It was superating very badly running down and standing in a pool in his stomach. She rolled up her sleeves and went to work on him" (Joseph B. Holt to wife, June 7, 1863, Box 2, Folder 27, Holt-Messer Papers, Schlesinger Library, Radcliffe Institute for Advanced Study, Cambridge, Mass.).

54. *HAC*, 242.

55. Kristie Ross, "Arranging a Doll's House: Refined Women as Union Nurses," in *Divided Houses: Gender and the Civil War*, ed. Catherine Clinton and Nina Silber (New York: Oxford University Press, 1992), 98, 100.

56. Jane E. Schultz, "The Inhospitable Hospital: Gender and Professionalism in Civil War Medicine," *Signs* 17 (Winter 1992): 377.

57. "Our Wounded Heroes–Letter from Mrs. Swisshelm," *New York Tribune*, May 13, 1863, p. 1; *HAC*, 242–51.

58. Various sources of tension existed between nurses and surgeons. Civil War doctors competed with each other for authority and respect, and that competition often damaged their relationships with subordinates. Nurses' inadequate training did not help matters. And the degree to which nurses held surgeons responsible for depersonalizing patients and tolerating corruption in the distribution of supplies only added to the tension. For discussions of these problems, see Schultz, "Inhospitable Hospital," 363–92; Ann Douglas Wood, "The War within a War: Women Nurses in the Union Army," *Civil War History* 18 (September 1972): 197–212. For Baxter's particular reasons for excluding women from his ward, see *HAC*, 254.

59. JGS to the *New York Tribune* and the *SCD*, May 19, 1863, in *Crusader and Feminist*, 233–34.

60. *HAC*, 251–53.

61. Ibid., 253–54. Not until October 29, 1863, did the surgeon general empower physicians to appoint nurses without Dix's authority (Schultz, "Inhospitable Hospital," 367).

62. *HAC*, 266–67. She apparently did not find her work in the quartermaster general's office particularly demanding and seems to have spent the hours before and after work tending to her patients (JGS to the *SCD*, July 12, 1863, in *Crusader and Feminist*, 239; JGS to the *SCD*, July 27, 1863, in *Crusader and Feminist*, 246; *HAC*, 297). In May 1864, she left her job as a clerk to work in a field hospital in Fredericksburg and on a transport ship run by the Sanitary Commission. It is not clear whether she applied for or was granted leave from the quartermaster general's office to do so (*HAC*, 306–13, 342–44).

63. Ross, "Arranging a Doll's House," 101–4.

64. *HAC*, 243, 245, 250, 255, 258, 262, 263. These were fairly typical duties; see Jane E. Schultz, "Race, Gender, and Bureaucracy: Civil War Army Nurses and the Pension Bureau," *Journal of Women's History* 6 (Summer 1994): 47.

65. *HAC*, 249, 285.

66. Ibid., 280, 285.

67. Ibid., 267, quotation on 285–86.

68. Ibid., 245–47.

69. Ibid., 264–65; see also 342–43.

70. Ibid., 265.

71. Ibid., 342–43.

72. Ibid., 300, 302.

73. Ibid., 323–25, quotations on 324–25.

Chapter 5

1. "Women and Politics," *PSV*, October 22, 1853, p. 53; see also "Women Dabbling in Politics," *PSV*, April 29, 1848, p. 2.

2. Paula Baker, "The Domestication of Politics: Women and American Political Society, 1780–1920," *American Historical Review* 89 (June 1984): 628.

3. Elizabeth R. Varon, "Tippecanoe and the Ladies, Too: White Women and Party Politics in Antebellum Virginia," *Journal of American History* 82 (September 1995): 494–521.

4. George S. Jackson, *An Uncommon Scold: The Story of Anne Royall* (Boston: Bruce Humphries, 1927); Alice S. Maxwell and Marion B. Dunlevy, *Virago! The Story of Anne Newport Royall (1769–1854)* (Jefferson, N.C.: McFarland, 1985).

5. Nancy A. Hewitt, *Women's Activism and Social Change: Rochester, New York, 1822–1872* (Ithaca: Cornell University Press, 1984); Lori D. Ginzberg, *Women and the Work of Benevolence: Morality, Politics, and Class in the Nineteenth-Century United States* (New Haven: Yale University Press, 1990); Wendy Hamand Venet, *Neither Ballots nor Bullets: Women Abolitionists and the Civil War* (Charlottesville: University of Virginia Press, 1991); Jean Fagan Yellin and John C. Van Horne, eds., *The Abolitionist Sisterhood: Women's Political Culture in Antebellum America* (Ithaca: Cornell University Press, 1994).

6. *HAC*, 91.

7. Peter F. Walker, *Moral Choices: Memory, Desire, and Imagination in Nineteenth-Century American Abolition* (Baton Rouge: Louisiana State University Press, 1978), 128–29; see also *HAC*, 93–94.

8. *HAC*, 105–6.

9. "Our Nod" and "Notice," *PSV*, December 20, 1847, p. 2.

10. December 20, 1847, was actually a Monday. Swisshelm acknowledged that the publication of the first edition of her paper had been "unavoidably delayed" and promised her readers that the *PSV* would appear regularly on Saturday ("Announcements," *PSV*, December 20, 1847, p. 2).

11. For examples of early advertising, see *PSV*, February 26, 1848.

12. "Our Nod," *PSV*, December 20, 1847, p. 2

13. *HAC*, 112; "Our Nod," *PSV*, December 20, 1847, p. 2.

14. "Our Politics" and "Notice," *PSV*, December 20, 1847, p. 2.

15. "Our Nod," *PSV*, December 20, 1847, p. 2.

16. *HAC*, 113–14; Lester Burrell Shippee identifies Prentiss as the editor of the *Louisville Journal* ("Jane Grey Swisshelm: Agitator," *Mississippi Valley Historical Review* 7 (December 1920): 212).

17. See, for example, *PSV*, January 22, 1848, p. 2; February 19, 1848, p. 1; May 27, 1848, p. 2; *HAC*, 115.

18. "To the Patrons of the Visiter," *PSV*, July 29, 1848, p. 2; see also "Messrs. Stevenson and Errett," *PSV*, September 2, 1848, p. 2; "Something or Nothing," *PSV*, January 25, 1851, p. 2.

19. David M. Potter, *The Impending Crisis, 1848–1861* (New York: Harper, 1976), 79–80.

20. "Our Duty," *PSV*, August 19, 1848, p. 2.

21. "An Explanation" and "Messrs. Stevenson and Errett," *PSV*, September 2, 1848, p. 2.

22. *HAC*, 162.

23. "Something or Nothing," *PSV*, January 25, 1851, p. 2.

24. "Salutory," *PSV*, January 20, 1849, p. 2; "Something or Nothing," *PSV*, January 25, 1851, p. 2.

25. "Prospectus" and "An Introduction," *PSV*, January 19, 1850, p. 2.

26. "Our Exchanges" and "Matters Personal," *PSV*, December 14, 1850, p. 190.

27. "Agencies," *PSV*, February 22, 1851, p. 18.

28. "Woman's Rights versus Babies," *Boston Daily Journal*, May 27, 1852, p. 2. Swisshelm turned the main editorial duties over to Riddle in mid-May (see "A Change" and "Explanatory," *PSV*, May 15, 1852, p. 66).

29. "Women and Office," *PSV*, June 5, 1852, p. 78.

30. "Explanatory" and "Valedictory," *PSV*, August 21, 1852, p. 122.

31. Potter, *Impending Crisis*, 142–43.

32. "Our Course," *PSV*, November 13, 1852, p. 170.

33. "Volume for 1853," *PSV*, December 25, 1852, p. 194.

34. "Pittsburgh Platform," *PSV*, February 19, 1853, pp. 18–19.

35. "The State Convention," *PSV*, April 23, 1853, p. 54.

36. "Free Democratic Nominations," *PSV*, July 2, 1853, p. 94.

37. Clarence D. Stephenson, *Indiana County 175th Anniversary History*, 5 vols. (Indiana, Pa.: A. G. Halldin, 1983), 1:389–92.

38. "Matters Personal," *PSV*, September 24, 1853, p. 143; "Non-Paying Subscribers," *PSV*, December 31, 1853, p. 193; "Our Future," *PSV*, January 28, 1854, p. 209.

39. "Our Future," *PSV*, January 28, 1854, p. 209.

40. Ibid.; *HAC*, 164.

41. Potter, *Impending Crisis*, 257.

42. *HAC*, 158.

43. Ibid., 170–71.

44. "Personal," *SCV*, December 10, 1857, p. 2. They did not finalize their arrangements for almost two months; see Brott-Swisshelm Agreement, February 3, 1858, MHS.

45. There is a great deal of literature on this topic. A good place to begin is John Mack Faragher, *Women and Men on the Overland Trail*, rev. ed. (New Haven: Yale University Press, 2001); Sandra L. Myres, *Westering Women and the Frontier Experience, 1800-1915* (Albuquerque: University of New Mexico Press, 1982); Peggy Pascoe, *Relations of Rescue: The Search for Female Moral Authority in the American West, 1874-1939* (New York: Oxford University Press, 1990); Susan Lee Johnson, *Roaring Camp: The Social World of the California Gold Rush* (New York: Norton, 2000), 280-89.

46. Herman Roe, "The Frontier Press of Minnesota," *Minnesota History* 14 (December 1933): 403-4.

47. *HAC*, 178.

48. "The Press," *SCV*, June 24, 1858, p. 1; "Definitive," *SCV*, January 14, 1858, p. 1.

49. "Prospectus," *SCV*, December 24, 1857, p. 1.

50. "Definitive," *SCV*, January 14, 1858, p. 1.

51. For a more detailed discussion of St. Cloud politics, see Kathleen Neils Conzen, "Pi-ing the Type: Jane Grey Swisshelm and the Contest of Midwestern Regionality," in *The American Midwest: Essays on Regional History*, ed. Andrew R. L. Cayton and Susan Gray (Bloomington: Indiana University Press, 2001), 91-110.

52. "History," *SCV*, June 24, 1858, p. 2; "History," *SCV*, July 22, 1858, p. 2; *HAC*, 179.

53. Minnesota Territorial Manuscript Census, Stearns County, Minnesota, 1857; U.S. Manuscript Census, Stearns County, Minnesota, 1860. The two black residents living in the Lowry household may have been the property of Lowry's brother-in-law, the Reverend Thomas Calhoun. For a discussion of Calhoun's slaveholding, see "To the Rev. Calhoun," *SCD*, September 10, 1858, p. 2. See also Conzen, "Pi-ing the Type," 95.

54. "A Change and the Reasons," *SCV*, February 18, 1848, p. 1.

55. "Stearns County Politics," *SCV*, March 3 [4], 1858, p. 2.

56. William B. Mitchell, *History of Stearns County*, 2 vols. (Chicago: H. C. Cooper Jr., 1915), 2:1405.

57. There is no extant copy of Shepley's lecture. His comments are summarized in Swisshelm's review, "Lectures," *SCV*, March 18, 1858, p. 2, and in *James C. Shepley and Mary F. B., His Wife, against N. N. Smith et al.*, Box 3, MFP.

58. Minnesota Territorial Manuscript Census, Stearns County, Minnesota, 1857; U.S. Manuscript Census, Stearns County, Minnesota, 1860.

59. "The Visiter," *SCV*, May 20, 1858, p. 2. Jane repeats this comment in "The Democrat," *SCD*, July 21, 1859, p. 3.

60. Norma Basch, "Marriage, Morals, and Politics in the Election of 1828," *Journal of American History* 80 (December 1993): 890-918; Robert V. Remini, *Andrew Jackson and the Course of American Freedom, 1822-1832* (New York: Harper and Row, 1981), 2:203-29; John F. Marszalek, *The Petticoat Affair: Manners, Mutiny, and Sex in Andrew Jackson's White House* (New York: Free Press, 1997); Kirsten E. Wood, " 'One Woman So Dangerous to Public Morals': Gender and Power in the Eaton Affair," *Journal of the Early Republic* 17 (Summer 1997): 237-75.

61. The issue of the *Visiter* in which this letter appeared is not extant. Copies of the letter appeared in other newspapers, however; see "Mrs. Swisshelm's Estimate of Daniel Webster," *The Liberator*, May 3, 1850, p. 70; "The Godlike" (excerpt), *Ashtabula (Ohio) Sentinel*, May 18, 1850, p. 3. Jane maintained that before she mailed the story to the *Visiter*, she confirmed it with Joshua Giddings, Gamaliel Bailey, and Mr. and Mrs. George Julian (*HAC*, 132). For responses to her letter, see "New York Tribune and Mr. Webster," *New York Daily Tribune*, May 13, 1850, p. 4; "Letter from Mrs. Swisshelm," *New York Daily Tribune*, May 28, 1850, pp. 1–2; "Mrs. Swisshelm—Mr. Webster," *Ashtabula (Ohio) Sentinel*, June 22, 1850, p. 1; "Daniel Webster" (excerpts from the *Lowell American* and the *Dundee Record*), *PSV*, May 25, 1850, p. 74; "Daniel Webster and the Ladies," *New York Daily Herald*, May 14, 1850, p. 2.

62. "Disgraceful Outrage at St. Cloud! Press Destroyed!" and "Copy of the Letter," *SCV*, May 13, 1858, p. 1; in her memoir published years later and written largely from memory, Swisshelm wrote that the letter said, "If you ever again attempt to publish a paper in St. Cloud, you yourself will be as summarily dealt with as your office has been" (*HAC*, 184). Walker, *Moral Choices*, 198, names the three guilty men. Shepley accepted responsibility for the attack in the *St. Paul Pioneer and Democrat*, April 2, 1858, p. 2; Jane charged Lowry with being present and dared him to sue her for libel (*Minnesotan*, September 13, 1859, p. 2). Violence against the press was not a particularly unusual phenomenon during the period before the Civil War. Indeed, historian John C. Nerone has chronicled a long and glorious history of antipress violence in the United States, which he argues was "systematic rather than episodic" and "an integral part of the culture of public expression" (*Violence against the Press: Policing the Public Sphere in U.S. History* [New York: Oxford University Press, 1994], 9–10).

63. For an account of the meeting, see "Border Ruffianism in Minnesota," *St. Paul Daily Pioneer and Democrat*, March 30, 1858, p. 1; *HAC*, 185–88.

64. "Border Ruffianism in Minnesota! Great Excitement!! Attempt to Stifle Free Speech!!! A Press Demolished!! Great Gathering of People, etc., etc., etc.," *SCV*, May 13, 1858, p. 1; "Disgraceful Outrage at St. Cloud! Press Destroyed!" [reprinted from the *St. Paul Times*, March 30, 1858], *SCV*, May 13, 1858, p. 1.

65. A copy of the complaint is in Box 3, MFP.

66. "To Subscribers," *SCV*, December 24, 1857, p. 1; "To Subscribers," *SCV*, January 14, 1858, p. 2. See also "Corn," *SCD*, December 9, 1858, p. 2.

67. The 1857 Minnesota territorial census did not list assets, although the 1860 U.S. Manuscript Census for Stearns County, Minnesota, did. Sixteen of her twenty-six supporters appeared in the 1860 census, with assets in real property totaling $37,300 and assets in personal property totaling $7,750.

68. "Cards and Coquetry," *SCV*, June 17, 1858, p. 2; the last part of this editorial was reprinted a week later; see "Corrections," *SCV*, June 24, 1858, p. 3.

69. George S. Hage, *Newspapers on the Minnesota Frontier, 1849–1860* (St. Paul: Minnesota Historical Society, 1967), 91.

70. *HAC*, 191.

71. "A Change," *SCV*, July 22, 1858, p. 2.

72. *HAC*, 185–95, quotations on 195. Shippee, "Jane Grey Swisshelm," 218, traces this chronology.

73. "Mrs. Swisshelm," *St. Paul Daily Pioneer and Democrat*, April 2, 1858, p. 2. A copy of the letter appeared in the *New York Tribune* on April 12, 1858, and was reprinted in the *SCV* on May 13, 1858.

74. "The Shepley Suit—Letter from Stephen Miller," *SCD*, August 5, 1858, p. 2.

75. List of Republican Party candidates, *SCD*, September 23–October 7, 1858, p. 2.

76. "Notice," *SCD*, September 30, 1858, p. 2.

77. "Glorious Democratic Victory," *SCD*, October 14, 1858, p. 2. Swisshelm had some help from an unexpected source in her attempt to destroy Lowry's political power. By the spring of 1862, Lowry began to exhibit signs of mental instability, a condition that had apparently plagued him periodically since adolescence. In May his family sent him to an insane asylum in Cincinnati ("General Lowry," *SCD*, May 8, 1862, p. 2; "Taken to an Asylum," *SCD*, May 29, 1862, p. 3; "Insane Patients," *SCD*, December 4, 1862, p. 3). He returned to St. Cloud after he was released. In the summer of 1864, he had a relapse, tried to kill his sister, and was arrested. He was released after posting a three hundred dollar bond to keep the peace. He died of a heart attack just before Christmas 1865 (William Bell Mitchell, "St. Cloud in the Territorial Period," *Collections of the Minnesota Historical Society* 12 [December 1908]: 641; "Attempt to Kill," *SCD*, July 28, 1864, p. 3; "Died," *SCD*, December 21, 1865, p. 3). James Shepley moved back to Maine in 1859. Fourteen years later, he migrated to Fresno County, California, where he worked as a sheep rancher. He was reportedly murdered there in 1874 (Mitchell, *History*, 2:1135).

78. "Democrat," *SCD*, October 14, 1858, p. 2.

79. "Minnesota Politics," *SCD*, May 19, 1859, pp. 1–2.

80. "Quit That" and "The Republican Convention," *SCD*, March 24, 1859, p. 2.

81. JGS to Alexander Ramsey, February 27, 1859, Alexander Ramsey Family Papers and Governor's Records, MHS.

82. "Republican Candidates," *SCD*, June 2, 1859, p. 2.

83. "Congressional Candidate," *SCD*, June 16, 1859, p. 2.

84. "Republican State Convention," *SCD*, July 28, 1859, p. 1; for a list of candidates, see p. 2.

85. JGS to Mr. Sherer, Central Committee of the Republican Party, September 21, 1859, Box 1, Republican Party of Minnesota State Central Committee Records, 1857–1956, MHS.

86. In his diary, Ramsey, for example, mentions attending one of her lectures, attending a party at her house, and writing letters to her (February 28, October 30, 1860, August 9, 13, 1861, Ramsey Family Papers; see also her correspondence with Ignatius Donnelly, Ignatius Donnelly Papers, MHS).

87. See endorsements, *SCD*, March 8–May 17, 1860.

88. "The Candidates," *SCD*, May 31, 1860, p. 2. Jane ran her endorsements in the *SCD* from August 23 to November 1, 1860.

89. "Disunion," *SCD*, March 15, 1860, p. 2.

90. "Disunion," *SCD*, November 22, 1860, p. 2.

91. "S[e]cession," *SCD*, November 27 [29], 1860, p. 2.

92. "Secession and Treason," *SCD*, December 27, 1860, p. 2.

93. JGS to Donnelly, October 26–31, 1862, Donnelly Papers.

94. JGS to Donnelly, August 13, 1862, Donnelly Papers. Donnelly noted his response at the end of her letter.

95. JGS to Ramsey, August 4, 1861, Ramsey Family Papers.

96. JGS to Ramsey, August 11, 1861, Ramsey Family Papers.

97. See, for example, "Thrilling Scenes—Burying the Dead at Manassas," *SCD*, September 19, 1861, p. 1; "A Fight on the Potomac," *SCD*, October 24, 1861, p. 2; "Ward Beecher on Emancipation," *SCD*, January 16, 1862, p. 2; "From South Carolina—A Noble Tribute to Negro Daring," *SCD*, December 11, 1862, p. 1.

98. "Lost," *SCD*, September 19, 1861, p. 2.

99. "The Silver Lining," *SCD*, April 24, 1862, p. 2; "The Proclamation," *SCD*, October 2, 1862, p. 1.

100. "State of Minnesota—Proclamation by the Governor" and "Republican District Convention for 3d Senatorial District," *SCD—Extra*, September 6, 1862.

101. *HAC*, 234. A more complete discussion of her position on the Dakota War appears in chap. 6.

102. She sold the paper for six hundred dollars. See Mitchell's note and payment schedule dated September 25, 1863, Box 3, MFP.

103. For a collection of these letters, see *Crusader and Feminist: Letters of Jane Grey Swisshelm*, ed. Arthur J. Larsen (St. Paul: Minnesota Historical Society, 1934).

104. For more on Reconstruction, see Eric Foner, *Reconstruction: America's Unfinished Revolution, 1863–1877* (New York: Harper and Row, 1988); Michael Perman, *The Road to Redemption: Southern Politics, 1869–1879* (Chapel Hill: University of North Carolina Press, 1984); Laura F. Edwards, *Gendered Strife and Confusion: The Political Culture of Reconstruction* (Urbana: University of Illinois Press, 1997).

105. "Prospectus," *The Reconstructionist*, February 10, 1866, p. 4.

106. In her memoir, she claims to have visited Sumner while he was recuperating from being attacked by Preston Brooks on the floor of the Senate in 1856 (*HAC*, 158). She mentions her acquaintance with Julian and his wife in connection with her stint as a reporter for Greeley's *New York Daily Tribune* in 1850 (*HAC*, 132). See also JGS to George Julian, February 3, 1877, and George Julian to JGS, February 14, 1877, Joshua Giddings and George Julian Papers, Library of Congress, Washington, D.C.

107. "Maj. Gen. C. C. Andrews and Negro Suffrage," *The Reconstructionist*, December 14, 1865, p. 1; "Wilson on Cowan" and "Reconstruction," *The Reconstructionist*, February 10, 1866, p. 1; "A Touching Appeal," *The Reconstructionist*, February 10, 1866, p. 2.

108. "Mr. Julian's Land Bill," *The Reconstructionist*, March 3, 1866, p. 2.

109. "Are These Things So?" *The Reconstructionist*, February 10, 1866, p. 1.

110. See, for example, "Speech of Hon. G. W. Julian," *The Reconstructionist*, December 14, 1865, p. 4; "A Loyal Voice from Louisiana," *The Reconstructionist*, February 10, 1866, p. 2; "A Disgraceful Harangue," *The Reconstructionist*, March 3, 1866, p. 1.

111. "The President and His Message," *The Reconstructionist*, December 14, 1865, p. 1.

112. "President Johnson," *The Reconstructionist*, March 3, 1866, p. 2.

113. "Gone Back," *The Reconstructionist*, February 10, 1866, p. 1.

114. The dismissal letter was dated February 26, 1866. See *The Reconstructionist*, March 3, 1866, p. 2.

115. "The Conspiracy," *The Reconstructionist*, March 10, 1866, p. 1.

116. Chester Hearn, *The Impeachment of Andrew Johnson* (Jefferson, N.C.: McFarland, 2000); Hans L. Trefousse, *Impeachment of a President: Andrew Johnson, the Blacks, and Reconstruction* (New York: Fordham University Press, 1999).

117. "Attempt to Burn the Office of the Reconstructionist," *Washington Daily Morning Chronicle*, March 27, 1866, p. 4. The *Chronicle*'s report was republished by the *St. Cloud Democrat*, April 12, 1866, p. 1. Greeley's *New York Tribune* picked up the story from the *Constitutional Union*. See "Incendiarism Frustrated," *New York Tribune*, March 28, 1866, p. 1. Jane provided a description of the arson attempt in her letter to the *New York Tribune* ("The Reconstructionist," *New York Tribune*, March 29, 1866, p. 10).

118. "The Reconstructionist," *New York Tribune*, March 29, 1866, p. 10. The *St. Cloud Democrat* reprinted this letter on April 12, 1866, p. 1.

119. *HAC*, 92.

120. See, for example, "Views of a Woman Suffragist," *Chicago Tribune*, February 27, 1874, p. 8; "Tribute to the Dead from Mrs. Jane Grey Swisshelm," *Chicago Tribune*, July 20, 1882, p. 7.

121. "The Democrat," *SCD*, July 21, 1859, p. 3.

122. Rebecca Edwards, *Angels in the Machinery: Gender in American Party Politics from the Civil War to the Progressive Era* (New York: Oxford University Press, 1997), 28–29; Margaret M. R. Kellow, "'For the Sake of Suffering Kansas': Lydia Maria Child, Gender, and the Politics of the 1850s," *Journal of Women's History* 5 (Fall 1993): 39–43; Chester Giraud, *Embattled Maiden: The Life of Anna Dickinson* (New York: Putnam's, 1951), 45–84; J. Matthew Gallman, "Anna Dickinson: Abolitionist Orator," in *The Human Tradition in the Civil War and Reconstruction*, ed. Steven E. Woodworth (Wilmington, Del.: Scholarly Resources, 2000), 93–110. For discussion of other politically active women involved in partisan politics, see Janet L. Coryell, "Superseding Gender: The Role of the Woman Politico in Antebellum Partisan Politics," in *Women and the Unstable State in Nineteenth-Century America*, ed. Alison M. Parker and Stephanie Cole (College Station: Texas A&M University Press, 2000), 84–112.

123. Conzen, "Pi-ing the Type," 99, says that "thanks in part to [Jane's] effort, Minnesota became Republican, her fellow Pennsylvanian Ramsey became the first governor to offer his troops to Lincoln, and her kinsman Miller" led troops at Gettysburg. For reference to the University of Minnesota, see Abigail McCarthy, "Jane Grey Swisshelm: Marriage and Slavery," in *Women in Minnesota: Selected Biographical Essays*, ed. Barbara Stuhler and Gretchen Kreuter (St. Paul: Minnesota Historical Society Press, 1977), 54.

Chapter 6

1. Lorton ended her story by saying that before leaving Louisville, Jane had purchased a young, light-skinned slave woman and educated and then freed her, only to have her run away after stealing Jane's watch, pocketbook, and silver spoons. There is no evidence to substantiate this part of Lorton's story. Given the financial straits in which the Swisshelms found themselves after James's bankruptcy, it is unlikely that Jane would have had the money to buy a slave even if she had wanted to do so.

2. Women were on the forefront of these efforts. For an introduction to the literature on women's reform and benevolent activities, see Anne F. Scott, *Natural Allies: Women's Associations in American History* (Urbana: University of Illinois Press, 1991); Lori D. Ginzberg, *Women and the Work of Benevolence: Morality, Politics, and Class in the Nineteenth-Century United States* (New Haven: Yale University Press, 1990); Mary P. Ryan, *Cradle of the Middle Class: The Family in Oneida County, New York, 1790–1865* (New York: Cambridge University Press, 1981); Nancy A. Hewitt, *Women's Activism and Social Change: Rochester, New York, 1822–1872* (Ithaca: Cornell University Press, 1984); Anne M. Boylan, *The Origins of Women's Activism* (Chapel Hill: University of North Carolina Press, 2002).

3. For references to that assurance and to her expectations, see "The Democrat," *SCD*, July 21, 1859, p. 3; JGS to Alexander Ramsey, February 27, 1859, Alexander Ramsey Family Papers and Governor's Records, MHS; *HAC*, 37.

4. *Crusader and Feminist: Letters of Jane Grey Swisshelm*, ed. Arthur J. Larsen (St. Paul: Minnesota Historical Society, 1934), 5; for examples of her opposition to the death penalty, see "Capital Punishment," *PSV*, July 14, 1849, p. 102; "Capital Punishment," *PSV*, July 21, 1849, p. 106; "Capital Punishment," *PSV*, September 1, 1849, p. 130. Some of her early essays were reprinted in Riddle's *Pittsburgh Daily Commercial Journal*; see, for example, "Capital Punishment—No. 2," *PDCJ*, March 20, 1848, p. 2.

5. David Brion Davis, "The Movement to Abolish Capital Punishment in America, 1787–1861," *American Historical Review* 63 (October 1957): 28–30; Louis P. Masur, *Rites of Execution: Capital Punishment and the Transformation of American Culture, 1776–1865* (New York: Oxford University Press, 1989), 143; Albert Post, "Early Efforts to Abolish Capital Punishment in Pennsylvania," *Pennsylvania Magazine of History and Biography* 68 (January 1944): 38–53.

6. "Capital Punishment," *PSV*, September 1, 1849, p. 130.

7. Post, "Early Efforts," 50; Davis, "Movement," 31.

8. For a discussion of changing drinking patterns, see W. J. Rorabaugh, *The Alcoholic Republic: An American Tradition* (New York: Oxford University Press, 1979), 25–149. For more on the early temperance movement, see Barbara Leslie Epstein, *The Politics of Domesticity: Women, Evangelism, and Temperance in Nineteenth-Century America* (Middletown, Conn.: Wesleyan University Press, 1981), 89–94; Steven M. Buechler, *Women's Movements in the United States: Woman Suffrage, Equal Rights, and Beyond* (New Brunswick, N.J.: Rutgers University Press, 1990), 15, 96–97.

9. "Horsewhips," *PSV*, April 28, 1849, p. 58.

10. "Our Junior's Opinion," *PSV*, May 26, 1849, p. 74.

11. "Messrs. Riddle and Greeley," *PSV*, June 23, 1849, p. 90. Jane eventually reversed her position on this issue. When those who participated in the 1874 Woman's Crusade began taking direct action against businessmen who trafficked in liquor, Jane wrote that they were engaged in "illegal warfare" and advised them to desist in their efforts. If they had worked to achieve their political rights, she argued, they would not have to break the law by trespassing and making spectacles of themselves. The key to fighting drunkenness was not demonstrations but getting the vote and then using it to stop the sale of alcohol. See JGS, "Views of a Woman Suffragist," *Chicago Tribune*, February 27, 1874, p. 2; JGS, "The Woman's Temperance War," *The Independent*, reprinted in the *Cincinnati Commercial*, March 20, 1874, p. 2; "The Temperance Crusade," *Atlanta Constitution*, March 10, 1874, p. 2.

12. *HAC*, 34. For more on the Presbyterian Church's position on slavery, see Victor B. Howard, "Presbyterians, the Kansas-Nebraska Act, and the Election of 1856," *Journal of Presbyterian History* 49 (Summer 1971): 133–56; Andrew E. Murray, *Presbyterians and the Negro: A History* (Philadelphia: Presbyterian Historical Society, 1966).

13. For more on the abolitionists, see Lawrence Friedman, *Gregarious Saints: Self and Community in American Abolitionism, 1830–1870* (New York: Cambridge University Press, 1982); James Brewer Stewart, *Holy Warriors: The Abolitionists and American Slavery* (New York: Hill and Wang, 1997); Julie Roy Jeffrey, *The Great Silent Army of Abolitionists: Ordinary Women in the Antislavery Movement* (Chapel Hill: University of North Carolina Press, 1998); Shirley J. Yee, *Black Women Abolitionists: A Study in Activism, 1828–1860* (Knoxville: University of Tennessee Press, 1992).

14. *HAC*, 51, quotation on 53–54.

15. Ibid., 54–55.

16. Ibid., 55–57, 59. For other descriptions, see "From the Ploughboy," *PSV*, November 3, 1849, p. 166; "Our Kentucky Experience," *PSV*, November 10, 1849, p. 170.

17. *HAC*, 52–53.

18. Ibid., 60, 63, 64.

19. "Mrs. Swisshelm and the Constitution," *PSV*, February 17, 1849, p. 18.

20. R. J. M. Blackett, "'Freedom, or the Martyr's Grave': Black Pittsburgh's

Aid to the Fugitive Slave," *Western Pennsylvania Historical Magazine* 61 (January 1978): 129; "Caught," *PSV*, February 22, 1851, p. 18.

21. "From the Commercial Journal," *PSV*, March 1, 1851, p. 22.

22. "Mr. Riddle," *PSV*, March 1, 1851, p. 22.

23. Articles about slavery and antislavery printed during the first year of the *Pittsburgh Saturday Visiter*'s publication include "The Presbyterian Advocate," *PSV*, January 1, 1848, p. 2; "Address of the First Presbytery of Mahoning to the Christian Public," *PSV*, February 5, 1848, p. 4; "The Slave Mother's Petition," *PSV*, February 26, 1848, p. 1; "Capture of Runaway Slaves," *PSV*, April 22, 1848, p. 2; "Slavery Debate in the Senate," *PSV*, May 6, 1848, p. 2; "The Great Question," *PSV*, June 3, 1848, p. 2; "The Hodges Slave Case," *PSV*, June 17, 1848, p. 1; "Address to the Friends of Liberty," *PSV*, July 22, 1848, p. 1; "The Pittsburgh Bloodhound," *PSV*, September 30, 1848, p. 2. In subsequent years, Jane followed a similar pattern, clipping articles about slavery from other newspapers as well as writing editorials of her own.

24. "To the Rev. Calhoun," *SCD*, September 30, 1858, p. 2.

25. "Letter to the Rev. Calhoun," *SCD*, November 11, 1858, p. 2.

26. "Frightful Accident," *SCD*, February 24, 1859, p. 2; "Rev. Thomas Calhoun," *SCD*, April 7, 1859, p. 1.

27. "Schools for Colored Children," *PSV*, September 29, 1849, p. 146.

28. JGS, "Social Equality," *Boston Commonwealth*, March 25, 1865, p. 2; JGS, "Social Equality," *Boston Commonwealth*, May 6, 1865, p. 2.

29. "Mr. Dana's Lecture on Woman," *PSV*, December 29, 1849, p. 198.

30. "The Syracuse Convention," *PSV*, September 25, p. 142.

31. "The Journal and the Bloomer Dress," *PSV*, October 4, 1851, p. 146.

32. "Woman's Right to Vote," *PSV*, August 11, 1849, p. 118.

33. "Mrs. Lydia Jane Pierson," *PSV*, December 15, 1849, p. 190.

34. "Deference to Women," *PSV*, July 12, 1851, p. 98. For more on this controversy, see E.C.S., "Mrs. Swisshelm," *The Lily*, July 1851, and "E.C.S. vs. Mrs. Swisshelm," *The Lily*, August 1851, in *Papers of Elizabeth Cady Stanton and Susan B. Anthony* [microfilm], ed. Patricia G. Holland and Ann D. Gordon (Wilmington, Del.: Scholarly Resources, 1991), ser. 3, reel 7, frames 99, 101, 102.

35. "Deference to Women," *PSV*, July 12, 1851, p. 98.

36. "The Bloomer Dress," *PSV*, September 27, 1851, p. 138.

37. Ibid.

38. "A Woman's Rights Convention," *PSV*, August 12, 1848, p. 1.

39. "Worcester Convention," *PSV*, August 31, 1850, p. 130. Given their troubled relationship, it seems odd that James was willing to support the idea of woman's rights. One explanation may be that by placing his signature next to hers, he was trying to preserve his reputation as a husband by assuring anyone who saw his signature that his wife's participation in the campaign was not an act of domestic rebellion.

40. "The Worcester Convention" and "Woman's Rights Convention at

Worcester, Mass.," *PSV*, November 2, 1850, p. 166; "Woman's Rights Convention at Worcester, Mass.," *PSV*, November 9, 1851, p. 170.

41. "Akron and the Convention," *PSV*, June 7, 1851, p. 78.

42. For coverage of the second Worcester Convention taken from the *New York Tribune*, see *PSV*, November 1, 1851, pp. 161, 164; November 8, 1851, pp. 166, 168; November 15, 1851, p. 172.

43. See *The Proceedings of the Woman's Rights Convention, Held at Syracuse, September 8th, 9th, & 10th, 1852* (Syracuse, N.Y.: J. E. Masters, 1852), v–vi; "The Syracuse Convention," *PSV*, September 25, 1852, p. 142; "Address on Woman's Rights," *PSV*, October 2, 1852, p. 145.

44. "The Worcester Convention," *PSV*, November 2, 1850, p. 166.

45. Parker Pillsbury, "Women's Rights Convention and People of Color," *PSV*, November 23, 1850, p. 178.

46. "Woman's Rights and the Color Question," *PSV*, November 23, 1850, p. 178. Her editorial prompted a response from Pillsbury, and their discussion of the issue was published in the *National Anti-Slavery Standard* as well as the *Anti-Slavery Bugle*; see the *Anti-Slavery Standard*, December 5, 1850, p. 112; see Jane's reference to the *Anti-Slavery Bugle*'s response in "The Anti-Slavery Bugle," *PSV*, January 25, 1851, p. 2.

47. "Akron and the Convention," *PSV*, June 7, 1851, p. 78; *The Proceedings of the Woman's Rights Convention Held at Akron, Ohio, May 28 and 29, 1851* (Cincinnati: Ben Franklin, 1851), 3, 6, 7, 8.

48. *HAC*, 142; "Rev. J. L. Hatch and the Women's Convention," *PSV*, November 13, 1852, p. 170.

49. "Akron and the Convention," *PSV*, June 7, 1851, p. 78.

50. "Odds and Ends: Aunt Fanny Again," *PSV*, August 30, 1851, p. 126; see also "From Mrs. Gage," *PSV*, January 3, 1852, p. 198; "Correspondence from Sundry Persons," *PSV*, January 3, 1852, p. 198.

51. "Woman's Rights Convention," *PSV*, October 11, 1851, p. 150. Jane also criticized Lucy Stone; see "Mrs. Swisshelm vs. Lucy Stone," *The Lily*, December 15, 1854, p. 183.

52. "Conventions Again," *PSV*, January 11, 1851, p. 206.

53. "Conventions," *PSV*, December 13, 1851, p. 186.

54. "Women's Conventions," *PSV*, January 10, 1852, p. 202. Despite her low regard for their usefulness, Jane claimed to have attended five conventions (*HAC*, 144), including the 1877 National Woman Suffrage Association convention held in Washington, D.C.; see Elizabeth Cady Stanton, Susan B. Anthony, and Matilda Joslyn Gage, eds., *History of Woman Suffrage*, 3 vols. (Rochester, N.Y.: Charles Mann, 1886), 3:60–61; *Washington Evening Star*, January 16, 1877, p. 4; January 17, 1877, p. 4; January 18, 1877, p. 4. For a response to her speech, see *Washington Evening Star*, January 23, 1877, p. 4.

55. "Better Education for Women," *PSV*, December 11, 1852, p. 186; "Employment for Women," *PSV*, May 14, 1853, p. 66.

236 NOTES TO PAGES 146–49

56. *HAC*, 157; "Female Typesetters," *PSV*, November 26, 1853, p. 173; "The Reconstructionist," *New York Tribune*, March 29, 1866, p. 10; "Female Compositors," *PSV*, September 24, 1853, p. 143.

57. "Female Employments," *PSV*, March 22, 1851, p. 36.

58. "Why Do Women Never Excel?" *PSV*, September 15, 1849, p. 138.

59. "Mrs. Lydia Jane Pierson," *PSV*, December 15, 1849, p. 190.

60. JGS, "Women Voting and Holding Office," *The Lily*, August 1850, p. 60.

61. JGS, "The Masculine Qualification for the Rights of Citizenship," *The Lily*, January 1851, p. 4.

62. "Woman's Legal Disabilities," *PSV*, October 25, 1851, p. 158.

63. *HAC*, 146–47.

64. See, for example, "Rights of Married Women," *SCV*, January 14, 1858, p. 2; "Petition," *SCV*, February 18, 1858, p. 2; "Fair Play for Women," *SCV*, May 27, 1858, p. 2; "Extension of Suffrage to Women," *SCV*, June 24, 1858, p. 1; "The Editor Abroad," *SCD*, March 3, 1859, p. 2; "Notices of the Editor's Lecture," *SCD*, March 15, 1860, p. 2. On February 5, 1862, Jane appeared in the State Senate to give a lecture favoring legislation that would give married women the right to their own property and custody over their children in case of separation. See John G. Riheldaffer Family Papers, Box 1, "Notes of Events" Folder, MHS. For examples of reports on her public lectures, see "The Editor's Lecture," *SCD*, January 30, 1862, p. 2, "Mrs. Swisshelm's Lecture," *SCD*, March 27, 1862, p. 1; "Mrs. Swisshelm's Lecture," *SCD*, April 3, 1862, p. 1.

65. Frances D. Gage to Elizabeth Cady Stanton, March 24, [1853?], and Elizabeth Cady Stanton to Susan B. Anthony, March 1, [1853], in *Papers of Stanton and Anthony*, ser. 3, reel 7, frames 585, 571; Stanton, Anthony, and Gage, *History*, 1:386–88; "Amelia Bloomer Comments on Jane G. Swisshelm," in Stanton, Anthony, and Gage, *History*, 1:844; E.C.S., "Mrs. Swisshelm," *The Lily*, July 1851, in *Papers of Stanton and Anthony*, ser. 3, reel 7, frame 99; "Woman's Rights:—Matilda Gage vs. Jane Swisshelm," *Chicago Tribune*, February 10, 1878, p. 13. For a reference to this letter, see *New York Daily Tribune*, February 14, 1878, p. 5.

66. For information on the post–Civil War woman's rights movement, see Eleanor Flexner, *Century of Struggle: The Woman's Rights Movement in the United States* (New York: Atheneum, 1972), 142–331; Aileen S. Kraditor, *The Ideas of the Woman Suffrage Movement, 1890–1920* (Garden City, N.Y.: Anchor, 1971); Nancy F. Cott, *The Grounding of Modern Feminism* (New Haven: Yale University Press, 1987), 13–50. For more recent studies, see Ellen Carol DuBois, *Harriot Stanton Blatch and the Winning of Woman Suffrage* (New Haven: Yale University Press, 1997); Marjorie Spruill Wheeler, *New Women of the New South: The Leaders of the Women's Suffrage Movement in the Southern States* (New York: Oxford University Press, 1993); Elna C. Green, *Southern Strategies: Southern Women and the Woman Suffrage Question* (Chapel Hill: University of North Carolina Press, 1997); Suzanne M. Marilley, *Woman Suffrage and the Origins of Liberal Feminism in the United States, 1820–1920* (Cambridge: Harvard University Press, 1996); Rosalyn Terborg-Penn, *African American Women in*

the Struggle for the Vote, 1850–1920 (Bloomington: Indiana University Press, 1998). For recent studies on the suffrage movement on the state level, see Barbara Stuhler, *Gentle Warriors: Clara Ueland and the Minnesota Struggle for Woman Suffrage* (St. Paul: Minnesota Historical Society Press, 1995); Genevieve McBride, *On Wisconsin Women: Working for Their Rights from Settlement to Suffrage* (Madison: University of Wisconsin Press, 1993); Mary Martha Thomas, *The New Woman in Alabama: Social Reforms and Suffrage* (Tuscaloosa: University of Alabama Press, 1992).

67. Hewitt, *Women's Activism*, 203–4, 23, 96, 232; Debra Gold Hansen, *Strained Sisterhood: Gender and Class in the Boston Female Anti-Slavery Society* (Amherst: University of Massachusetts Press, 1993), 9, 97, 102, 116–17.

68. *HAC*, 223.

69. Glenda Riley, *Women and Indians on the Frontier, 1825–1915* (Albuquerque: University of New Mexico Press, 1984), 1–81.

70. *HAC*, 223.

71. Linda K. Kerber, "The Abolitionist Perception of the Indian," *Journal of American History* 62 (September 1975): 271–95; Robert Winston Mardock, *The Reformers and the American Indian* (Columbia: University of Missouri Press, 1971), 8–9.

72. JGS to the *SCD*, March 10, 1860, in *Crusader and Feminist*, 63.

73. Kerber, "Abolitionist Perception," 295.

74. An exception to this generalization would be her friendship with "the celebrated civilized Chippewa" Tanner, whose son's wedding she attended in November 1862 ("Indians in St. Cloud," *SCD*, November 20, 1862, p. 2).

75. "Indians," *SCD*, December 9, 1858, p. 2; see also "The Indians," *SCD*, November 24, 1859, p. 2; "Driving off the Indians," *SCD*, December 15, 1859, p. 2; "Indian Depredations," *SCD*, August 30, 1860, p. 2.

76. "Indian Massacre," *SCD*, November 10, 1859, p. 2.

77. For a more detailed description of the rebellion and its consequences, see Gary Clayton Anderson, *Kinsmen of Another Kind: Dakota-White Relations in the Upper Mississippi Valley, 1650–1862* (Lincoln: University of Nebraska Press, 1984); David A. Nichols, *Lincoln and the Indians: Civil War Policy and Politics* (Columbia: University of Missouri Press, 1978), 65–128; Kenneth Carley, *The Sioux Uprising of 1862* (St. Paul: Minnesota Historical Society, 1961); June Namias, *White Captives: Gender and Ethnicity on the American Frontier* (Chapel Hill: University of North Carolina Press, 1993), 204–61; Micheal Clodfelter, *The Dakota War: The United States Army versus the Sioux, 1862–1865* (Jefferson, N.C.: McFarland, 1998), 35–67. For accounts of the rebellion from the Dakota point of view, see Gary Clayton Anderson and Alan R. Woolworth, eds., *Through Dakota Eyes: Narrative Accounts of the Minnesota Indian War of 1862* (St. Paul: Minnesota Historical Society Press, 1988); Gary Clayton Anderson, *Little Crow: Spokesman for the Sioux* (St. Paul: Minnesota Historical Society Press, 1986). For a more detailed discussion of Jane's response to the rebellion, see Sylvia D. Hoffert, "Gender and Vigilantism on the Minnesota Frontier: Jane Grey Swisshelm and the U.S.-Dakota Conflict of 1862," *Western Historical Quarterly* 29 (Autumn 1998): 343–62.

78. Carley, *Sioux Uprising*, 24.

79. Nichols, *Lincoln and the Indians*, 76–77.

80. "Notice," *SCD*, July 12, 1860, p. 3.

81. See, for example, "Indian Rising" and "Indian Raid: Massacre at Acton," *SCD*, August 21, 1862, p. 2.

82. "Address," *SCD—Extra*, September 6, 1862.

83. "Indian Amusements," *SCD*, September 18, 1862, p. 2.

84. "Hanging Indians," *SCD*, January 8, 1863, p. 2; "Peace with the Sioux," *SCD*, November 13, 1862, p. 2; "The Sioux War," *SCD*, November 6, 1862, p. 2.

85. "Scalps," *SCD*, September 11, 1862, p. 2.

86. "The Indian Wrongs," *SCD*, September 18, 1862, p. 2.

87. "Indian War," *SCD*, October 16, 1862, p. 2.

88. Nichols, *Lincoln and the Indians*, 93–128.

89. *HAC*, 234.

90. JGS to the *SCD*, February 23, 1863, in *Crusader and Feminist*, 184.

91. JGS to the *SCD*, March 19, 1863, in ibid., 191.

92. JGS to the *SCD*, May 1, 1863, in ibid., 227.

93. "Letter from Mrs. Swisshelm," *SCD*, August 27, 1963, p. 1.

94. "The Indian Wrongs," *SCD*, September 18, 1862, p. 2, emphasis added.

95. JGS to the *SCD*, September 7, 1863, in *Crusader and Feminist*, 269.

96. *Special Senate Report of the Commissioner of Education on the Condition and Improvement of Public Schools in the District of Columbia* (Washington, D.C.: U.S. Government Printing Office, 1871), 233.

97. It is not clear when Jane became an active member. She is listed as the secretary of the Ways and Means Committee on a flyer dated February 11, 1865. See a copy of a fund-raising appeal in Jane Grey Swisshelm File, Consolidated Correspondence File, RG 92, Box 1100, Quartermaster General Papers, National Archives and Records Administration, Washington, D.C.

98. Cox had fled to Virginia at the beginning of the war to support the cause of state's rights and was then serving as a major in the Confederate Army (*Special Senate Report*, 234). See also *First Annual Report of the National Association for the Relief of Destitute Colored Women and Children* (Washington, D.C.: McGill and Witherow, 1864), 7; *Annual Report of the National Association for the Relief of Destitute Colored Women and Children, 1865* (Washington, D.C.: Chronicle, 1866), 7. Richard S. Cox is misidentified as S. E. Cox in "Local News," *Washington Star*, January 11, 1865, p. 1.

99. *Special Senate Report*, 233–35; *Senate Report on Charities and Reformatory Institutions in the District of Columbia* (Washington, D.C.: U.S. Government Printing Office, 1898), 126–27.

100. For descriptions of Maria Mann, see Adelia Doolittle Bauer to Robert L. Straker, February 27, 1938, Robert L. Straker Collection of Horace Mann Letters, Antiochiana Collection, Olive Kettering Library, Antioch College, Yellow Springs, Ohio; Albert G. Browne Jr. to Elizabeth P. Peabody, February 11, 1865, and Mary Mann to Dorothea Dix, January 18, 1864, Robert L. Straker Collection of Peabody

Letters, Antiochiana Collection; *Special Senate Report*, 237. Peabody, Mary Mann, and Maria Mann held life memberships in the orphan home association (*First Annual Report*, 18). On Peabody and Mary Mann's activities on behalf of the orphans, see Louise Hall Tharp, *The Peabody Sisters of Salem* (Boston: Little, Brown, 1950), 291, 292; Mary Mann to H. C. Badger, January 14, 1864, and Mary Mann to Mrs. Moncure Conway, [November 1864], Straker Collection of Peabody Letters.

101. *First Annual Report*, 7–8; Lucy N. Colman, *Reminiscences* (Buffalo: H. L. Green, 1891), 61; Mary Mann to H. C. Badger, January 14, 1864, and Elizabeth P. Peabody to W[illiam]. C[ullen]. Bryant, [October 1864], photostat, Straker Collection of Peabody Letters.

102. *Special Senate Report*, 237; *First Annual Report*, 8.

103. Colman, *Reminiscences*.

104. Elizabeth P. Peabody to Mary Mann, February 12, [1865], Straker Collection of Peabody Letters.

105. Colman, *Reminiscences*, 62; "Local News," *Washington Evening Star*, January 11, 1865, p. 1.

106. Elizabeth P. Peabody to W[illiam]. C[ullen]. Bryant, [October 1864], photostat, Straker Collection of Peabody Letters. For another reference to this incident, see Elizabeth P. Peabody to Mary Mann, February 12, [1865], Straker Collection of Peabody Letters.

107. Unless otherwise noted, the story that follows comes from "Local News," *Washington Evening Star*, January 11, 1865, p. 1.

108. *Special Senate Report*, 236. For reference to Colman's superintendency, see Colman, *Reminiscences*, 63. After her resignation, Colman continued to campaign to get Mann removed from her position (*Reminiscences*, 62).

109. Elizabeth P. Peabody to W[illiam]. C[ullen]. Bryant, [October 1864], photostat, Straker Collection of Peabody Letters.

110. Colman, *Reminiscences*, 62.

111. "William Channing," *Dictionary of American Biography*, ed. Allen Johnson and Dumas Malone (New York: Scribner's, 1930), vol. 2, pt. 2, pp. 9–10. For Jane's impression of Channing, see JGS to the *SCD*, August 6, 1863, in *Crusader and Feminist*, 242.

112. JGS to Mary C. Mitchell, March 7, 1865, Box 1, MFP.

113. JGS to the editor, *Washington Evening Star*, January 17, 1865, p. 3.

114. *Special Senate Report*, 237, 240. Maria Mann remained in Washington for about ten years, left temporarily to spend some time in the West promoting the kindergarten movement, and then returned to the capital city, where she found employment as a private teacher. She died in Washington on November 17, 1894 (Ruth M. Baylor, *Elizabeth Palmer Peabody: Kindergarten Pioneer* [Philadelphia: University of Pennsylvania Press, 1965], 116; Adelia Doolittle Bauer to Robert L. Straker, February 27, 1938, Straker Collection of Mann Letters; obituary of Maria Mann, *Washington Star*, November 19, 1894).

115. By this time, Jane's nephew owned and operated the *Democrat*. He pub-

lished the novel in weekly installments from December 3, 1868, through June 3, 1869.

Chapter 7

1. Elizabeth Davison and Ellen McKee, eds., *Annals of Old Wilkinsburg and Vicinity: The Village, 1788–1888* (Wilkinsburg, Pa.: Group for Historical Research, 1940), 390.

2. Stuart M. Blumin, "The Hypothesis of Middle-Class Formation in Nineteenth-Century America: A Critique and Some Proposals," *American Historical Review* 90 (April 1985): 299–338, establishes criteria for defining membership in the middle class.

3. Richard L. Bushman, *The Refinement of America: Persons, Houses, Cities* (New York: Knopf, 1992), xii–xix. On the influence of etiquette books in setting the standard for gentility, see John F. Kasson, *Rudeness and Civility: Manners in Nineteenth-Century Urban America* (New York: Hill and Wang, 1990), 34–37. On the problems associated with the rise of gentility, see also Karen Halttunen, *Confidence Men and Painted Women: A Study of Middle-Class Culture in America, 1830–1870* (New Haven: Yale University Press, 1982). For a literary description of the struggle to achieve gentility, see Margaret Bayard Smith, *What Is Gentility? A Moral Tale* (Washington, D.C.: Pishy Thompson, 1828).

4. *HAC*, 132–33, 158, 104–5, 235, 236–37, 129, 205–6. See also JGS to George Julian, February 3, 1877, and George Julian to JGS, February 14, 1877, Joshua Giddings and George Julian Papers, Library of Congress, Washington, D.C.; JGS to Charles Sumner, January 28, 1858, Charles Sumner Papers, Houghton Library, Harvard University, Cambridge, Massachusetts.

5. Jane was skilled in portraiture and painted flowers on canvas. She was also a seamstress (JGS, "Material and Making up of Dresses," in *Letters to Country Girls* [New York: J. C. Riker, 1853], 142–47). Jane knew that the durability of a dress depended on the quality of the fabric from which it was made (JGS, " 'That Dress of Mine'; Wherein It Appears That No End of Education Will Improve an Ungrateful Frock," an article originally published in the 1880s and reprinted in the *Cheney Silk News* 1 [July 1930], clipping in Box 3, MFP).

6. JGS, " 'That Dress of Mine.' "

7. *HAC*, 165.

8. These letters were republished by other newspapers. See, for example, "Letters to Country Girls," *Petersburg (Virginia) Kaleidoscope*, February 21, 1855, p. 48; March 7, 1855, p. 63; "Plain Advice to Country Girls," *New England Farmer*, September 29, 1849, p. 282, which was republished from the *Ohio Cultivator*. In 1853, Jane published this series of essays in *Letters to Country Girls*.

9. JGS, "City Belles, Peach Butter, and Catchup," in *Letters to Country Girls*, 131–33. See also JGS, "Reading," in *Letters to Country Girls*, 148–54.

10. Lydia Maria Child, *The American Frugal Housewife Dedicated to Those Who Are Not Ashamed of Economy*, 8th ed. (Boston: Carter and Hendee, 1832), 93.

11. JGS, "Lectures for Ladies—Peach-Trees," in *Letters to Country Girls*, 9–10.

12. JGS, "Woman's Work and Man's Supremacy," in ibid., 79–80.

13. JGS, "Wire Fences and Hedges," in ibid., 83.

14. JGS, "Personal Cleanliness," in ibid., 89, 91; for another reference to personal cleanliness, see, JGS, "Bathing and a Case of Consumption," in ibid., 207–8.

15. JGS, "Fingers and Faces," in ibid., 16–18.

16. JGS to ECM, March 27, 1867, Box 1, MFP.

17. Jane filed her lawsuit in January 1867 and moved into the little cottage on March 28 (JGS to ECM, March 27–31, 1867, Box 1, MFP). It is not clear what book she is referring to. It has been alleged that Jane was the author or coauthor of the autobiography of a Washington, D.C., seamstress, Elizabeth Keckley, called *Behind the Scenes: Thirty Years a Slave, and Four Years in the White House* (New York: G. W. Carleton, 1868); see "Bizarre Lincoln Story Traced," *Washington Star*, November 11, 1935, p. A-10, Elizabeth Keckley File, MHS. It is just as likely, however, that Jane's "book" is "Margaret Merlyn," the novel she wrote after leaving Washington in 1866.

18. Davison and McKee, *Annals*, 397.

19. JGS to Mary C. Mitchell, January 30, 1869, Box 1, MFP.

20. JGS to Henry Z. Mitchell, July 29, 1872, Box 1, MFP.

21. JGS to Henry Z. Mitchell, October 14, 1872, Box 1, MFP.

22. "A Pen Picture," *St. Cloud Journal Press*, November 26, 1874, p. 3.

23. Zo Swisshelm to Bertie Holt, May 5, [?], Box 2, Folder 32, Holt-Messer Papers, Schlesinger Library, Radcliffe Institute for Advanced Study, Cambridge, Mass.

24. Ibid.

25. Zo Swisshelm to Bertie Holt, March 5, [?], Box 2, Folder 32, Holt-Messer Papers.

26. JGS to William B. McClelland, March 21, 1876, Box 8, Folder 11, McFP.

27. JGS to William B. McClelland, May 7, 1876, Box 8, Folder 11, McFP; JGS to ECM, May 10, 1876, Box 2, MFP.

28. Stanley Sadie, ed., *The New Grove Dictionary of Music and Musicians* (Washington, D.C.: Grove's Dictionary of Music, 1980), 10:634–42.

29. JGS to ECM, May 10, 1876, and JM to Mrs. H. C. Burbank, May 28, 1876, Box 2, MFP.

30. See, for example, "Mrs. Swisshelm: Her Experiences over the Sea," *Chicago Tribune*, June 5, 1876, p. 8.

31. JGS to ECM, May 10, 1876, JM to Mrs. H. C. Burbank, May 28, July 2, 1876, and JM to ECM, August 10, 1876, Box 2, MFP.

32. JM to Mrs. H. C. Burbank, May 28, July 2, 1876, Box 2, MFP.

33. JM to ECM, August 10, 1876, Box 2, MFP.

34. JM to Mrs. H. C. Burbank, October 28, 1876, Box 2, MFP.

35. Halttunen, *Confidence Men*, 33–43.

36. JGS to William B. McClelland, May 7, 1876, Box 8, Folder 11, McFP.

37. JGS to ECM, May 10, 1876, Box 2, MFP.

38. JM to Mrs. H. C. Burbank, May 28, 1876, Box 2, MFP.

39. JM to ECM, October 1, 1876, Box 2, MFP. Part of the reason for Jane's return to the United States was that she had instructed her lawyer to supervise her application for a patent for a home ventilation system, and the process was not going smoothly. See patent application and correspondence in the McFP; see also JGS to William B. McClelland, May 7, 1876, Box 8, Folder 11, McFP.

40. JM to ECM, October 1, 1876, Box 2, MFP.

41. Ibid.; JM to Mrs. H. C. Burbank, October 28, 1876, Box 2, MFP.

42. JM to ECM, December 1876, JM to Mrs. H. C. Burbank, December 25, 1876, March 1, 1877, Box 2, MFP.

43. JM to Mrs. H. C. Burbank, November 13, 1876, Box 2, MFP.

44. The girls probably left in early May. Jean's last extant letter from Leipzig is dated April 27, 1877 (JM to Mrs. H. C. Burbank, April 27, 1877, Box 2, MFP).

45. JM to Mrs. H. C. Burbank, March 1, 1877, Box 2, MFP.

46. Excerpted review from the *Pittsburgh Commercial*, March 15, 1878, reprinted in the *St. Cloud Journal Press*, March 28, 1878, p. 2.

47. JGS to William B. McClelland, July 1, 1878, Box 8, Folder 11, McFP.

48. JGS to Mrs. Stockhum, August 20, 1878, Holt-Messer Papers.

49. *St. Cloud Journal Press*, December 8, 1881, p. 3.

50. *SCD*, November 7, 1861, p. 3; *SCD*, December 26, 1861, p. 3; Gertrude B. Gove, "St. Cloud No Longer Frontier Town in 1862," *St. Cloud Daily Times*, July 17, 1962, clipping, Stearns County Historical Society, St. Cloud, Minnesota; "Mrs. Swisshelm," *Chicago Tribune*, December 24, 1881, p. 11.

51. "Jane Gray [*sic*] as a Mother-in-Law," *St. Cloud Weekly Press*, January 4, 1882, p. 4.

52. "Mrs. Swisshelm," *Chicago Tribune*, December 24, 1881, p. 11.

53. JGS, untitled poem, May 17, 1881, Box 2, MFP.

54. "Allen-Swisshelm," *St. Cloud Journal Press*, December 22, 1881, p. 3.

55. For a general discussion of Chicago's social and cultural life during the 1870s and 1880s, see Bessie Louise Pierce, *A History of Chicago*, vol. 3, *The Rise of a Modern City, 1871–1893* (New York: Knopf, 1957), 20–63, 444–500.

56. JGS to ECM, n.d. [1882], Box 2, MFP.

57. JGS to ECM, June 27, 1882, Box 2, MFP; see "Mrs. Swisshelm," *Chicago Tribune*, December 24, 1881, p. 11.

58. JGS to ECM, June 27, 1882, Box 2, MFP.

59. Halttunen, *Confidence Men*, 112–14, 167; using Washington, D.C., as an example, see Catherine Allgor, *Parlor Politics: In Which the Ladies of Washington Help Build a City and a Government* (Charlottesville: University Press of Virginia, 2000), 120–24.

60. Allgor, *Parlor Politics*, 121.

61. JGS to ECM, n.d. [1882], Box 2, MFP.

62. JGS to ECM, June 27, 1882, Box 2, MFP.

63. JGS to ECM, n.d. [1882], Box 2, MFP.

64. JGS to ECM, June 27, 1882, Box 2, MFP.

65. JGS to ECM, n.d. [1882], Box 2, MFP.

66. Ibid.

67. JGS to ECM, June 27, 1882, Box 2, MFP.

68. JGS to Zo Swisshelm Allen, August 7, 1882, Box 2, MFP.

69. Ernest S. Craighead, "The Swisshelm Home in Edgewood" (speech delivered on December 9, 1948, at the annual meeting of the Edgewood Historical Society), pp. 14–19, Historical Society of Western Pennsylvania, Pittsburgh; see also Davison and McKee, *Annals*, 398.

70. *Golden Progress: History and Official Program of the Fiftieth Anniversary Celebration of Swissvale, Pennsylvania, 1898–1948* (n.p.: Executive Committee for the Fiftieth Anniversary Celebration, 1948), 9–10, 13.

71. JGS to ECM, June 20, 1883, Box 2, MFP.

72. *Golden Progress*, 10–12.

73. Davison and McKee, *Annals*, 397.

74. S. J. Fisher, "Reminiscences of Jane Grey Swisshelm," *Western Pennsylvania Historical Magazine* 4 (July 1921): 165.

75. Craighead, "Swisshelm Home," 14.

76. JGS to ECM, February 18, 1883, Box 2, MFP.

77. It is not clear exactly when Zo gave birth. JGS to ECM, June 20, 1883, Box 2, MFP, refers to Zo's daughter as having cut two teeth.

78. Zo Swisshelm Allen to ECM, July 23, 1883, Box 2, MFP.

79. JGS to ECM, April 8, 1884, Box 2, MFP.

80. Davison and McKee, *Annals*, 398; Ernest Allen to JM, July 22, 1884, Box 2, MFP; "Passing Away: A Great Mind Losing Its Hold on Earth," *Pittsburgh Commercial Gazette*, July 22, 1884, p. 4; "Jane Grey Swisshelm Dead," *Pittsburgh Daily Post*, July 23, 1884, p. 4; unsigned to husband, July 25, 1884, Box 2, MFP.

81. "In Her Grave: Jane Grey Swisshelm Laid at Rest," *Pittsburgh Commercial Gazette*, July 25, 1884, p. 2; Craighead, "Swisshelm Home," 14.

82. "Mrs. Swisshelm's Funeral," *Pittsburgh Commercial Gazette*, July 24, 1884, p. 2. Jane's obituary appeared in a wide variety of newspapers outside the Pittsburgh area. In Minnesota, see, for example, *St. Cloud Journal Press*, July 24, 1884, [p. 2]; *St. Paul Daily Globe*, July 23, 1884, p. 4, July 26, 1884, p. 4; *Minneapolis Evening Journal*, July 22, 1884, [p. 2]; *St. Paul and Minneapolis Pioneer Press*, July 23, 1884, p. 4. All three widely circulated New York newspapers ran her obituary on July 23 (*New York Times*, p. 5; *New York Daily Tribune*, p. 5; *New York Herald*, p. 10). For obituaries in Chicago, see *Chicago Evening Journal*, July 24, 1884, p. 2; *Chicago Tribune*, July 23, 1884, p. 1; *Chicago Daily News*, July 22, 1884, p. 1; *Chicago Daily Sun*, July 23, 1884, p. 3; *Chicago Times*, July 23, 1884, p. 2. Notices of her death also appeared in the *Wash-*

ington Post, July 24, 1884, p. 1, and the *Louisville Courier Journal*, July 27, 1884, p. 11. Zo apparently returned to Chicago with her husband after her mother's funeral. Between that time and her death a few years later, she bore another daughter. Her husband remarried after she died and eventually moved with his new wife and his two daughters to New York, where then he died. After his death, the girls reportedly lived much of the time abroad with their stepmother (George T. Fleming, "Bits of Biography—Jane Grey Swisshelm," *Pittsburgh Gazette Times*, August 3, 1919, clipping in Jane Swisshelm File, Pittsburgh Authors, Pennsylvania Room, Carnegie Library, Pittsburgh).

83. *HAC*, 35.

84. Ibid.

85. "Lady Jane," *Pittsburgh Commercial Gazette*, July 25, 1884, p. 2.

Afterword

1. "Opinions of the Press," *PSV*, February 19, 1848, p. 2.

2. Patricia Okker has identified more than six hundred nineteenth-century female editors (*Our Sister Editors: Sarah J. Hale and the Tradition of Nineteenth-Century American Women Editors* [Athens: University of Georgia Press, 1995], 171–220).

3. See, for example, "Mrs. Swisshelm's Recollections," *New York Times*, August 8, 1880, p. 8; "Mrs. Swisshelm's Reminiscences," *New York Tribune*, July 20, 1880, p. 6. The more conservative *New York Herald* was less enthusiastic ("Half a Century," *New York Herald*, August 16, 1880, p. 5).

4. Mott's granddaughter, Anna Davis Hallowell, published a collection of her letters (*James and Lucretia Mott: Life and Letters* [Boston: Houghton, Mifflin, 1884]). Stone's daughter wrote her biography (Alice Stone Blackwell, *Lucy Stone, Pioneer of Woman's Rights* [Boston: Little, Brown, 1930]). Friend and fellow suffragist Ida Husted Harper put together a collection of Anthony's papers and speeches in *The Life and Work of Susan B. Anthony*, 3 vols. (Indianapolis: Bowen-Merrill, 1898–1908). Stanton's children, Theodore Stanton and Harriot Stanton Blatch, published *Elizabeth Cady Stanton as Revealed in Her Letters, Diary, and Reminiscences* (New York: Harper and Brothers, 1922). And Howe's children literally made a cottage industry out of memorializing their mother; see Maud Howe Elliott, *The Eleventh Hour in the Life of Julia Ward Howe* (Boston: Little, Brown, 1911); Florence Howe Hall, *Julia Ward Howe and the Woman Suffrage Movement* (Boston: Dana Estes, 1913); and Laura E. Richards and Maud Howe Elliott, *Julia Ward Howe, 1819–1910*, 2 vols. (New York: Houghton, Mifflin, 1915).

5. Keith E. Melder, *Beginnings of Sisterhood: The American Women's Rights Movement, 1800–1850* (New York: Schocken, 1977); Ellen Carol DuBois, *Feminism and Suffrage: The Emergence of an Independent Women's Movement, 1848–1869* (Ithaca: Cornell University Press, 1979; Sylvia D. Hoffert, *When Hens Crow: The Woman's Rights Movement in Antebellum America* (Bloomington: Indiana University Press, 1995); Aileen S. Kraditor, *The Ideas of the Woman Suffrage Movement, 1890–1920* (New

York: Columbia University Press, 1965); Marjorie Spruill Wheeler, *New Women of the New South: The Leaders of the Woman Suffrage Movement in the Southern States* (New York: Oxford University Press, 1993); Rosalyn Terborg-Penn, *African American Women in the Struggle for the Vote, 1850–1920* (Bloomington: Indiana University Press, 1998).

6. Quoted in Sherilyn Cox Bennion, *Equal to the Occasion: Women Editors of the Nineteenth-Century West* (Reno: University of Nevada Press, 1990), 85.

7. There was so much anxiety about gender issues at the turn of the century that some historians of gender have called the period between about 1880 and 1920 a time of "crisis" for men; see, for example, Peter G. Filene, *Him/Her/Self: Gender Identities in Modern America*, 3d ed. (Baltimore: Johns Hopkins University Press, 1998), 74–99; Michael Kimmel, *Manhood in America: A Cultural History* (New York: Free Press, 1996), 81–188; Gail Bederman, *Manliness and Civilization: A Cultural History of Gender and Race in the United States, 1880–1917* (Chicago: University of Chicago Press, 1995).

8. "Personal Reminiscences," Chicago *InterOcean* newspaper clipping, Harpel Scrapbook, vol. II, p. 146, Chicago Historical Society, Chicago.

9. For a discussion of the "New Woman," see Carroll Smith-Rosenberg, "The New Woman as Androgyne: Social Disorder and Gender Crisis, 1870–1936," in *Disorderly Conduct: Visions of Gender in Victorian America* (New York: Oxford University Press, 1986), 245–96.

ACKNOWLEDGMENTS

I wish to express my thanks to many colleagues and friends, including Anne Butler, Wendy Gamber, Michael Green, Barbara Harris, Nancy Hewitt, Joy Kasson, Roger Lotchin, Laurie Maffly-Kipp, Don Mathews, Theda Perdue, Anne Firor Scott, Sarah Shields, Linda Wagner-Martin, Harry Watson, Margaret Wiener, and an anonymous reader for the University of North Carolina Press. Some read and critiqued all or parts of this book; others wrote supporting letters for my grant proposals. Institutional support from the Minnesota Historical Society, Southwest Missouri State University, the Institute for the Arts and Humanities, and the University of North Carolina at Chapel Hill has been generous and very much appreciated. My thanks to the Western History Association and the University of Nebraska Press for allowing me to republish parts of chapters 5 and 6. Archivists from the American Antiquarian Society, Antioch College, the Carnegie Library in Pittsburgh, the Chicago Historical Society, the Historical Society of Western Pennsylvania, the Houghton Library, the Indiana County (Pennsylvania) Historical Society, the Library of Congress, the Minnesota Historical Society, the National Archives, the Schlesinger Library, the Stearns County Historical Society, the Western Reserve Historical Society, and the Wisconsin Historical Society were enormously helpful. Chris Catalfamo, Meganne Fabrega, Carlton Fletcher, Stan Harrold, Michael Murphy, Michael Pierson, and Clarence Stephenson all offered encouraging words at times when I was much in need of them. Chuck Grench, senior editor at the University of North Carolina Press, read more than one draft of the manuscript. His attention to detail and excellent advice were extremely valuable. And last, I thank my husband for his unfailing support.

Sylvia D. Hoffert

Chapel Hill, North Carolina

INDEX

Cannon, Thomas, Jr., 1, 9; dies, 2, 18, 212
(n. 34); born and apprenticed, 15;
moves family to Wilkinsburg, 16;
moves family to Pittsburgh, 17;
indebtedness of, 63–64
Cannon, Thomas, Sr., 15
Cannon, William, 15, 17, 18, 20
Capital punishment, 135
Catholics, 13, 25–29, 30–31, 123, 203
Celibacy, 57
Chancellorsville, battle of, 98
Chancery courts. *See* Equity courts
Channing, William Ellery, 158
Channing, William Henry, 158
Charles I (king of England), 11, 12
Charles II (king of England), 12
Chase, Salmon P., 94
Chicago, Ill., 176–77
Chicago Tribune, 148
Child, Lydia Maria, 130, 149, 164–65
Chippewa. *See* Ojibwa
Churchill, Carline Maria Nichols, 196
Clay, Cassius M., 124
Clerks, government, 94–97
Colman, Lucy N., 156–58
Compromise of 1850, 139
Courtship, 38, 41–42
Covenanter Presbyterianism, 11, 16, 23,
31–32, 38–39
Covenanters, 10, 11–15, 18, 19, 23, 103,
104, 137, 188
Coverture, 64–65
Cox, Richard S., 155, 238 (n. 98)
Cromwell, Oliver, 12

Dakota Sioux, 5, 126, 149, 150–54, 194
Declaration of Sentiments, 216 (n. 38)
Democrats, 110, 114–21, 123–24
Denver Queen Bee, 196
Dickinson, Anna, 130
Dickson, John, 185
Dickson-Steward Coal Company, 184,
185

Divorce, 49, 51, 53–55, 57
Dix, Dorothea, 98, 101
Donnelly, Ignatius, 123, 124–25
Double, Daniel, 175–76
Douglass, Frederick, 191
Dress Reform. *See* Bloomers

Eaton, John, 117–18
Eaton, Peggy, 117–18
Edgar Thompson Steel Works, 184
Edgeworth School, 19, 37
Edwards, Rebecca, 130
Elizabeth I (queen of England), 12
Equity courts, 65
Errett, J. E., 107, 108
Evangelicals, 10–11
Ewalt, Samuel, 64

Family Journal and Saturday Visiter, 26,
111
Femininity, 7, 82, 88, 116
"Femme covert," 215 (n. 18)
Fessenden, William Pitt, 97
Field, Marshall, 176
Fleeson, Reese, 90, 105
Fredericksburg, Va., 101
Free Democrats, 107–8, 109–11, 122
Free Soil Party, 107–8, 110
Frémont, John C., 111, 126, 130
Fugitive Slave Act, 139

Gage, Frances, 144–45, 147
Gage, Matilda Joslyn, 148
Garrison, William Lloyd, 136, 149, 191
Gender, 209 (n. 1)
Gender relations: among covenanters,
23, 104; during courtship, 38, 41–42;
and marriage, 38–41, 42–43; and
property ownership, 61, 62–63, 64–
77; and work, 80, 81–102; and politics, 106–7, 111, 112–21, 130, 131; on
frontier, 112, 115
Gentility, 83, 162–63, 164

as a child, 2, 18; in Louisville, 2, 45–46, 84, 120, 133, 137–38; marriage of, 2, 38, 40, 43, 47; attacks Daniel Webster, 3, 118, 228 (n. 61); in Washington, D.C., 3, 5, 94–101, 118, 126–29; writes columns for *New York Tribune*, 3; becomes mother, 4, 109, 202; edits *St. Cloud Democrat*, 4, 120, 126; edits *St. Cloud Visiter*, 4, 112–20; moves to St. Cloud, Minn., 4, 53, 71, 111; press destroyed, 4, 118–19, 228 (n. 62); and Republicans, 4, 111, 121–29, 131; in Chicago, 5, 76, 169, 170, 176, 185–86; conflict over property, 5, 53, 61, 64–76, 204–6; edits *The Reconstructionist*, 5, 127–29; as government clerk, 5, 80, 94–97, 129; as nurse, 5, 80, 97–102; writes for *Chicago Tribune*, 5, 130, 171, 181, 191; death of, 6, 76, 186; religious background of, 10, 11–15, 18–19, 31–32; spiritual life of, 15–17, 19–21, 22–23; education of, 19; relationship with James Swisshelm, 20–21, 22, 37, 43–47, 52–55, 58–59, 61–62, 66–68, 69, 70–76, 205–6; attitude toward Methodism, 21–23, 44, 46–47; relationship with Mary Elizabeth Swisshelm, 22, 46, 47, 66, 73, 205; attitude toward gender, 23–25, 45–46, 141–43; attitude toward Catholics, 25, 26–31, 203; on Bloomers, 29–30, 100–101, 141–42; described by others, 31, 103, 133, 147–48, 161; attitude toward divorce, 33, 48–49, 54–55; on Marriage, 33, 40, 50, 51; characteristics of, 34, 35–36, 115, 130, 135, 194–95; courtship of, 37–38; as teacher, 46, 47; writes fiction, 48–50, 159; attitude toward motherhood, 51–52, 109, 202–4; on child custody, 55, 236 (n. 64); sexuality of, 57; sells *Pittsburgh Saturday Visiter*, 70; relations with co-workers, 84, 85–89, 90–97, 100–102; social class of, 84,

163–64, 187, 193–94; on female printers, 92–93; on clerks, 95–97; on female nurses, 100–101; and politics, 104–31, 194; and Liberty Party, 105, 106, 107; and Democrats, 106, 110, 114–16, 121; and Whigs, 106, 110; and Free Democrats, 109–10, 111, 122, 123; struggle with Sylvanus Lowry, 112–21; on Lincoln, 124, 126; on secession, 124; and Dakota Sioux, 126, 149–55; attitude toward Andrew Johnson, 127–29; edits *Reconstructionist*, 127–29; political significance of, 131; and capital punishment, 135–36; and integration, 140–41; and woman's rights conventions, 142–45; and married women's property, 145, 236 (n. 64); and woman's suffrage, 146–47; and National Association for the Relief of Destitute Women and Children, 155–59, 238 (n. 97); and Maria Mann, 158–59; attitude toward social class, 164–66, 181, 187–88, 192, 193–94; publishes "Letters to Country Girls," 164–66; relationship with Zo, 166–76, 181–84, 185–86, 202–4; in Leipzig, Saxony, 170–73; in Princeton, N.J., 174; funeral of, 186–87. See also *Half a Century*

Swisshelm, John, 20, 36, 62, 67
Swisshelm, Mary Elizabeth, 34, 43, 51; and Methodism, 21, 22; marries, 36; meets Jane, 37; relationship with Jane, 46, 47, 66; and John Swisshelm's will, 62; sells part of Swissvale, 74; dies, 213 (n. 1)
Swisshelm, Mary Henrietta. *See* Allen, Mary Henrietta Swisshelm
Swisshelm, Nettie. *See* Allen, Mary Henrietta Swisshelm
Swisshelm, Samuel, 36, 43, 63
Swisshelm, William, 36, 51, 63, 70, 75, 87, 108